DEVELOPMENT ETHICS:

A GUIDE TO THEORY AND PRACTICE

For Mary Ann Glendon,
fellow ethicist,
theorist, and
practitioner.

Denis Goulet

Books by Denis Goulet

Ethics of Development (in Spanish and Portuguese) (1965/1966)

The Cruel Choice: A New Concept in the Theory of Development (1971)

A New Moral Order: Development Ethics and Liberation Theology (1974)

The Myth of Aid: The Hidden Agenda of the Development Report (with Michael Hudson) (1975)

Looking at Guinea-Bissau: A New Nation's Development Strategy (1976)

Survival with Integrity: Sarvodaya at the Crossroads (1981)

Mexico: Development Strategies for the Future (1983)

The Uncertain Promise: Value Conflicts in Technology Transfer (2nd edition) (1989)

Incentives for Development: The Key to Equity (1989)

DEVELOPMENT ETHICS:

A GUIDE TO THEORY AND PRACTICE

DENIS GOULET

University of Notre Dame

The Apex Press

New York

Zed Books Ltd

London

For L. J. Lebret

Development Ethics was first published in the Americas
by The Apex Press, an imprint of the Council on International and Public Affairs, 777 United Nations Plaza,
Suite 3C, New York, NY 10017, USA (800/316-2739;
914/271-6500), and in the rest of the world by Zed Books
Ltd., 7 Cynthia Street, London N1 9JF, UK (171/837-
4014), in 1995.

Library of Congress Cataloging-in-Publication Data:

Goulet, Denis.
     Development ethics : a guide to theory and practice
       p.   cm.
     Includes bibliographical references and index.
     ISBN 0-945257-65-1 (hard) : ISBN 0-945257-64-3 (pbk.)
       1. Economic assistance—Developing countries—Moral and
ethical aspects. 2. Technical assistance—Developing countries—
Moral and ethical aspects. I. Title.
HC60.G627 1995   94-38517
174—dc20   CIP

A catalogue record for this book is
available from the British Library.

Zed Books Ltd. edition
ISBN 1-85649-385-7 hard
ISBN 1-85649-386-5 soft

Cover design by Warren Hurley
Typeset and Printed in the United States of America

CONTENTS

PART III. ETHICAL STRATEGIES: ILLUSTRATIVE SECTORS

A Note on Background Sources

Portions of the chapters in this volume have drawn on writings of the author appearing in earlier books and journals, to which acknowledgement is hereby made:

Chapter 2   "Three Rationalities in Development Decision-Making," *World Development*, 14:2, 1986, pp. 301-317; "Tasks and Methods in Development Ethics," *Cross Currents*, XXXVIII:2, Summer 1988, pp. 146-163, 172.

Chapter 3   "An Ethical Model for the Study of Values," *Harvard Educational Review*, 41:2, May 1971, pp. 205-227.

Chapter 4   *The Cruel Choice: A New Concept in the Theory of Development*, New York: University Press of America, 1985, Chapter 3.

Chapter 5   *Ibid.*, Chapter 6.

Chapter 6   *The Uncertain Promise: Value Conflicts in Technology Transfer*, New York: New Horizons Press, 1989, Chapter 7.

Chapter 7   *Mexico: Development Strategies for the Future*, Notre Dame, IN: University of Notre Dame Press, 1983, Chapter 1.

Chapter 8   "Participation in Development: New Avenues," *World Development*, 17:2, February 1989, pp. 165-178.

Chapter 9   *The Uncertain Promise, op. cit.*, Chapter 8, pp. 174ff.

Chapter 10 "Development Ethics and Ecological Wisdom," in J. Ronald Engel and Joan Gibb Engel, eds., *Ethics of Environment and Development*, London: Belhaven Press, 1990, pp. 36-49.

Chapter 11 "Cultural Resistance in Latin America: Future Prospects," in E. Masini, ed., *The Futures of Culture*, Vol. 2, Paris: UNESCO, 1992, pp. 100-111.

Chapter 12 "Notes on the Ethics of Developmental Assistance," in Krishna Kumar, ed., *Bonds Without Bondage: Explorations in Transcultural Interactions*, Honolulu: University Press of Hawaii for the East-West Center, 1979, pp. 177-206.

Chapter 13 "The Human Dilemma of Development," in Charles K. Wilber and Kenneth P. Jameson, eds., *The Political Economy of Development and Under-Development*, Fifth edition, New York: McGraw-Hill, Inc., 1992, pp. 469-477.

Chapter 14 "Obstacles to World Development: An Ethical Reflection," *World Development*, 11:7, July 1983, pp. 609-624.

Chapter 15 *The Cruel Choice, op. cit.*, Chapter 10.

Chapter 16 "Development Experts: The One-Eyed Giants," *World Development*, 8:7/8, July/August 1980, pp. 481-489.

PREFACE

This introductory guide to development ethics is written for students of development and for practitioners of that art—national and international policy-makers, program planners, project managers, field workers, and local "communities of need" who are the presumed beneficiaries of development. Development ethics has recently emerged as a new field of study and action from a heightened awareness of social issues and the recognition that something more than the application of "normal ethics" is needed to deal with a new set of complex multi-dimensional value problems. In ever-new and ever-changing settings, development poses ancient philosophical questions: what is the good life (and the relation between *having* goods and *being* good), what are the foundations of life in society, and what stance should human groups adopt toward nature? "Development" provides one particular answer to these questions. Merely to engage in applied ethics, however, is tantamount to harnessing ethics in *instrumental* fashion to the uncritical pursuit of development. Yet the very goals of modern development and the peculiar answer it offers to the ancient philosophical questions are themselves at issue. Accordingly, ethics is summoned to a task beyond mere instrumental norm-setting in development processes. What is needed is a critical questioning of the very nature of development and of its declared goals: a better human life and societal arrangements that provide a widening range of choices for people to seek their common and individual good.

In formulating this new discipline, the pioneers of development ethics have traveled two separate but now converging roads. The first road runs from engagement as planners or change agents in development practice to the formal articulation of ethical strategies. The second road originates in an internal philosophical critique of conventional ethical theory and moves outward to the elaboration of a distinctive ethics of development as normative *praxis*. Both modes of "doing" development ethics go beyond instrumental application to a reformulation of ethical theory itself, this in accord with the inner exigencies of the development *problématique*.

The present work travels down the first of these two roads: the ethical strategies proposed herein are derived from the development practice of varied national societies, of opposition social movements experimenting with alternative counter-strategies, and of the author's own activities as a development ethicist.[1] The basic mode of study employed is phenomenological analysis, *i.e.*, the methodical "peeling away" of values and counter-values contained, usually implicitly and in latent form, in the policies, programs, and projects proposed and carried out by development agents.

Readers will not find in these pages a comprehensive manual of development ethics, a specialized domain of theory and practice which is expanding rapidly and linking up with environment, world order, and numerous other realms as peaks in a common mountain chain of intellectual concerns.

Among the many ethical issues *not* treated in this introductory guide are:

- the detailed foundational justification of rights, needs, and entitlements;

- the ethical assessment of policies as these affect special categories of persons victimized or marginalized by current development practices (women, children, dispersed and nomadic populations, ethnic and cultural minorities);

- evaluations of competing economic, political, and social systems;

- new conceptions of security posed by the militarization of societies, environmental stresses across national boundaries, new patterns of large-scale migratory and refugee flows; and

- issues of economic justice arising from the growing practice of "social dumping," the unfair trade advantages derived by countries which deny their workers basic rights or treat the environment irresponsibly.

These and a broad array of cognate issues—strategies of economic liberalization and the operation of transnational corporations, the ethics of intervention (the role of "insiders" and "outsiders"), the merits of democracy or autocracy in promoting development, and disputes over the control of biogenetic resources—constitute the subject matter and the formal object of study by that second stream of development ethics proceeding from an internal critique of general ethical theory to the framing of a specific practice-oriented development ethics.

On the other hand, what *is* covered in this work is the delineation and justification of development ethics:

- as a new discipline with its proper nature, distinctive methods, and research rules;

- as the constitutive source of general principles that serve as criteria guiding the formulation of ethical strategies;

- as operational guides or ethical strategies in four selected, illustrative sectors of development decision-making and action; and

- as the source of normative standards for evaluating development performance.

Some of the materials found in these pages have appeared, in vastly different form over a span of thirty years, thus representing and illustrating the gestation of development ethics as an embryonic discipline. In addition to new materials, what appears here is a distillation and synthesis of three kinds of writings:

- unpublished reports prepared by the author on specific value conflict issues in development;[2]

- *ad hoc* exploration into development issues bearing a high valence of value significance. These were written for: economic planning bodies, social change agents, specialists in political science, sociology, anthropology, public administration, geography, technology, ecology, theology, and development education;[3] and

- excerpts from two earlier books by the author on development ethics.[4] Unlike these earlier extended formal treatises on development ethics, the present work is a brief pedagogical compendium and guide to decision-makers.

Part I of this work portrays development ethics as a new discipline that straddles and overlaps, as it were, intellectual spaces occupied by multiple diagnostic, policy, and normative sciences (Ch. 1). The nature, methods, and research procedures proper to development ethics are described and illustrated (Ch. 2, 3).

Part II critically surveys the goals of development (Ch. 4) and the principles shaping diverse strategies adopted for pursuing it (Ch. 5), this in accord with basic options (Ch. 6) taken along diverse pathways (Ch. 7) which associate beneficiary populations to development decisions and actions (Ch. 8).

In Part III, four ethical strategies are presented, justified, and illustrated. Chapter 9 analyzes value conflicts surrounding technology, viewed as the key to success in development, and policies for its selection, acquisition, use, and dissemination. Environmental issues, which generate value clashes with development both at theoretical (how to reconcile human freedom with nature's integrity) and practical levels (how to arbitrate competing principles of resource use), form the subject matter of Chapter 10. Through the scientific and technological rationality it carries, modern development shatters that *vital nexus* which is present in traditional cultures and which links their signifying (or symbolic meaning) values with their operational (normative) values. This conflict is examined in Chapter 11. And Chapter 12 inquires whether aid or development assistance is an ethically good thing, and whether it contributes effectively to development.

In Part IV, development performance is evaluated on several registers: the measure of costs paid to develop (Ch. 13), an assessment of obstacles to development (Ch. 14), and criteria for judging whether development enhances human well-being (Ch. 15).

In conclusion, the development adventure is presented as a grandiose historical task which either stifles or liberates humans to pursue their fulfillment in transcendence (Ch. 16).

Acknowledgement is gladly made of a stimulating exchange of ideas with David Crocker, which has aided me in planning this work. Over the years, Louis Xhignesse has helped me to understand development as a larger process of constructing human civilizations. Ward Morehouse's attentive reading of an earlier version of this book and his illuminating suggestions for revision are greatly appreciated. I have been the beneficiary of enlightened secretarial and editorial assistance from Marti Dincolo. And my wife, Ana Maria, continually provides me with a living testimonial of what authentic human development can be. My gratitude to these persons engages none of them in responsibility for errors or imperfections found in this work; for these, I alone am accountable.

INTRODUCTION

Development is an ambiguous term used both *descriptively* and *normatively* to depict a present condition or to project a desired alternative. Descriptive usage prevails in the growing body of testimonial writings on development,[1] in statistical and policy reports issued by international financing agencies, and in the voluminous academic literature in many disciplines. Normative usage of the term appears in works of advocacy[2] whose authors employ value-laden language to criticize development as now conducted or to advocate an alternative vision deemed ethically or politically superior. Moreover, the same term "development" refers either to the ends of social change or to the means for reaching these ends: to the vision of a better life (one materially richer, institutionally more "modern," and technologically more efficient), or to an array of means to achieve that vision. Means range from economic planning to mobilization campaigns, from comprehensive social engineering aimed at altering values, behaviors, and social structures to sectoral interventions of many sorts.

Development practice is likewise fraught with ambiguities. Under the banner of development parades a bewildering, and at times contradictory, assortment of policy prescriptions:

- a "big push" into self-sustained economic growth or rapid shock-treatment reform of the economic system;

- the Westernization of social institutions and practices;

1

- the repudiation of Westernization in favor of an "endogenous" model of change;

- the mobilization of national resources and energies around "giant projects"; or conversely

- the glorification of the "small is beautiful" strategy based on small, locally controlled projects.

Originally, development was viewed as a proper topic of study in the field of economics. But, as the editors of a book series on development and underdevelopment observed:

> [T]he nature of the subject matter has forced both scholars and practitioners to transcend the boundaries of their own disciplines whether these be social sciences, like economics, human geography or sociology, or applied sciences such as agronomy, plant biology or civil engineering. It is now a conventional wisdom of development studies that development problems are so multi-faceted and complex that *no* single discipline can hope to encompass them, let alone offer solutions.[3]

Development is all these things—simultaneously and inextricably an economic and political matter, a social and cultural one, an issue of resource and environmental management, a question of civilization.

The present work takes the development *problématique* in this wider sense: as a question of defining the good life, the just society, and the relations of human communities to nature. The new pluridisciplinary field of development ethics allies diagnostic (analytic) sciences to policy (applied) sciences and to normative sciences. The raw materials of its reflection are supplied by two sources: the lived experience of those undergoing "development" and the numerous formal disciplines studying development.

PART I

DEVELOPMENT ETHICS

1.

A NEW DISCIPLINE

Ethicists are late arrivals on the stage of development studies. For many years development's value dilemmas were treated only peripherally by a small number of economists.[1] Gunnar Myrdal's 1968 study *Asian Drama* acknowledges development to be a value-laden operation.[2] And a 1968 textbook by economist Benjamin Higgins asserts that "the philosopher needs to be added to the development team; without a clear concept of the philosophy of development, the team becomes a simple *ad hoc* mission."[3] Incidental discussion of development's value questions was likewise conducted by a few post-World War II sociologists and anthropologists studying social change—Daniel Lerner, Edward Banfield, George Dalton, Bert Hoselitz, Georges Balandier, Manning Nash, and Clifford Geertz.[4]

The systematic *ex professo* study of development ethics, however, except by a few philosophers working in isolation,[5] had to await the birth in 1987 of IDEA (International Development Ethics Association) in San José, Costa Rica. IDEA's founders represented three streams of ethical theory: Yugoslav *praxis* humanists searching for a non-dogmatic brand of Marxism,[6] Central American analytical philosophers applying methods of symbolic logic to issues of technology and social transformation,[7] and U.S. analytical philosophers looking beyond Western theoretical sources to craft applied ethical norms to guide action in spheres of global change and public policy.[8] The three

5

groups share a common view of the proper mission of ethics: to diagnose vital problems facing human societies, to guide public policy
choices, and to clarify value dilemmas surrounding these problems
and policies. They undertook to conduct this threefold reflection around
value questions posed by development. With the creation of IDEA,
development ethics gained formal recognition as an interdisciplinary
field in development studies and philosophy.[9]

Twenty years earlier the political scientist David Apter had observed that the study of modernization "brings us back to the search
for first principles and rapid-fire developments in social theory and
the breakthroughs in the biological sciences, not to speak of the re-
treat of philosophy into linguistics, have combined to render us philosophically defenseless and muddled."[10] The reason for the muddle is
that Machiavelli[11] in politics in the sixteenth century and Adam Smith[12]
in economics two centuries later had stripped ethics of its norm-setting role in society. Thereafter, all philosophies fell into disrepute as
socially irrelevant,[13] nowhere more totally so than in economics. Now,
however, a growing number of economists are working to restore value
questions to the center of their theoretical, methodological, and the-
matic concerns.[14]

Louis Joseph Lebret, founder of the Economy and Humanism
movement in 1941, defined development as a basic question of values
and the creation of a new civilization.[15] He considers his definition to
be anchored in essential human values and, consequently, to be valid
for all cultures and social groupings. Lebret described development
as:

> . . . the series of transitions, for a given population and all the
> sub-population units which comprise it, from a less human to
> a more human phase, at the speediest rhythm possible, at the
> lowest possible cost, taking into account all the bonds of soli-
> darity which exist (or ought to exist) among these popula-
> tions and sub-populations.[16]

Hence the discipline of development is the study of how to achieve
a more human economy.[17] The expressions "more human" and "less
human" must be understood in the light of a vital distinction between
plus avoir ("to have more") and *plus être* ("to be more"). Societies
are more human or more developed, not when men and women "*have*

more" but when they are enabled "to *be* more." The main criterion of development is not increased production or material well-being but qualitative human enrichment. Economic growth and quantitative increases in goods are doubtless needed, but not any kind of increase nor growth obtained at any price. According to Lebret, the world remains underdeveloped or falls prey to an illusory anti-development so long as a few nations or privileged groups remain alienated in an abundance of luxury (facility) goods at the expense of the many who are thereby deprived of essential (subsistence) goods.

In the decades following 1945, as development gained formal recognition as a subdiscipline of economics, it came to be viewed as a technical issue of resource planning and social engineering to launch national societies into self-sustained economic growth capable of providing mass consumption to their citizens.[18] Increasing the size of the economic pie was uncritically assumed to be a self-validating goal synonymous with the pursuit of the good life. Thousands of economists, administrators, and engineers emerged from academic and professional enclaves to become social architects of a new world, serving as expert midwives who would transfer the institutions, practices, and technology of industrialized countries' to "underdeveloped" nations. To these early "developers," it seemed self-evident that economic growth, as speedily as possible and with little regard for social or human costs, was a good thing for everyone everywhere. With cavalier self-assurance, they set about reshaping every culture and value system. While economists and engineers pursued these promethean endeavors, philosophers were withdrawing ever further from social arenas into intellectual ghettos where they indulged in elaborate word games analyzing the meaning of meaning.

Development ethics borrows freely from the work of economists, political scientists, planners, agronomists, and specialists of other disciplines. Ethics places each discipline's concept of development in a broad evaluative framework wherein development ultimately means the quality of life and the progress of societies toward values expressed in various cultures. *How* development is pursued is no less important than *what* benefits are gained. Although development can be fruitfully studied as an economic, political, technological, or social phenomenon, its ultimate goals are those of existence itself: to provide all humans with the opportunity to live full human lives. Thus understood, development is the ascent of all persons and societies in their total humanity.[19]

The dual nature of development as an array of competing images of the good life and as a social change process is best understood by focusing on the value conflicts it poses. These conflicts, which make up the subject matter of development ethics, are found in four different arenas:

- debates over *goals*: economic growth, the provision of basic needs, cultural survival, ecological balance, transfers of power from one class to another;

- divergent notions of power, legitimacy, authority, governance, competing *political systems*;

- competition over resources and over rules of access to resources, competing *economic systems*; and

- pervasive conflicts between *modern* modes of living (with their peculiar rationality, technology, social organization, and behavior) and *traditional* ways of life.

Development ethics functions as a kind of "disciplined eclecticism." Four traits characterize any intellectual discipline: the *systematic* pursuit of knowledge in ways which are *cumulative, communicable,* and *verifiable*. Development ethics is *eclectic* in its choice of subject matter, but in this fourfold sense *disciplined* in its study of it. Behind all its operations lies a clear unifying mission: to diagnose value conflicts, to assess policies (actual and possible), and to justify or to refute valuations placed on development performance.

The present book is organized around this triangular axis: diagnosis, policy, and values in development (see Figure 1: The Pedagogical Triangle). It explores the linkages or circulation systems that connect or fail to connect these three elements across a wide spectrum of issues.

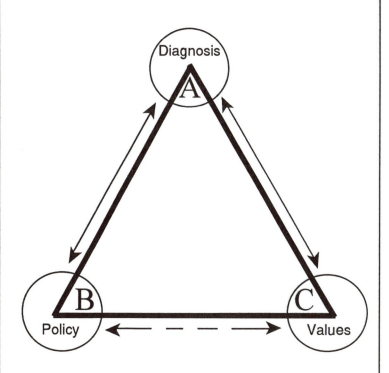

Figure 1:
THE PEDAGOGICAL TRIANGLE

A = Diagnosis.   Key Questions: What Is the Problem?
                                   Why (Causes)?

B = Policy.   Key Questions: Boundaries of Policy Arena,
                                   Actors, Actions, Effects, *etc.*

C = Values.   Key Questions: Whose Values? How Do They
                                   Interact with A & B, *etc.*?

Arrows = Circulation systems which link (or fail to link) the three
         vertices.

2.

NATURE AND METHODS

Development ethics critically explores development's competing goals, alternative strategies for reaching these goals, and the criteria invoked for assessing costs in pursuing desired social changes. The present chapter, after examining the various levels at which ethical discourse is conducted, sets forth the epistemological foundations, subject matter, methods, and tasks of development ethics.

Levels of Ethical Discourse

Ethical discourse is conducted at four distinct levels: general ends, criteria which specify when these ends exist in concrete situations, systems of interrelated means which constitute strategies for pursuing the ends sought, and individual means taken separately.

In questions of social change the sharpest ethical disagreements arise in the two middle realms—criteria specifying when desired goals are effectively reached, and the system of means deployed to obtain targeted objectives.

Discussion over general ends rarely engenders debate because such ends are deemed to be universal and are easily disguised behind verbal smokescreens. Even tyrants profess to cherish freedom and warmongers to seek peace. Hence many apparent debates over general ends—ideal conceptions of justice, freedom, reciprocity, equity—are, in truth, controversies over the concrete marks or institutions by which the presence of these ideals can be detected. In reality, therefore, they are debates over the second level of ethical discourse, *viz.*, specifying criteria. And the fourth level, that of individual means, breeds little discord because each means, taken in isolation, can usually be put to a good or to a bad use and cannot be characterized as ethically good or bad except by reference to diverse circumstances, motivations, constraints, and consequences. That most arguments should rage at the two middle levels is not surprising once it is recalled that methodological differences often mask ideological divergences. One's ethical stance on ends is dramatically revealed in the means one adopts to pursue them. Consequently, development ethics as "means of the means" requires not that moralists pose ideal goals and pass judgement on the means used by others to pursue these or other goals, but rather that decision-makers, versed in the constraints surrounding vital choices, promote the values for which oppressed and underdeveloped groups struggle: greater justice, a decent sufficiency of goods for all, and equitable access to collective human achievements in technology, organization, and research. Indeed, development practitioners ought to adopt as their "moral imperative in development" those strategies that harness existing social forces to implement the values to which they give their allegiance. This means preferring strategies, programs, and projects (and even modes of reaching decisions) that assign more importance to ethical considerations than to mere technical criteria of efficiency.

In ideal circumstances, ethicists would share responsibility for the practical consequences of joint decisions taken by teams of development planners, economists, and technicians. Unless economists, planners, and technicians assess the ethical import of their decisional criteria from inside the dynamics of their respective specialties, however, they will fall prey to the determinisms of "pure technique." Conversely, ethicists need to receive critical input from problem-solvers if they are to avoid purely extrinsic moralism. Only dynamic interaction between the two categories of critical interlocutors can lead to the formulation of ethical strategies which operate as a "means of the means."

Development ethicists need to have a clear view of their tasks and functions. Their first task is to raise high certain banners to proclaim certain values:

- the primacy of needs over wants;

- obligations incumbent on favored nations and populations to practice effective solidarity with those less favored, based in justice and not merely in charity;

- an insistence that the demands of justice are structural and institutional, not merely behavioral or reducible to policy changes; and

- an exegesis of politics as the art of the possible which defines the role of development politics as that of creating new frontiers of possibility and not merely manipulating resources (of wealth, power, information, and influence) within given parameters of possibility.

Development ethicists must present a convincing rational case for the values just enunciated. They must offer persuasive reasons why solidarity and not some version of enlightened self-interest should be the ethical norm.

The second essential task of development ethics is to formulate ethical strategies for multiple sectoral domains, ranging from population policy to investment codes, from aid strategy to norms for technology transfers and criteria for evaluating human rights compliance.

Ethicists can strategize only by entering into the technical and political constraints of any problem domain and rendering explicit the value costs and benefits of competing diagnoses and proposed solutions to problems. They must also establish criteria and procedures by which technical, political, and managerial decision-makers may choose wisely, and implement at the lowest cost possible, what Berger calls making the calculus of pain and the calculus of meaning.[1]

Three rationalities or basic approaches to logic converge in decision-making arenas: technological, political, and ethical rationality.[2] Each has a distinct goal and a preferred *modus operandi* (Figure 2: Three Rationalities). Problems arise because each rationality tends to treat the other two in reductionist fashion, seeking to impose its peculiar view of goals and procedures on the entire decision-making process (Figure 3: Interaction of Three Rationalities—What Is). The resulting decisions may be technically sound but politically foolish or ethically repulsive; or in other cases, ethically sound but technically inefficient or politically impossible. The three rationalities ought to operate in a circular rather than a vertical pattern of interaction. This is the only way to avoid reductionism and guaranteed bad decisions (Figure 4: Interaction of Three Rationalities—What Ought To Be). No less than economic planners and other developmental problem-solvers, ethicists must earn their right to speak theoretically and nor-matively about development by engaging in action, or at least in con-sultation, with communities of need. More consciously and intention-ally than other development specialists, ethicists need to undergo a professional revolution of attitudes or conversion that weans them away from elite values and allegiances to the values and allegiances of those who are left powerless and stripped of resources by the "nor-mal" operations of resource transfers.[3] It is from within the con-straint systems enveloping all development decisions that ethicists must establish the phenomenology of values at play in those decisions and actions.

Epistemological Foundations[4]

Development ethics rests on the epistemological premise that the study of the human condition is valid only when it takes place simul-taneously on the level of positive science and on the evaluative level of philosophy.

If dialogue between social scientists and philosophers is to be fruitful, both must make a first global approach to the reality studied. This pre-scientific and pre-philosophic approach is "existential" in the sense that one engages in it with everything one is—one's intelli-gence, sensitivity, affective powers, and entire experience. Inasmuch as any individual's experience is situated in a given place, this experi-ence is necessarily limited, conditioned, and subjective. Nevertheless, this first attempt to approach a human experience embues researchers with the sense of the whole which they must never thereafter lose. In the next step, it becomes incumbent upon scientific reflection to con-trol all the elements of this totality lying within its specialized capa-bilities. Critical philosophical reflection, in turn, needs to make a twofold use of the initial findings in its own critical elaboration: the findings observed as a vital whole, and the findings as analyzed with rigor by each specific scientific discipline.

It is on this common foundation, and on all specialized studies

Figure 2:
THREE RATIONALITIES

DEFINITION OF RATIONALITY:

- A mode of thinking.
- A universe of cognitive assumptions and methodological procedures.
- A body of criteria to establish truth or validity.

TECHNICAL RATIONALITY:

Goal: Get something done, accomplish a concrete task. Apply scientific knowledge to problem-solving.

Approach: Treat everything except the goal instrumentally. Eliminate obstacles and use aids efficiently. *Hard* logic.

POLITICAL RATIONALITY:

Goal: Assure survival of institutions, preserve rules of the game, maintain power position.

Approach: Compromise, negotiate, accommodate, "navigate." *Soft* logic.

ETHICAL RATIONALITY:

Goal: Promote, create, nurture, or defend certain values for their own sake.

Approach: Inherently judgmental: good or bad, fair or unfair, just or unjust. Relativizes all other goals and means. Logic can be *hard* or *soft* (ethic of acts, of intentions, of consequences).

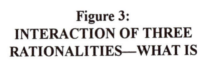

Figure 3:
INTERACTION OF THREE
RATIONALITIES—WHAT IS

(Vertical Pattern: *Reductionism)*

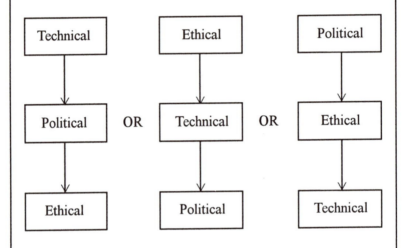

Assumption: Each rationality seeks to assert itself and win
assent from others as to the priority of its goals
and approach.

Figure 4:
INTERACTION OF THREE
RATIONALITIES—WHAT OUGHT TO BE

(Circular Pattern: *Mutuality)*

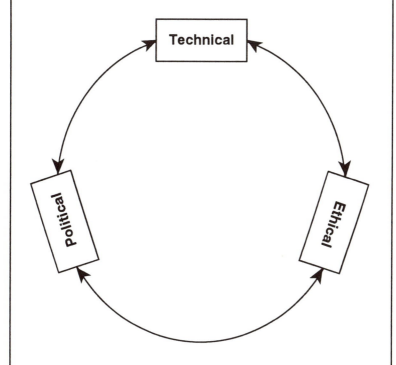

Assumption: Any form of knowledge is partial and risks mistaking itself for the whole, or dominating discourse with other forms.

undertaken from this point on, that all interdisciplinary work in development must be built.[5] This cognitive effort is a "journey along a common path." Specialists of individual disciplines should not try to persuade others of the conclusions of their own science or philosophy, but all should accept to retrace in the presence of others the description of their own personal formulation. As they listen to each one, others in the pluridisciplinary dialogue begin to perceive better than before how to relate their own viewpoint to that of others; new perceptions enter into play and critiques are formulated. What is achieved at the end of the road is a unified approach to a complex human reality. Social scientists who limit themselves simply to extracting a few testable hypotheses, which they can utilize from the original holistic data, inevitably distort these data. The reason is that the properly philosophical research on values formulates its own hypotheses at another level, one which is not immediately transposable into social science research hypotheses. More importantly, to insist on looking first of all merely for testable hypotheses is to miss the whole point of the problem, which is *primarily a problem of epistemology*; that is, of the critical study of different types of human cognition. Like all sciences, social scientists must question their own assumptions in terms of a critique of knowledge and of the requirements of action.

One cannot short-circuit or dispense with this sequence of operations lest one fall into the trap of bypassing the real problem in studying values, namely, the kind of construction to be wrought among all modes of knowing with a view to guiding development in the most human way possible.

Two types of bias are to be avoided. First is the bias of a latent and unavowed philosophical position. One must always be conscious of this danger and, in effect, science has proved very helpful in this domain by striving after objectivity even before it attempts to explain reality. Indeed, philosophy is above all an interrogation of reality and, as far as possible, of total reality. Second, there also exists the bias of a scientific hypothesis that runs the risk of interfering surreptitiously with facts and even of distorting them.

When it abstracts, science necessarily fragments reality. This procedure needs to be challenged in the specific case of value studies, although not in general terms; the reason is that values involve evaluational totality by definition, and not merely valuational fragments.

Social scientists become guilty of provincialism when, in the name of rigor, they limit the use of the term methodology solely to matters of quantitative technique applicable to empirical research situations. Methodology in the broad sense governs the larger facets of the scientific enterprise: the logic of theory construction and the derivation of analytic propositions from abstract concepts. If the subjective component in *value* is central, it follows that values cannot be reduced to mere objects of study.[6]

After scientific observation has been conducted, there follows a stage of "post-reflection" consisting of a phenomenological/philosophical treatment going far beyond mere correlational analysis or statistical inference. In addition to reducing ethnocentrism and empiricist bias, this treatment protects populations from having social change imposed upon them (wittingly or unwittingly) by elitist groups—native or foreign—in a manner which unduly raises the cost to them in human suffering and value destruction. Moreover, this procedure places researchers in a position of vulnerability toward the people they study.[7] No less importantly, it thrusts the values of researchers into the same arena of critical discourse as the values of the populace studied. Above all else, this method incorporates analysis into a larger framework wherein all syntheses are repeatedly tested against vital experiential perceptions.

Subject Matter

The Brazilian economist Celso Furtado judges that "economic development is, in the strict sense, a means. Nevertheless, it constitutes an end for its own sake, an irreducible element of the new generation's way of thinking."[8]

For the U.S. economic historian Robert Heilbroner, development is:

> . . . the first real act of world history. Certainly in size and scope it towers over any previous enterprise of man. . . . For the Great Ascent is not merely a struggle against poverty. The process which we call economic development is also, and in the long run primarily, a process through which the social, political, and economic institutions of the future are being shaped for the great majority of mankind.[9]

Ethical values are usually treated as categories subordinate to economic considerations. Thus human resource planners typically speak of upgrading manpower and increasing the pool of trained personnel in order to boost production or render bureaucracies more efficient. Human beings are not treated as something qualitatively different from other inputs in a productive machine: capital or raw materials. It is true that men and women must be treated instrumentally, but they must not be treated *only* as instruments, this in recognition of their non-instrumental self-validating worth as persons.

As presently conducted, development *absolutizes means, materializes value,* and *creates structural determinism.*

Absolutization of Means.   Ellul has analyzed the drive toward autonomy inherent in technology and denounced the fatalism with which instruments of destruction are used, simply because they exist and must be tried.[10] Similarly many economists, although they privately denounce the folly of treating development in economic terms alone, publicly recommend policies which grant absolute primacy to one particular manifestation of economics—namely, industrialized mass-consumption. Psychologists, sociologists, and anthropologists have likewise been seduced into lending their talents to the cause of promoting rapid social change regardless of human costs.[11] Those ends characterizing "underdeveloped" societies are relegated to the ashcan: personal communion as it is time-consuming, contemplation of nature's beauty for it is useless, community ritual because it is not functional. Upon first visiting New York City, the Swiss architect Le Corbusier complained that "skyscrapers are greater than their architects."[12] While building towering edifices, the architects of economic prosperity have shown themselves to be puny human beings. The fault lies not in their ambition—for economic well-being is an eminently good thing!—but they forget that a high standard of living, like "the Sabbath, was made for man, not man for the Sabbath!"[13]

Development Models Materialize Value.   Current models assume the sole motivational relevance of self-interest, the profit motive, personal mobility, the need for absolute power. Under such stimuli, it becomes practically impossible for developing societies to practice austerity. Instead come ostentation, bloated military or propaganda expenditures, showcase projects which do little to improve the lot of the masses.

There exist two kinds of materialism. One form is healthy and prevents religion or spiritual preoccupations from becoming the opium of the people (although Mumford remarks, not without irony, that in nineteenth-century England, it was opium that became the religion of the workers).[14] This brand of materialism is a needed safeguard against the idealist trap of regarding material wants as unimportant, or misery as a condition willed by the gods. Such outlooks imagine purity of soul to reside in indifference to matter. Nevertheless, because it is in matter —in their flesh and blood—that people suffer, virtue cannot reside in closing one's eyes to the materialities of life.

On the other hand, a second type of materialism dehumanizes: it turns human beings into manipulators and reduces their "being" to their "having,"—substituting worth (measurable in monetary terms) for value. In the words of Paul Goodman, this system "excludes human beings rather that exploits them."[15] This mindless and morally insensitive system believes that the "culture of poverty" is inferior to that of the middle class, and that poverty cannot be morally superior to depersonalized abundance. The social critic August Hecksher comments wryly that the more leisure modern urban man acquires, the more space he needs simply to store his gadgets: "[H]e is islanded in an encroaching sea of things. The closets are merely to take the unmanageable excess."[16]

Creation of Structural Determinism. Nations easily become prisoners of their myths as well as of their interests. The instrumentalization of ends reduces responsibility and freedom—the twin foundations of ethical choice. One can readily imagine, fifty years hence, a world in which poverty will have been abolished at the price of closing off value options to humans. Skinner's *Walden Two* can become the prototype of a bread-and-circus civilization on a planetary scale, faultlessly managed by social engineers relying on infallible reward mechanisms. The danger is real, for the very drive toward development tends to consecrate efficiency and productivity as absolute goals. Frustrations bred by widening inequalities constitute a strong temptation for desperate victims to resort to violence in the most efficient *(i.e.,* the most destructive and amoral) ways possible. Can ethics survive if humans thus continue to abdicate responsibility and freedom?

Not that we are irrevocably trapped: Goodman still sees "hope for reconstruction through conflict."[17] Nevertheless, whatever theoretical chances for success exist, only a massive effort of will—preceded by true comprehension of development's terms—can render a likely solution. Ellul pessimistically assesses humankind's chances of making this monumental effort of will. Three conditions must be filled for politics to be just, he argues: long-term foresight, the ability to posit acts which here and now do not seem necessary, and generosity. Regarding the second, Ellul contends that:

> ... a just solution can be found only if there is a considerable range of solutions. If, as a result of some development, choices have been progressively eliminated and, eventually, only one solution remains, inexorably imposing itself, such a solution will always be an expression of the strongest power supporting it, and *never* can be just. A solution imposed by necessity in political affairs cannot be just.[18]

Methods

Development thrusts three basic moral questions to the surface:

- What is the relation between the fullness of good and the abundance of goods?

- What are the foundations of justice in and among societies?

- What criteria should govern the posture of societies toward the forces of nature and technology?

Providing satisfactory normative and institutional answers to these questions is what makes a country developed. It follows, therefore, that not every nation with a high per capita income is truly developed. What renders these ancient moral questions specifically developmental, and the old answers to them obsolete, is the unique cluster of modern conditions.

The first modern condition is the vast scale of most human activities. In the size of its cities, bureaucracies, and factories, and in the sheer volume of images and fantasies which assault its senses, humankind has reached the point where a quantitative difference produces a qualitative change.

The second feature of modernity is technical complexity and the specialized division of labor which ensues therefrom. No single set of skills—manual, intellectual, or artistic—can equip us to cope adequately with all our needs for unity, integration, and openness to change. We crave new facts but are crushed by information overload and can find no wisdom to match our science, no unifying threads through which to weave the countless strands of our expanding knowledge. In such a world it becomes almost impossible to answer such disarmingly simple questions as: What is the good life? What is the relation between goods and good? What is the basis of justice and equity? What is the right stance toward nature and technology?

A third contextual feature of modern life is the web of interdependence that transforms local happenings into global events and causes international conflicts to impinge on local destinies. The growing interdependence of nations, communities, and individuals is a two-edged sword, simultaneously a good and a bad thing.[19] Starving populations in Somalia are rescued by food airlifted from Nebraska in the wake of a television report. But American weapons can also be used to kill innocent peasants in Guatemala for reasons unrelated to their local decisions or those of their national leaders.

The fourth and most dramatic modern condition is the ever-shortening time lag between changes proposed or imposed on human communities of need, and the deadline these communities face for reacting to these changes in ways which protect their integrity. Mass media, modern medicine, and technology constantly affect the consciousness, values, and destinies of people, leaving them scant time to take counsel with themselves, their traditions, or their images of the future in order to shape a wise response.

Thanks to these four distinctively modern conditions, the moral questions all societies faced in the past have now become contemporary developmental questions. By and large, however, these normative questions have been ignored by development experts and ethicists alike. Galbraith laments that "[T]he final requirement of modern development planning is that it have a theory of consumption . . . A theory of consumption—a view of what the production is ultimately for—has been surprisingly little discussed and has been too little missed

. . . More important, what kind of consumption should be planned?"[20] Should productive capacity be employed to produce a decent sufficiency of essential goods to meet the basic needs of all, or should it produce whatever goods will be bought by those who possess effective purchasing power? Most development experts avoid such value-laden questions, branding them unscientific or subjective. Ethicists, in turn, rarely take development processes and conflicts as the raw materials of their moral reflection. By remaining outside the dynamics of social change, however, they risk imprisoning themselves within sterile forms of moralism that are useless or positively harmful. Answers to the normative questions posed by development do not pre-exist in any doctrine, nor are they easy to supply. Neither ancient wisdoms interpreted in static fashion, nor uncritical modern scientific approaches suffice. Sound answers can issue only from new dialogues between ancient wisdoms and modern rationality in modes which avoid ethnocentrism, dogmatism, and ideological manipulation.

Ethics as "Means of a Means"

Not every way of articulating ethics is adequate to the task of integrating development's diagnostic and policy domains with its value realms. No abstract deductive ethics can serve, for the discipline of development is an art and not a science: it deals with decisions and actions taken in domains of high uncertainty, not with orderly or perfect patterns of logic or design. Great practical wisdom is required in development affairs. Wisdom brings unity out of multiplicity only after facing contradiction and complexity. In this, it is distinguished from naiveté, which is reached by avoiding contradiction and complexity. On the contrary, development ethics must pay attention to political and economic imperatives while recognizing that these operate in highly diverse settings marked by varied cultural antecedents, resource endowments, and explanatory meaning systems. In a word, development ethics must become a "means of the means." What does this enigmatic phrase signify?

In a critical study of Nietzsche published in 1975, the French philosopher Gustave Thibon reinstates:

> . . . the Nietzschean ideal of the sanctification of power. Here
> tofore power and purity could coexist, one separate from the

other. It was possible, without causing too much damage, for the first to remain spiritually impure and the second materially ineffectual simply because power had but limited means at its disposal: the worst whims of Caesars did not totally threaten the equilibrium and survival of humanity. But nowadays power disposes of almost infinite means of destruction; therefore, can we seek salvation elsewhere than in the union of force with wisdom?[21]

What Thibon seeks is not the legitimation of political power, but some way of converting power to a higher ethic.

Ethics cannot exorcise evil from realms of political power simply by preaching noble ideals: development ethics wields no prescriptive power unless it takes us beyond moralism.[22] Ethics must somehow get inside the value dynamisms of the instruments utilized by development agents and itself become a "means of the means."[23] Ethicists do not discharge themselves of their duty merely by posing morally acceptable values as ends of economic action. Nor does it suffice for them to evaluate, in the light of some extrinsic moral rule, the economic and political instrumentalities employed to pursue those ends. Rather, ethicists must analyze and lay bare the value content of these instrumentalities from within their proper dynamism. To illustrate, they must ask whether a policy of export promotion favors economic equity or not, whether it consolidates fragile local cultures or not. Ethicists must conduct a phenomenological "peeling away" of the value content—positive and negative—latently present in the means chosen by development decision-makers. Any moral judgement must relate in realistic terms to the technical data pertinent to the problem under study. Moreover, such a judgement must utilize those data in ways which professional experts can recognize as faithful to the demands of their discipline. It is in this sense that ethics must serve as a "means of the means," as a moral beacon illuminating the value questions buried within the instrumental means to which decision-makers and problem-solvers of all kinds resort.

Many ethicists who comment on social justice rest content with portraying ideal ends and passing adverse judgement on the means used by politicians, planners, or others to mobilize social energies. This approach fails because it remains outside the real criteria of decisions invoked by those who, in plying their craft as decision-makers, make and unmake social values.

Genuine ethics is a kind of praxis[24] which generates critical reflection on the value content and meaning of one's social action. Unlike the mere extrinsic treatment of means, ethical praxis conditions choices and priorities by assigning relative value allegiances to essential needs, basic power relationships, and criteria for determining tolerable levels of human suffering in promoting social change. Alternative development strategies, programs, and projects have varying impacts on populations victimized by poverty, economic exploitation, or political domination. For this reason, an ethic of social justice needs to harness concrete instruments in support of the struggle conducted by social classes at the bottom of the stratification ladder. It is a hollow exercise to speak rhetorically about human dignity unless one builds social structures fostering human dignity and eliminating obstacles to its attainment—endemic disease, chronic poverty, unjust systems of land tenure, and political powerlessness. A vital nexus links any society's basic value choices to its preferred development strategy and to the criteria it applies in all arenas of specific policy, be it employment, investment, taxes, or education.

Ethics is centrally concerned with the means of human action, but as Ginsberg notes: "[I]t is concerned also with the relative worth of the different ends in relation to the costs involved in attaining them, and this task it cannot fulfill adequately without inquiry into the basic human needs and grounds of our preferences and choices."[25] Certain values stand as ends worthy for their own sakes. Even if they cannot fully command action, these ends guide and orient, and the choice of appropriate means remains crucial. Ethics strives untiringly to become a "means of the means" by transmitting selected value allegiances and value criteria from inside the very instrumentalities and constraints surrounding decisions and actions. The greatest danger faced in this enterprise is that development ethicists will fall into the role played by plantation preachers in the days of slavery—namely, assuring good conscience to the rich while providing spiritual, "other-worldly" solace to the victims of unjust structures. Therefore, development ethicists cannot discharge their function merely by harnessing human aspiration or values to such developmental imperatives as growth, modernization, or even structural change. To do so is to treat human values in instrumental fashion as mere aids or obstacles to development goals uncritically accepted as self-validating values.

Ultimately, the whole development enterprise itself needs to be critically subjected to the value tests of justice, human enhancement, and spiritual liberation. It is these values which must pass judgment on development, not vice versa. These values can only judge development choices, however, by getting inside the concrete specificity of these choices. A sound epistemological reason exists for this: namely, that the closer any knowledge comes to human subjects—especially in their social context—the more difficult it becomes to sustain any real difference between the observed connections among phenomena and the organization of the ends of action.

The Essential Task

The essential task of development ethics is to render development actions humane to assure that the painful changes launched under the banners of development not produce anti-development, which destroys cultures and exacts undue sacrifices in individual suffering and societal well-being, all in the name of profit, an absolutized ideology, or some alleged efficiency imperative. The discipline of development ethics is the conceptual cement that binds together multiple diagnoses of problems with their policy implications through an explicit phenomenological study of values which lays bare the value costs of alternative courses of action.

Most fundamentally, however, the mission of development ethics is to keep hope alive. By any purely rational calculus of future probabilities, the development enterprise of most countries is doomed to fail. Poor classes, nations, and individuals can never catch up with their rich counterparts as long as these continue to consume wastefully and to devise ideological justifications for not practicing solidarity with the less developed. In all probability, technological and resource gaps will continue to widen and vast resources will continue to be devoted to destructive armaments and wasteful consumption. Catastrophes generated by environmental or demographic folly,[26] to say nothing of nuclear or radiation poisoning, are likely scenarios of despair. And in all likelihood, exacerbated feelings of national sovereignty will continue to co-exist alongside an ever-more urgent need to institute new forms of global governance and problem-solving. In any plausible scenario projected over the next fifty years, development will remain the privilege of a relative few, while underdevelopment will continue to be the lot of the vast majority. Only some transrational calculus of hope, situated beyond apparent realms of possibility, can elicit the creative energies and vision which authentic development for all requires. This calculus of hope needs to be ratified by ethics. Ellul writes eloquently of the need for hope in a time of abandonment.[27] He speaks in an openly theological vein, arguing that human beings cannot count on some *Deus ex machina* salvation from whatever gods they believe in. Only the human race can extricate itself from the human impasses—nuclear, ecological, economic, and political—it has itself created. Yet human beings will despair of even attempting to create a wisdom to match their sciences, says Ellul, unless they have hope and grounds for hope in some God who has entrusted the making of history to them.

In analogous fashion, development ethics must summon human persons and societies to become their best selves in order to create structures of justice and of what Ivan Illich calls conviviality[28] to replace exploitation and aggressive competition. There is hope for improvement, however, and the dismal scenario is not ineluctable. The basis for hope is provided by René Dubos and other sociobiologists, who remind us that only a tiny fragment of human brainpower has been utilized up to the present.[29] This means that Africans, Asians, and Latin Americans are capable of inventing new and more authentic models of development. They need not become the consumers of a single pattern of modern civilization in order to become "developed." In *The Coming Dark Age*, Robert Vacca[30] gloomily forecasts a world with no future. Development ethics offers a corrective view by insisting that human futures are not foreordained. Indeed, the most important banner to be raised high by development ethics is that of hope, hope in the possibility of creating new possibilities.[31] Although modern men and women have grown skeptical of facile utopias, they also understand that far more changes than were ever anticipated are possible.

Development ethics pleads normatively for a certain reading of history, one in which human agents are makers of history even as they bear witness to values of transcendence.[32] Marx expressed a profound truth in asserting that until the present we have only witnessed pre-history. The beginning of authentic developmental human history does indeed come with the abolition of alienation. And development's true task is precisely this: to abolish all alienation—economic, social, political, and technological.

3.

A RESEARCH MODEL

One approach to the study of values, little known in English-speaking development circles, is derived from long reflection on experiments in community development, educational planning, and the mobilization of urban and rural populations in several African countries, the Middle East, and Latin America. Its author is Georges Allo,[1] the late French social philosopher and rural community organizer. Allo's research method is based on a value critique undertaken by the populace itself.

The basic premises of his research orientation are that:

- all formulations used in studying values should be made in the language and symbols of the people being studied;

- value studies must focus on integrated patterns of total value orientations in a human community;

- total integrated patterns of value cannot be obtained if people are treated as mere *objects* of observation or of interrogation. They must engage in the process of studying their own values as *subjects*, as active judges of the study undertaken;

- images and conscious profiles of themselves held by individuals and groups express their values more adequately than descriptions, measurements, correlations, or classifications dealing with their economic activity, political life, kinship structure, or societal roles;

- while they are under study, members of developing societies should be allowed to appraise the value changes they are undergoing or which can be anticipated;

- empirical research procedures used by cross-cultural social science disciplines must be allied to philosophical and phenomenological modes of reflection. If the distortion produced by the fragmentation of value patterns is to reduced, this reflection should be conducted jointly by researchers and members of the culture studied;

- fruitful generalizations about values and scaled needs can be gained only from a permanent and disciplined dialogue among representatives of many value systems in the process of being challenged by modernity.

Values as they are experienced by living communities are distorted unless the hypotheses and research instruments used to study them are derived from a holistic view of these values in their pre-scientific human existential setting. Scientific fragmentation is inappropriate in this special domain because by definition values refer to *evaluational* totality as well as to *valuational* fragments. Whenever subjects "evaluate," they situate their values in an overall framework of standards they deem important. In order to do this, they must posit a reflective act and, at least implicitly, refer to a total pattern of meaning and worthwhileness. On the other hand, when they merely "valuate," subjects do not engage in this reflective action nor do they make a critical or judgmental reference to their total universe of standards. To "valuate" means simply that they make a selective preference to which they join some judgment about the suitability of their preference and of its object. It is because values contain an essentially subjective component that one cannot reduce them to being mere objects of study. Any procedure adopted to study values must respect the complex nature of values both as integral and integrative entities. Hence one cannot validly examine the values of an individual or society unless one understands the relative position of all that individual's or society's values in their totality. Abstraction and analysis are not thereby ruled out, but they become legitimate only at certain moments in a specified sequence. Indeed, fidelity to this sequence imposes itself as a normative principle. *The goal of a comprehensive research sequence is to achieve permanent evaluative synthesis of dynamic value profiles and to capture the meaning of the evolution of these profiles.* The stages in this process of permanent synthesis are as follows:

Preliminary Synthesis. The investigator solicits from acknowledged leaders in a community—and from popular spokespersons having no influence beyond their limited kinship or affective circles—their perception of what their total human existential situation is, what it means, and what it ought to be. Information is also obtained as to which changes are affecting them, how society's members assess these changes, what their understanding is of issues lying outside the purview of their daily concerns, and what degree of relevance or interest they attach to these issues. In order to obtain such testimonies, it is evident that researchers must engage in intimate and prolonged immersion in the environment under study. More importantly, they must establish relations of confidence with informants. Confidence comprises both trust and the willingness of interlocutors to confide or divulge intimate thoughts. From this phase of "pre-reflection," which precedes systematic empirical study, researchers obtain preliminary global notions of what is valuated and what is evaluated by a populace.

Systematic Observation. Under ideal conditions, systematic observation should then take place at four different levels. The first is primary groups or subsystems that constitute natural units of daily life. General observation can be conducted, for instance, on all aspects of life in a village or among an itinerant tribe. A second level of observation examines some limited sector of activity, such as work, recreation, worship, or familial relations. Third, there is the cultural system as a whole, whether it be the belief system (cognitive values), the set of norms, patterns of interaction, or the total network of social forces affecting cohesion and disruption. A fourth level touches upon the broad worldview or philosophy of life.

In these studies, social science disciplines are to play a major role. But, Allo contends, these studies can be valid only if areas of study are chosen and hypotheses derived from the psychic universe revealed to investigators in the first step of the research sequence, what is here termed the pre-reflection. This global first approach is the matrix from which empirical research orientations are to flow.

Reflective Synthesis by the Research Team.   The third stage in the process is the elaboration by the research team of a reflective and critically conscious synthesis, as distinct from the naive or unreflective synthesis of the first stage. Ideally, the research team ought to include members of the society under observation as well as trained outside investigators. All those who have taken the pulse of the populace in Stage 1 and conducted systematic study at any of the four levels in Stage 2 should then confront their findings as a group. The purpose of these sessions is to begin formulating a reflective synthesis of the value universe of the human group under study. This synthesis is not ingenuous or uncritical as it was in Stage 1, inasmuch as it is formulated at a more explicit level of consciousness than the earlier one. Moreover, it is elaborated only after the investigators themselves have influenced the consciousness of the population. The elements of this new systemization are drawn from findings obtained in prior stages, examined in the light of all available secondary documents and relevant parallel studies. Inasmuch as diverse interest groups, classes, partisans, and ideologies are represented, the resulting reflective value syntheses necessarily vary. Each partial synthesis is made to confront all the others in order to test the critical survival value of each and to probe inductively for possible generality, partial or total.

Feedback of Reflective Synthesis to Populace.   The final stage of the normative sequence consists in resubmitting the critical syntheses obtained in Stage 3 to the informants who provided the naive synthesis in Stage 1. The choice of appropriate terms and symbols to be used evidently depends on prolonged interaction between the research team and a representative portion of the interested populace. Informants of the initial phase may reject the synthesis elaborated, correct it, or accept it tentatively as a new outlook to be considered in their growing awareness of their own values and value evolution. They may endorse it, with or without qualifications, or they may not understand it.

Never must the research team arrogate to itself the right to interpret the problems of the native populace, which holds the final veto over the value synthesis elaborated. This synthesis delineates existing value constellations, interprets the significance of challenges posed (or proposed) to these constellations, and explores alternatives in terms of probable futures.

Allo's normative sequence launches a dynamic process of continuous synthesizing among values held, values proposed, and values newly embraced. Allo's endeavor is premised on the underlying belief that social science can best formulate hypotheses on value change after conducting a pre-reflection or global approach. The findings of empirical research are then subjected to a treatment that is not abstract or analytical, but critical and "dialogical" in nature. And finally, all knowledge obtained is to be tested through pedagogical action, which itself leads to mobilization.

PART II

ETHICAL STRATEGIES: GENERAL PRINCIPLES

4.

GOALS OF DEVELOPMENT

Achieving development is not a self-validating absolute goal but a relative good, desirable only with reference to a particular view of the meaning of life. It is the failure to perceive this relativity that leads many to equate the process of developmental change with its goal, thus mistaking an instrumental for a consummatory end. Although under certain aspects development is sought for its own sake, at a deeper level it is subordinated to the good life. As the UNDP's *Human Development Report 1992* observed:

> Human development is thus a broad and comprehensive concept. It covers all human choices in all societies at all stages of development. It broadens the development dialogue from a discussion of mere *means* (GNP growth) to a discussion of the ultimate *ends*. . . . The concept of human development does not start with any predetermined model. It draws its inspiration from the long-term goals of a society. It weaves development around people, not people around development.[1]

Nevertheless, as Harbison and Myers note, "there need be no conflict between the economists and the humanists. . . . The development of man for himself may still be considered the ultimate end, but economic progress can also be one of the principal means of attaining it."[2]

Development for What?

Developed economies are usually contrasted with subsistence economies, wherein life is shorter and is judged, in many respects, to be qualitatively "less human." Judgments about the greater or lesser quality of life can be made, however, only with reference to what constitutes human happiness and, more fundamentally, to what being human means. The human being has been variously defined as a feeble emergence of spirit, a rational animal, a potential freedom wrestling with absurdity, a network of stimulable ganglia, an illusion summoned to discover true self by liberation from self. This definitional diversity has generated multiple prescriptions for human happiness. Therefore, the question, "development for what?" necessarily elicits a host of answers. It also raises a multitude of new questions. Must relativity reign? Is the quest for a general answer illusory? If it is not, is agreement to be reached only be accepting some lowest common denominator linking all particular answers to questions of ultimate meaning?

The pluralism of answers given to these questions is not merely a fact to be tolerated, but is itself a value to be prized. Accordingly, although the goals of development are variously conceived, divergent answers can be meaningful even across boundaries of ideology, discipline, or historical circumstances. The reason is that at times identical goals are pursued for different reasons. To illustrate, Gandhi sought to improve India's standard of living in order to release his fellows from material cares and free them to cultivate spiritual wisdom. In contrast, Nehru pursued the same objective because he judged material well-being to be a constitutive ingredient of human happiness. Notwithstanding diversity over ultimate goals, there was agreement over proximate goals.

There are two levels at which one may pose the question, "development for what?": the level of ultimate meanings and that of practical choices. At the ultimate level, it is illusory to expect consensus. Action need not be paralyzed, however, because agreement is possible at the pragmatic level. Notwithstanding disagreement over ultimate meanings, all can agree that providing basic needs for all should enjoy priority over the satisfaction of capricious wants for a privileged few. All can likewise agree that excessive manipulation of "desire mechanisms" breeds senseless frustration and stifles freedom. Most individuals, both instinctively and reflectively, value life as a good, or at least as a lesser evil than death or annihilation. Mass misery is universally seen as destructive of life and as an evil. It is legitimate to state, therefore, that one of development's general goals is to foster life. Disagreements arise when we move beyond the confines of life-sustaining goods and seek to justify development on the grounds that it "enriches" life or makes it more "human." Here "culture filters" abound and render all answers problematic.

Even people alerted to the dangers of ethnocentrism, however, cannot avoid speaking of development in their own value terms. Those labeled as "universal" geniuses in literature bear the distinctive stamp of their particular culture: Dante is unmistakably Italian, Lao-Tze Chinese, Dostoyevsky Russian. Yet their art speaks to us in evocative tones that are not provincially or exclusively Italian, Chinese, or Russian. So too with "philosophers of development." As they strive to give expression to development's "universal" goals, they inevitably speak in registers clearly identifiable as Indian, Nigerian, Brazilian, or Egyptian. To illustrate, Cheikh Hamidou Kane's novel *Ambiguous Adventure*[3] depicts the anguish of a young Senegalese Muslim over the challenge posed to his values by the introduction of a modern school in his village. Yet Kane's message touches hearts which are neither Muslim nor African. So too with *Child of the Dark*,[4] Carolina Maria de Jesus' diary of life in a São Paulo *favela* (slum). So poignantly does Carolina capture the central emotions of life in the culture of poverty, that she speaks eloquently to Asians and Africans as well as to Latin Americans.

Consequently, one need not fear to speak in one's own value register as one strives to answer the question, "development for what?" Such overt value explication may indeed constitute a surer safeguard of "objectivity" than hiding behind some allegedly "value-free" mode of speaking impersonally and objectively. This very mode of "value-free" discourse bears the unmistakable brand of "Western" rationalism whenever it moves beyond the realm of purely descriptive empirical statements. No special mode exists which would enable one to speak non-ethnocentrically about development's ultimate purposes. One must enunciate one's value judgements and allow those from other cultures and value universes to respond with varying degrees of receptivity to one's proffered ideas. This being said, the claim now made is that development deals most centrally with the content given to the question, "what is the good life?"

Whenever development is studied as a particular kind of social change process, *quantitative* indicators are stressed—measures of income, productivity, output, literacy rates, occupational structure. When it is treated as a goal, however, development evokes an image of life deemed *qualitatively* better than its opposite, underdevelopment. Although planners and policy-makers frequently take goals for granted, their uncritical acceptance breeds confusion. Instead one should ask whether higher material living standards, self-sustained economic growth, technological efficiency, and specialized modern institutions (the uncritically assumed goals of development) are good in themselves or necessarily constitute the highest priorities of social effort.

The African-American social philosopher Robert S. Browne considers development to be an irreversible process. Nevertheless, he asks:

> What is our moral license to alter people's lives irreversibly in so fundamental a fashion? What evidence do we have that what we conceive of as development is an absolute good, or even an improvement over what those we "develop" now have? In view of population projections and the attendant ills anticipated from this explosion, ills not restricted to our ability or inability to feed the increased numbers but ills having to do with the very quality of life as the pressure of even greater numbers presses upon a fixed land area, can we be certain that even massive saving of life is justified?[5]

What are the goals of a society, regardless of its degree of development? Although no *a priori* claim is made here that universal goals exist, it is worth recalling with the anthropologist David Bidney that, "All absolutes are not necessarily ethnocentric, and all cultural ideologies are not of equal value. Belief in trans-cultural absolutes, in rational norms and ideals which men may approximate in time but never quite realize perfectly, is quite compatible with a humane policy of tolerance of cultural differences."[6] Bidney distinguishes "cultural universals" from "cultural absolutes" and supports Malinowski's view that there are cultural universals because there are universal human needs. All advocates of development, however they define it, pursue certain common objectives relating to the good life. *More impor-*

tantly, even societies which reject development can be shown, upon examination, to pursue this same goal—the good life.

The Good Life

In subsistence economies, life is short, disease rampant, poverty generalized, and opportunity limited. All these conditions readily appear to be, and are, "less human" than those that prevail after higher material levels of living are achieved. Most people are instinctively repelled by the "inhuman" quality of mass misery found in the streets of Calcutta or among the *fellahin* of Egypt. Paradoxically, however, the interpersonal relationships one observes in subsistence groups may appear more humanly satisfying, less impersonal, and more closely attuned to satisfying important human needs than the impersonal, anonymous mode of life in large cities. To use the term "less human" here is to assume that different qualities in human life can be detected and that certain visible signs point to what is "more human." Any judgment about the greater or lesser quality of life is impossible except with reference to what constitutes human happiness. Any culture or subculture may have "culturally absolute" values; the real problem is to discover whether there exist, in Bidney's terms, any "cultural universals." Do certain goods exist which development claims to provide and which are desired by all societies, developed and non-developed alike? Such goods need not enjoy the same relative importance on the scale of values of all societies: it is simply required that they be present in all. It is not necessary here to undertake an examination of all possible conceptions of development itself, or even of the good life. It suffices to ask whether we can identify common values which all societies desire and which development claims to foster.

In my view, three such values are goals sought by all individuals and societies: optimum *life-sustenance, esteem,* and *freedom.* These goals are properly universalizable, although their specific modalities vary in different times and places. They refer to fundamental human needs capable of finding expression in all cultural matrices and at all times.

Life-Sustenance. The nurture of life is treasured by sane men and women everywhere. Even in societies where human sacrifices were offered to propitiate deities or where female infanticide was practiced by parents desiring sons, the rationale for such violation of life was its putative contribution to overall vitality in the community or family. Moreover, all objects that satisfy a person's basic requirements for food, shelter, healing, or survival are life-sustaining "goods." There is a compelling truth in Mumford's assertion that:

> . . . real values do not derive from either rarity or crude man-power. It is not rarity that gives the air its power to sustain life, nor is it the human work done that gives milk or bananas their nourishment. In comparison with the effects of chemical action and the sun's rays, the human contribution is a small one. Genuine value lies in the power to sustain or enrich life . . . the value lies directly in the life-function; not in its origin, its rarity, or in the work done by human agents.[7]

The strongest argument invoked by "conservative" peasants in resisting proposed innovations (fertilizer, new seed, modern tilling practices) is precisely that life-sustenance is too important and too precarious to warrant "risk-taking" on their part. Modernizers, in turn, allege that these same innovations possess superior power to assure and maintain life. Underlying contradictory prescriptions regarding the vital activity of food-growing, we discover a common value, life-sustenance.

For this reason, no argument arises over the importance of life-sustaining goods. Developed and non-developed societies alike acknowledge that death control, a by-product of better nutrition and medicine, renders life more human by the simple fact that it allows more life to exist. Death control is unhesitatingly endorsed even by societies that reject birth control. Accordingly, wherever there is a dearth of life-sustaining goods—food, medicine, adequate shelter, and protection— absolute underdevelopment exists. One of development's most important goals is to prolong and render human lives less "stunted" by disease, harmful exposure to nature's elements, and defenselessness against enemies. Nevertheless, longer life appears *desirable* to people only after they become aware of its *possibility*. So long as people remain convinced that it is the will of the gods that their children die in infancy or to combat certain diseases is a sacrilegious act, people will accept hard, brutish reality and in their quest for wisdom will seek equanimity in doing so. The most shocking feature of stunted or shortened human life is precisely that it is unnecessary. The carriers of modern medicine's demonstration effects—tourists, missionaries, government health agents, development workers—have now reached the most remote areas of the world and brought to their inhabitants visible proof that life can be prolonged. Indeed, the average life-expectancy of a people is usually taken to be one of the main indicators of development. This acceptance reflects the salience of life-sustenance as a universal goal of development.

Esteem. A second universal component of the good life is esteem, every person's sense that he or she is respected as a being of worth and one that others cannot use as a mere tool to attain their purposes without regard for one's own purposes. Every individual and every society seeks esteem, identity, dignity, respect, honor, recognition. Poor "underdeveloped" societies with a profound sense of self-esteem suffer in their contacts with economically and technologically advanced societies because material prosperity has now become a widely accepted touchstone of human worthiness. Because of the status attaching to material success in "developed" countries, esteem is nowadays increasingly conferred only on those who possess material wealth and technological power—in a word, on those who have "development."

The universal human need for esteem explains both the frenetic desire of some societies to achieve development and the resistance by others to development's innovations. The first seek development in order to receive some of the esteem so prodigally dispensed to nations already developed. The second resist development because they feel deeply wounded in their own sense of worth, independently of levels of material living.

Galbraith comments with irony on the difference between poverty in England two centuries ago and poverty in the United States today. After citing William Pitt's remark that "poverty is no disgrace but it is damned annoying," Galbraith counters that in the United States, "it is not annoying but it is a disgrace."[8] "Underdevelopment" is the lot of the majority of the world's populations. As long as esteem was dispensed on grounds other than material achievement, it was possible for a society to resign itself to poverty without feeling disdained. Once the essential ingredient of the good life becomes material welfare, however, it becomes difficult for the materially "underdeveloped" to feel respected. One may deplore the materialistic bias of prevailing standards governing status attribution, but it is nonetheless true that the poor need to climb out of their wretched condition in order to gain the esteem of others so crucial to the preservation of their own internal sense of worth. Just as nineteenth-century Japan embarked on the path of industrialization in order to avoid humiliation by technologically and militarily superior "barbarian" Western powers, today Third World countries pursue development in order to gain the esteem denied to societies living in a state of disgraceful "underdevelopment." Once the deprivation of esteem reaches an intolerable point, a society is quite ready to begin desiring material "development." Obviously, wealth can also be sought for motives other than esteem. Nevertheless, as long as esteem is not associated with material abundance by a populace, that populace is apt to remain indifferent to the material benefits of "development."

In the dominant worldview of most traditional societies, the fullness of *good* (some ideal image of the good society and the worthwhile human life) is distinct from, when not opposed to, the abundance of *goods*. Although this view need not romanticize misery, it profoundly mistrusts individual acquisitiveness and challenges the ethical merits of the systematic and competitive pursuit of wealth by an entire population. Therefore, under the pressure to improve their capacity to sustain life, and prodded by the need to gain respect in a world where modern technology and material abundance enjoy monumental prestige, traditional societies launch their quest for abundance. Thus they legitimize development as a goal because it is an indispensable way of gaining esteem. In certain other cases, however, that very same need for esteem is the reason why societies resist development. If the impact strategy consciously or unconsciously employed by change agents humiliates a community, its need for self-respect leads it to reject change. In this sense, esteem, like life-sustenance, is a universal goal of societies: whether they accept or reject development the same value lies behind the choice made.

Freedom. A third transcultural component of the good life, valued by developed and non-developed societies alike, is freedom. Although countless meanings attach to this word, at the very least it signifies an expanded range of choices for societies and their members, along with the reduction of constraints in the pursuit of some perceived good. To regard freedom as a general goal of developed and non-developed societies is not to assume, however, that all communities seek political freedom to govern themselves, or that all individuals wish to determine their own personal destinies. As Erich Fromm warns, even in "developed" societies most people seek to "escape from freedom."[9] The escape from freedom's responsibility is usually associated with an individual's desire for security. At the societal level, however, security can be conceptualized as freedom *from* unforeseen or uncontrollable dangers, although it is not necessarily freedom *for* self-actualization or for the exploration of some possibly exhilarating unknown good. Most individuals wish to have only that degree of freedom which they need to engage in spheres of activity for which they feel competent and wherein the use of their skills is satisfying. Inasmuch as for most people these spheres comprise a very circumscribed orbit, to step outside them is to flirt with unmanageable anxiety.

Whatever holds true at this psychological level, however, it can nevertheless be claimed that development is perceived as one way to emancipate oneself from the structural servitudes of ignorance, misery, perhaps even of exploitation by others. To this extent at least, it is a search for a *freedom from*, even if not a *freedom for* actualization of one's self and group. Admittedly, the proposition that freedom is enhanced by development is not self-evident.

Hannah Arendt, alert to the new constraints that must be imposed if development is to be successfully launched, believes that under no circumstances can economic growth "lead into freedom or constitute a proof for its existence."[10] One cannot isolate this dimension of freedom, however, from two others no less crucial: (a) the prior degree of freedom (economic, psychological, and political) extant in a society before it launches itself into development, and (b) the realistic alternatives open to one in the global context of competing forces.

As for the first, societies pay a high price for remaining underdeveloped: unnecessary deaths, exploitation of masses by privileged classes, low occupational mobility for most people. The Brazilian economist Celso Furtado explains:

> . . . the masses in the underdeveloped countries have not generally put the same high valuation on individual liberty that we do. Since they have not had access to the better things of life, they obviously cannot grasp the full meaning of the supposed dilemma between liberty and quick development . . .

the liberty enjoyed by the minority in our society is paid for by a delay in general economic development, hence is at the expense of the welfare of the great majority. . . . Very few of us have sufficient awareness of these deeply inhuman characteristics of underdevelopment. When we do become fully aware, we understand why the masses are prepared for any sacrifice in order to overcome it. If the price of liberty for the few had to be the poverty of the many, we can be quite certain that the probability of preserving freedom would be practically nil.[11]

Real Choices

A basic disagreement pits those who base their definition of freedom on external political forms against those who grant primacy to emancipation from alienating material conditions of life or psychological constraints. Notwithstanding Arendt's case against freedom, however, it is difficult to disagree with W. Arthur Lewis' contention that the "advantage of economic growth is not that wealth increases happiness, but that it increases the range of human choice."[12] Wealth makes it possible for men and women to gain greater control over their environment than if they remained poor, to choose greater leisure, to have more goods and services.

Development also imposes new disciplines, however, and in the long run may even place people at the mercy of technological determinisms over which they have little control. Of greater import, however, is the range of real alternatives available to them. Most societies have little choice but to come to terms with development: they simply are not free to reject it outright. For as Lewis commented over forty years ago: "[T]he leaven of economic change is already working in every society—even in Tibet—thanks to the linkage of the world which has been achieved in the past eighty years by steamships, by imperialism, by airplanes, by wireless, by migration, by Hollywood, and by the printed word."[13] Aspirations rise faster than the production needed to satisfy them, and death rates decline more rapidly than birth rates. These two occurrences introduce elements of imbalance into non-developed societies, making it impossible for them to postpone decisions regarding the kind and speed of development they may contemplate. It may perhaps be aesthetically satisfying to keep a portion of the world "pure" and free from modernity—a kind of cultural game preserve for human beings analogous to our wild-fowl sanctuaries. But in real life, no group can long remain beyond the reach of the disruptive influences unleashed by development.

Throughout the world, isolated communities are being denied the alternative of shielding themselves from development. The issue then becomes: what margin of freedom can they conquer to fulfill even their minimal purposes, such as survival and the protection of cultural identity? Whether they choose to pursue development at full speed, to resist it, or simply to postpone it, they do so in order to protect or enhance some perceived freedom to be and to do. The most pressing question for them becomes, therefore, the relationship between freedom and economic well-being.

Although within modern societies it is widely assumed that freedom increases as humans possess more goods, this view contradicts numerous traditions for whom wisdom consists in minimizing one's desires. Sahara Bedouins, for instance, look with scorn upon individuals who "need" a multitude of encumbering objects; they believe a person's freedom is inversely proportional to the quantity of goods one needs to have. Gypsies in southern Spain pass similar judgment on those who are not "free" to roam at will because they are "tied down" *to* their possessions and, ultimately, *by* them. Does greater freedom result from having fewer or more goods? Much depends on what level of freedom is at issue. The point is that freedom is valued both by those who pursue development and by those who reject it. This is why freedom, along with life-sustenance and esteem, must be included as a universalizable component of the good life.

Irrespective of its possible other purposes, development has for all groups at least the following objectives:

- to provide more and better life-sustaining goods to members of societies;

- to create or improve material conditions of life related in some way to a perceived need for esteem; and

- to free men and women from servitudes (to nature, to ignorance, to other men and women, to institutions, to beliefs)

considered oppressive. The aim here may be to release individuals from the bondage of these servitudes and/or to heighten
their opportunities for self-actualization, however conceived.

This analysis of development goals suggests that a wide range of
judgments is possible as to the degree to which "development" or some
component of it—*e.g.*, the rationalization of work procedures to raise
productivity, merit systems of status conferral, or large-scale urbanization—does in fact lead to a "better" life or not. Development, as
generally practiced, implies one particular image of the good life. Yet
there is no guarantee that, *all things considered,* this image is more
appropriate or more satisfying than others. The qualifying phrase
"all things considered" acknowledges that individuals in developed
societies can control disease, prolong life, and provide themselves with
defense against the ravages of the weather and natural catastrophes.
Nevertheless, no evidence exists that "developed" persons are either
happier or more "human" than their "underdeveloped" counterparts.
It is only because of their greater ability to influence events that developed societies have been able to impose a disjointed economy characterized by domination and structural vulnerability on societies which,
although poor and perhaps even economically stagnant, formerly enjoyed considerable social cohesion and some form of harmony with
nature's cosmic forces. Similarly, it is only because of their greater
power that rich industrial countries can portray "development" itself
to the Third World as necessary, if not as desirable. The cohesion and
harmony just evoked cannot long survive the onslaught of forces which
have been unleashed by the "developed" agents and which impinge on
societies already wounded by those agents. Hence the ancient goals
of protecting life, of nurturing esteem, and of freeing oneself as much
as possible must now become the criteria against which development
itself is to be judged. It is not these goals which must be judged by
development.
    Much confusion over goals arises because its champions assume
that development necessarily enhances life-values, esteem, and freedom. The larger processes at work in the world today, however, place
Third World countries in a vulnerable position in which their most
cherished conceptions of esteem and freedom are attacked.[14] Even if

they perceive development's material "benefits" as enhancing their capacity to sustain life, they understandably fear that development may destroy their esteem in a highly competitive world and that it will free them from some constraints only to plunge them into others.

Conflicting Goals

What significance one attaches to development matters greatly. At a gathering of scholars in Rheinfelden, Switzerland, in 1960, the French political philosopher Raymond Aron argued that even if material scarcity could be universally abolished, societies would place different interpretations on the meaning of their material prosperity.[15] George Kennan, his American counterpart, argued that developed societies can do little more than provide members with a "reasonable stake of choices" with which to occupy their leisure time. This remark led the Swiss philosopher Jeanne Hersch to object that human life goes far deeper than the range of choices available for achieving cultural or personal fulfillment. In her view, human life includes mysterious tragic elements, and no degree of "development" can truly solve problems of identity and meaning. Hersch feared that exaggerated material development could render people powerless to make profound value choices because they will have become "distracted" (in Pascal's sense, "diverted") by the abundance of goods and activities from properly human considerations.[16]

Development, therefore, no less than does underdevelopment, poses profound value problems. Any concept of human fulfillment is highly relative. Although development's general goals are optimal life-sustenance, esteem, and freedom, no priority ranking among these goals can be established except as a function of some particular image of the worthy or the fulfilled human life. Even this formulation remains ambiguous since for many the exercise of freedom is itself taken to be the highest form of human actualization. The interplay among development's goals is dialectical: life-sustenance, esteem, and freedom interact in ever-shifting patterns of mutual reinforcement or conflictual tension. A high degree of freedom from wants and of self-esteem is compatible with a society having low life-sustenance or low out-group esteem, provided disruptive effects from outside are weak. If a materially poor society is sheltered from competing images of the good life, and if its wants remain few and simple, it can subsist with a high degree of social cohesion and member satisfaction. "Remote" cultures are doubtless finding it ever more difficult to isolate themselves from modernity. Nevertheless, the basic options any society takes as to goals affect its central institutions: its form of government, educational system, and economic incentives.

Conversely, economic abundance and high prestige are compatible with low levels of genuine want-satisfaction, low self-esteem, and low freedom. A "developed" society's wants may increase so rapidly as to be insatiable. The combination of expanding wants, industrial power, and technological modernity can bring prestige to such a society while leaving its members profoundly dissatisfied and insecure as to their identity. Numerous combinations of the three factors are possible. An important qualitative difference must be recognized between freedom *from* wants and freedom *for* wants. The first exists when genuine human needs are adequately met, the latter when men and women control the dynamisms by which their wants are multiplied. The essential point is not how many wants can be met, but the degree of mastery individuals exercise over the forces by which their wants are generated. If entry into mass-consumer economic patterns is achieved in alienating fashion, it creates a society wherein a contradiction exists between happiness and freedom.

One source of trouble is the discontinuous and unequal development enjoyed by countries and social classes. Countries once colonized or now dominated, economically or culturally, need to assert their nationalism virulently in order to wage war against underdevelopment. Developed nations, on the other hand, must limit their sovereignty if harmful structural domination effects are to be neutralized. Identical norms cannot be applied to all types of nations. It is likewise with tariffs: non-industrial countries need high tariffs to nurture fragile incipient industry, whereas industrialized countries should lower tariffs to admit Third World goods to buyers' markets. Until all countries accept global solidarity and complementarity on the basis of acknowledged need-priorities, double standards in politics or trade will appear irrational or unjust to some. And given the present disparities among nations, authentic solidarity among them cannot be gained without serious conflict. Consequently, the manner in which conflict is envisaged takes on decisive importance.

Within consensus models of society, harmony is presumed to be normal and conflict is deemed subversive. Such models assume that existing institutions are just. Where underdevelopment prevails, however, and notwithstanding a facade of legality, existing structures are often structurally unjust and often devoid of legitimacy. When this is the case, conflict may be necessary to challenge established disorder. The history of revolutionary movements attests to their potent institution-building role. The sociologist Orlando Fals-Borda has described the transformations wrought in Colombia's rural society in the wake of guerrilla activity.[17]

Not all conflicts arise from armed revolution, however; they may emerge from campaigns to politicize peasants, to organize urban workers into a labor union, or to launch a cooperative. Resulting conflicts generate more developmental energies than does placid social harmony.[18] Conflict enables peasants to "integrate" themselves to urban society, thereby expanding their networks of solidarity. The general lesson is that where the domination of the strong relies for its maintenance on the apathy of the weak, conflict is a breeding ground for the growth of *solidarity* among those who hitherto formed an inactive mass. True solidarity grants powers of self-disposition to those who practice it. Consequently, disharmony is often a necessary prelude to the solidarity required for development.

The history of relations between underdeveloped and developed nations has rendered social scientists increasingly skeptical of consensus theories. Horowitz considers that "dissensus, while dysfunctional with respect to the ruling powers, is quite functional for the newly emergent nations."[19] Consensus based on mass apathy or the manipulation of a populace by an elite is sham consensus. And solidarity founded on threats to those who "rock the boat" of social equilibrium is fragile. "Any serious theory of agreements and decisions must at the same time be a theory of disagreements and the conditions under which decisions cannot be reached."[20] Because it expresses social needs and aspirations, conflict is a prerequisite for solidarity. Even radical Marxists view class warfare as the political vehicle for achieving non-conflictual solidarity within the entire society after the Communist revolution is over. What is thus stated in the language of one ideological system is true of all: whether conflict is judged to be disruptive or constructive, it is always viewed as disruptive or constructive in relation to some terminal condition of solidarity.

The practical question then becomes: how much solidarity is feasible at any given time? Where little solidarity has existed in the past, or where it has been based on the power monopoly of rulers strong enough to "paper over" dissent, the creation of genuine solidarity requires disruption of old rules of "cooperation." To succeed in this disruption, however, dissenters need to forge bonds of in-group solidarity far deeper than those imposed from above by superordinate rulers. Limitless sacrifices are required of genuine "subversives," who must subject personal ambitions to a larger cause and view the exploitation of others as an attack upon their own humanity. Even enemies are to be "re-educated," not destroyed or suppressed. The internal solidarity nurtured among partisans exemplifies the terminal solidarity of society as a whole after revolution triumphs. The dynamism of conflict turns out to be a luminous principle of development.

5.

STRATEGIC PRINCIPLES

Strategic principles are normative judgments as to how development goals ought to be pursued. They provide standards both for devising solutions to specific problems and for appraising performance.

The first strategic principle in development ethics states that, although human beings must surely "have" enough goods if they are to "be" good, the good life is not the abundance of goods. The second principle asserts the need for global solidarity to achieve development. Development is the integral ascent of all men and women and of all societies: it is the quintessence of cultural, spiritual, and esthetic maturation as well as of economic and social improvement. Solidarity is meaningless, however, if it is restricted: development's benefits are to extend to all societies and to every person in society.

First Principle: To "Have Enough" in Order to "Be More"

Abundance of goods and fullness of good are not synonymous: one may *have* much and *be* mediocre or *have* little and *be* rich. Nevertheless, we need to have a certain quantity of goods in order to be fully human, and certain kinds of goods enhance our being more than others. These statements cannot be understood unless we first explain why humans need to "have" goods at all.

All living organisms must go outside themselves to be perfected.

A fully perfect being would have no desires at all; or if it had them, it could draw upon its own inner existential wealth to satisfy them. Needs felt by human beings express the particular dynamism of their conditioned existence in time and space. The ontological significance of needs resides in this: if humans were fully perfect, they would not need to need. If, on the other hand, they were totally imperfect, they would be incapable of needing certain goods. An illustration is found in comparing a withered hand, incapable of feeling a burn, to a healthy one, which senses the painful stimulus caused by fire and reacts to protect itself. Humans have needs because their existence is perfect enough to be capable of development, but not perfect enough for them to realize all their potentialities at one time or with their own resources. Humans need to draw other beings into their orbit in order to sustain their own precarious act of existence, for unless their existence is nurtured they revert to nothingness.

Biological needs dictate the assimilation of outside elements: air, food, water. Beyond survival, however, humans also seek goods capable of enriching and enhancing their existence. By desire, choice, action, passion, and fulfillment they add new qualities to their naked act of being. The "need" humans feel for non-essential things is a summons for them to be more: when they "have" things they "are" more fully than they were previously. "To have" helps them "to be." So true is this that unless they "have" minimum goods, they cease to "be" altogether. Even when they have enough to be, however, they feel stunted in their being until they *have more*, this in order *to be more*.

"To have," in the ontological sense, is not to own in economic or juridical terms, but to assimilate for vital inner purposes. Juridical and economic notions of property are derivative. It does one no good to legally "own" such vital goods as air or food unless one can use and absorb them. And it makes no difference who legally "owns" these goods, provided the one in need has access to them and effective use of them. Legal possession or economic property becomes relevant only to the extent that scarce objects cannot be interiorized or assimilated by a living being unless they are first "possessed." Possession is a relational term: an object is possessed only with reference to someone who is excluded from use. Clearly, this has nothing to do with possessing internal riches, such as knowledge, talent, virtue, or health. Internal riches are distinct as a category from external goods, the kind presently under discussion. At any given time, humans *are* less than what they can *become*; and what they can become depends largely on what they can *have*. In order to become more, we must have "enough." The central questions thus become: How much is enough? And does the term "enough" have any objective meaning?

How Much Is Enough? "Enough" is a relative term when applied to some quantity of goods deemed necessary to human fulfillment. No one can say how much is enough without first stating what a person's capabilities are and how important it is for one to develop these capabilities.[1] Notwithstanding the multiple relativities brought to light by anthropologists and psychologists, we can make sense out of the seemingly unmanageable question, "How much is enough?" General agreement exists that "excessive" poverty stunts human lives—misery is hell, and disease, apathy, and escapism diminish humanity. To have "enough" must therefore mean, at a minimum, that the basic biological needs of humans are met sufficiently so that they can devote part of their energies to affairs beyond subsistence.

Human life, however, is considerably more than mere survival, a full stomach, or a warm body. If the goals of development are optimal life-sustenance, esteem, and freedom, men and women need those goods without which they cannot gain secure sustenance, esteem and freedom. An even wider range of goods may be psychologically and socially necessary to live the "good life." Although we swim here in the high seas of linguistic and conceptual relativity, it nonetheless remains true that most humans, once they awaken to modern possibilities, desire some share in the collective knowledge and discovery of the world's mastery over nature, which their fellow humans have achieved. Accordingly, educational and informational needs acquire new importance even for humble farmers, pastoralists, and artisans. Consequently, such people may genuinely come to "need" newspapers, books, radios, and television sets.

Needy human beings lack "enough," not only relative to what affluence others possess but in absolute terms as well. Regardless of what others have, millions of people lack enough goods to live lives worthy of the human condition. Whatever the theoretical difficulties of defining "enough," none can deny that millions of paupers in Bangladesh or Sudan do not have "enough" to live human lives. And who can seriously affirm that there is no difference between the struggle for survival waged by a Guatemalan sharecropper or a Tamil tea estate worker and the placid need-satisfaction of prosperous business executives or professionals? After surveying living conditions of factory workers a century and a half ago, Engels protested that "workers' dwellings of Manchester are dirty, miserable and wholly lacking in comforts. In such houses only inhuman, degraded and unhealthy creatures would feel at home."[2]

It is not moral passion but the knowledge of factual conditions which leads us to view extreme poverty as an "inhuman" state of affairs. There is manifestly something anomalous in world economic structures which allow millions to live in squalor while others tax their ingenuity to find new ways of wasting goods. While millions suffer deficiency diseases caused by malnutrition, a favored few fall prey to hitherto unknown degenerative diseases induced by excessive food and drink. Under such circumstances, it is foolish to claim that the notion of "enough goods" is a purely relative one not amenable to analytical or operational precision. The stark illogical fact is that millions do not have enough food, medicine, clothing, and shelter to live human lives. Their quest for full humanity is thwarted by an absolute insufficiency of goods. Persons driven by chronic hunger are either obsessed with food or grow apathetic. When one has no defense against sickness or death, one either clings to life with animal ferocity or one vegetates in resigned expectation of fate. In both cases, one becomes something less than human. Although even destitute individuals may at times display remarkable wisdom, lucidity, fortitude, and creativity, such exceptional moral triumphs testify to the indomitable strength of the human spirit, not to the adequacy of their social conditions.

This absolute dearth of necessities is aggravated by a growing awareness among the world's poor of shocking inequalities and of technology's power to abolish misery. The poor instinctively comprehend, as did Gandhi, that there are enough goods in the world to meet the needs of all, but not enough to satisfy the greed of each one. The question, "how much is enough?" now takes on a surprising new dimension and is transformed into another and different question: Can rich individuals or affluent societies live worthy human lives in a world where masses lack essential goods?

No facile answer will do ever since Veblen and other analysts have convincingly traced the role of prosperity and leisure in producing culture.³ Great collective works of art and the seven wonders of the world have all been borne in travail on the backs of toiling slaves or exploited servants. And, as Galbraith once quipped, "wealth is not without its advantages and the case for the contrary, although it has often been made, has never been proved widely persuasive."⁴ One hesitates, therefore, to posit some absolute ceiling on wealth beyond which each additional possession would diminish the moral quality of its owner. For centuries, Western tradition has taught that "superfluous" wealth is morally acceptable if its owner puts it to a noble use or enjoys it in a noble spirit. Nevertheless, the possession of great wealth easily leads people to rationalize their insensitivity to the pressing needs of others. What we need to know is whether any essential ethical difference exists between "superfluity" as it was conceptualized in the past and as it is in the present. Contemporary global consciousness adverts to two facts: (a) the mass of men and women lack "enough" basic goods to live fully human lives; and (b) the technological means for eliminating misery exist. These means have not yet been harnessed to social institutions capable of achieving the goal of creating conditions that allow all to live human lives. In such circumstances, can the existence of "superfluous" wealth in the hands of a few individuals, classes, and nations be ethically justified?

Two divergent traditions as to the legitimacy of "superfluous" goods have co-existed within Christianity. One expresses "truth" in static terms, the other in dynamic evolutionary fashion. According to the static tradition, every individual has a "station in life" within which a given level of consumption is deemed to be morally acceptable. A king or princess may spend as befits a king or princess, but a modest yeoman's style of life should be that of one's yeoman peers. Anyone acquiring wealth beyond what is required to "maintain" oneself at one's proper "station in life" is morally bound to give part of his/her superfluous wealth to needier individuals or groups. As time passed, authorized interpreters of this principle introduced upward mobility into the concept of one's "station in life." A further refinement of the doctrine judged rich persons' moral worth by their overall contribution to the welfare of society, rather than by any specific allocation of wealth they made to the poor. Both schools of interpretation agreed with the ethical judgment of superfluous wealth formulated by early Fathers of the Christian Church, notably Basil the Great and John Chrysostom. The cardinal principle of this ethic declares that all wealth, natural and manmade, is destined by God to serve the needs of all. Consequently, one is permitted to "appropriate" wealth only in order to serve the common needs of humanity. Basil and Chrysostom minced no words, accusing the wealthy of having "stolen" whatever goods they possessed over and above their own needs.[5] Centuries later Gandhi also declared that pervasive poverty has a terrifying effect on those who enjoy wealth. "Whenever I live in a situation where others are in need," he said, "whether or not I am responsible for it, I have become a thief."[6] The Church Fathers taught that by giving alms the wealthy simply restitute what rightfully belongs to the poor. These and similar arguments were usually based on scriptural texts. They assumed that all Christians believed in a Creator who is the final judge of one's "stewardship" of wealth.

Abundance and Destitution.   Although a critical evaluation of these positions is not without historical interest, it is more pertinent here to analyze the notion of "superfluity" in the context of a secular world where plural views as to the origin and destiny of the universe compete. What is needed, in a word, is an inquiry into the basis for a *rational ethic* of the relations between abundance and mass destitution.

That absolute want co-exists alongside relative superfluity is an incontestable fact: over half of the human race lives in chronic deprivation while a small percentage of people wastes prodigiously. The relative excess of goods enjoyed by the minority contrasts sharply with absolute want in the majority. Does relative surfeit lessen the quality of human existence, however? Or, to state the question in different terms, does alienation flow from misplaced abundance as surely as it does from destitution?

The perpetuation of relative superfluity alongside absolute insufficiency for most people necessarily entails a collective stunting of the human race. Because contacts are unavoidable, the desires of the poor are constantly aroused (and frustrated) by demonstration effects. Predictably, the poor will not tolerate huge disparity if they suffer absolute want. If those in abundance continue regarding their own affluence as justified, they will perforce become insensitive to others' pressing needs. Now that the poor articulate their demands, one cannot in good faith close one's eyes to their misery. The privileged and the needy share a common faith in the power of technology to abolish misery. Yet, as Myrdal observes, the poor, "put part of the blame of their poverty on the rest of the world and, in particular, on the countries which are better off—or, rather they attribute the inequalities to the world economic system which keeps them so poor while other nations are so rich and becoming richer."[7]

As with individuals who are undernourished, insensitive individuals are stunted human beings. "Human quality" consists in perceiving reality as it truly is and in feeling compassion for fellow humans. One consequence of the rebellion by the wretched of the earth is to show humankind's privileged members that under pain of dehumanization, they can no longer adopt attitudes of equanimity and self-justification in the face of disparities which in former times seemed acceptable. Even if they have not been "guilty" of producing it in the past, the rich have now become "responsible" for abolishing absolute want in others. The distinction here invoked between responsibility and guilt is of crucial importance. Responsibility looks to the present and the future, and it presupposes freedom—that is, the possibility of responding to an exigency that is perceived and accepted. Responsibility is founded on the belief that human agents are not always subject to absolute determinisms, but rather that they can respond to the solicitation of goals perceived by them as humanly worthy. Precisely because we are human, we are "responsible" for creating conditions that optimize the humanization of life. Guilt, on the contrary, is the negative burden of past fault or injustice. Guilt is something passive and recriminating, not active and creative. In an illuminating essay on "collective responsibility," the French ethicist Pierre Antoine argues:

> . . . individuals, groups and nations which, even by ethical means, have secured for themselves an advantageous, strong and prosperous position in the world, and by so doing have impeded the economic development or the social promotion of other individuals or other peoples (even if only indirectly, because goods available on this planet are limited) are responsible to the latter for the deprivation and they ought to remedy it, by making use of the very possibilities which their better position confers on them . . . *an obligation rooted in justice can exist, as a consequence of our acts, even when no fault of injustice has been committed.*[8]

The "responsibility" of rich classes and nations for creating justice does not rest on some scapegoat theory of history branding them "guilty" of the unequal distribution of riches. Recent experiences between black and white communities in the United States demonstrate that the desire of well-meaning whites to redeem "guilt" feelings is the worst basis on which to base cooperative action with blacks. Moreover, a qualitative difference exists between neurotic guilt and what Maslow designates as "real" or "humanistic" guilt.[9] Because the rich are responsible for abolishing the absolute poverty of their fellow human beings, they refuse to do so only at the price of stunting their own humanity. For this reason, the maintenance of superfluity alongside massive absolute want is dehumanizing both for those who have and for those who have not.

Paradoxically, the very dynamics of social conflict, which permits a few individuals to increase surplus wealth, also work dialectically to pressure them to share that wealth. Countervailing energies released by untrammeled accumulation generate powerful demands for economic compensation. As privileges mount, so does the rebellious spirit of victims: exploitation and conspicuous consumption can be pushed only so far before marginalized people assert their claims by rebelling. If pushed too far, those who are desperate will tear down the old order even if they have no hope of building a new order. This dialectic interplay between the insensitive accumulation of superfluous wealth and perpetuated misery is neither fatalistic destiny nor nature's moral vengeance on human hardness of heart. Rather, it is the natural outcome of dynamisms operative in society ever since the first technological revolution maximized, concurrently with the accumulation possibilities of the few, the hope of emancipation from need in the many. To state that such a suicidal and destructive climax to the pursuit of wealth destroys human value is also to assert that the attitude of privilege, which exacerbates this condition, is itself dehumanizing.

There is a further reason why superfluous wealth can prove socially destructive. Economic goods surreptitiously tend to substitute themselves for human goods. To be a good person easily comes to mean, in a society where the pursuit of economic goods is dominant, to own more goods. The spread of conspicuous consumption in advanced countries has already revolutionized the image of the good life in the world. The notion of "being more" increasingly comes to mean "having more." As long as one desired more goods from a low initial plateau of possession and consumption, "having more" represented genuine progress toward "being more." And it is surely idle to posit any "absolute" threshold of superfluity above which one is automatically dehumanized. Nevertheless, the unbridled surrender to processes aimed at generating more goods poses special value problems. The reason is that economic goods by nature are instrumental goods. Thanks to the wily imperialism of consumption, however, useful goods tend to arrogate to themselves the attributes of absolute or self-validating goods.[10] This monumental inversion of values—in full course within "developed" countries—augurs a disturbing future, for it obscures the difference among priorities in needs. Worse still, it sows unrealistic hopes in underdeveloped populaces while preventing advanced countries from making structural changes in world market mechanisms and their productive systems demanded by worldwide development. "Developed" countries refuse to redirect their own economic progress or revise their overall economic effort in terms of priority needs.

For economists, it matters not whether consumers spend wisely or wastefully: to them all expenditures express "preferences." Insofar as they are responsible social critics, however, even economists are troubled by wasteful and compulsive consumption. Although he warns his readers not to be deluded by Socialist utopias of wealth redistribution, Alfred Marshall nonetheless refuses to acquiesce in wealth inequalities. "The drift of economic science during many generations has been with increasing force toward the belief that there is no real necessity, and therefore no moral justification for extreme poverty side by side with great wealth."[11] Marshall judges it desirable to lower the wealth level of those at the highest rung if this helps raise the level of those at the lowest rung. Clearly, a monumental difference exists between imposed and voluntary austerity.[12] Austerity cannot be imposed on the world's poor nations unless developed societies also accept a measure of voluntary austerity. To be sure, judiciously selective austerity must contribute to the transformation of world structures with a view to the development of all peoples. Critical examination must be made of the extent to which different levels of material abundance affect one's freedom and capacity for growth. A major ethical crisis may be in the making because, in Lebret's words: "[T]he rich are covetous, desiring more than they need; and this covetousness is rapidly spreading to poorer peoples. A greedy world can only be a divided world, ethically sordid, heading toward barbarism."[13]

The dynamism of acquisition is useful in stimulating people to start acquiring things they genuinely need. These same dynamisms, however, may leave them unfit to exercise freedom in the pursuit of other goods. A theory of priority needs is mandatory; a later chapter outlines such a theory. What is asserted here is the importance of reappraising in normative fashion and in a developmental setting the notions of "superfluous" and "enough."

The analysis just conducted yields several conclusions, namely:

- all individuals need certain goods in order to realize themselves as human beings;

- some objective basis exists for deciding what is "enough";

- both the absolute insufficiency of goods and relative excess dehumanize the quality of life;

- an explicit theory of priority needs must be elaborated.

These conclusions are encapsulated in the first strategic principle of any development ethics, which states that underdeveloped people "need to *have* enough in order to *be* more."

Second Principle: Universal Solidarity

Pervasive communications now render isolation impossible. Over thirty-five years ago, the French economist François Perroux concluded that the "technical conditions for the establishment of a planetary economy now exist."[14] No country can erect walls around itself without thereby destroying the international foundations of technology. Thanks to systematic research and organization and also to the widespread consumption of their fruits, technological production has unified the globe. Everywhere human aspirations and lifestyles have felt the standardizing impact of technology: the homogenization of behavior is well under way. Business executives, professionals, technicians, and bureaucrats in Japan, Turkey, India, or the United States have more in common with one another than with their fellow nationals who are not executives or technicians.

More important than identical patterns of consumption, however, are the general *images*[15] gaining ascendancy throughout the world. Everywhere one finds the same confidence in the human ability to master nature, a sense of the importance of earthly life, and the notion that all people should be judged according to their performance. These ingredients of "modernization" are rapidly becoming generalized values. The environment within which information is processed as well as the "receptors" of information become more homogenous. Beyond technology's unifying effect, however, lie deeper bases for human solidarity.

A Common Humanity, Planet, and Destiny.   All persons are one by their common humanity. Although philosophies differ widely over the meaning of what is "human," each makes universal claims. All agree that beyond differences of race, nationality, culture, or social organization a common "human-ness" is present. This factual unity of a shared humanity is the first ontological basis for solidarity among humans.

A second foundation is the common occupation by all humans of a single planet. Throughout its physical extension the earth is governed by identical laws and is subject to the same determinisms and indeterminisms. Notwithstanding local variations in climate, relief, and geography, this planet has a specific identity distinct from other cosmic bodies. All humans dwell on this *one* planet[16] and the symbiosis between them and "nature" presupposes an intimate link between the two. Each human is part of nature and the world of objects. Were it otherwise, he or she could not be treated as a mere "object" by others. Moreover, physical occupation of this planet is the lot of all humans, not only of some. Even when humans do not interact directly with other humans, they are related at least indirectly to these others, thanks to their common links to the same planetary system. The prospects opened up by recent space exploration in no way modify the organic relations tying all humans to this planet as to their cosmic home so long as they are born on this earth and dwell here. Were permanent emigration to other planets to take place in the future, human solidarity would simply acquire an expanded basis—namely, the unity of cosmic planetary systems instead of a single planet. In either case, humans are interdependent because of identical ties to one system, planetary or cosmic.

Along with their common humanity and their common ties to a single cosmic environment, a third basis of solidarity exists: human beings' unity of destiny. Whatever be their personal occupational identities—as farmers, clerks, miners, taxi drivers, factory workers, politicians, artists, goat-herders, technicians, or managers—all must fulfill themselves in a properly human mode. All philosophies and systems of thought postulate, at least implicitly, a common destiny for humans: the fate of one is the fate of all. Hence the universality of human destiny represents no sectarian point of view but the common patrimony of human thought.

Only rarely, however, do humans translate their existential solidarity into cooperative behavior; on the contrary, they consistently act as though they were not bound together in webs of solidarity. Partial claims assert themselves as though they were of supreme importance. Classes and nations strive to dominate other classes and nations. Lip service is given to the "common good of humanity," but global development problems continue to be defined through prisms of parochial mercantile, strategic, and ideological interests. Even within international organizations, solidarity is often sacrificed to narrow political interests. Humans have not yet learned how to respond, institutionally or behaviorally, to the exigencies of solidarity. Nevertheless, only through the practice of universal solidarity can development be achieved for all. The Independent Commission on International Development Issues chaired by Willy Brandt appeals to solidarity as an ethical solution to global underdevelopment. In its report on *North-South: A Program for Survival*, the Commission declares:

> History has taught us that wars produce hunger, but we are less aware that mass poverty can lead to war or end in chaos. While hunger rules peace cannot prevail. He who wants to ban war must also ban mass poverty. Morally it makes no difference whether a human being is killed in war or is condemned to starve to death because of the indifference of others.

> Mankind has never before had such ample technical and financial resources for coping with hunger and poverty. The immense task can be tackled once the necessary collective

will is mobilized. What is necessary can be done, and must be done, in order to provide the conditions by which the poor can be saved from starvation as well as destructive confrontation.

Solidarity among men must go beyond national boundaries: we cannot allow it to be reduced to a meaningless phrase. International solidarity must stem both from strong mutual interests in cooperation *and* from compassion for the hungry.[17]

It is unrealistic to expect problems to be solved by some hidden hand which arbitrates competing interests. Ironically, genuine solidarity can be won only after much conflict, because worldwide community can be established only if the rules presently governing exchange and access to power are totally revised. The implantation of world solidarity, therefore, faces great obstacles.

Technology's unifying effects will ultimately prove disastrous unless humans allocate resources, access to information, and decision-making power on grounds of world equity and not on the basis of prior occupancy or greater political influence. Technology divides more than it unites unless it operates in conditions where self-development of societies can flourish. As stated above, the "ontological roots" of solidarity are common humanity, mutual occupancy of one planet, and identical destiny. Disaster will ensue if these roots are not translated into rules effectively obeyed. Humans may prove unable to express universal solidarity except by digging a common grave for themselves as a monument to their failure of will. On grounds of efficiency and economy, planned use of resources is the only rational policy of global development. It is irrational to pretend that national sovereignty is a beneficent myth; at best, nationalism provides limited sanctuary to vulnerable societies.

Survival and Solidarity.   The Bengali sage Rabindranath Tagore believed that only what is compatible with the universal has permanent survival value, and anything less is doomed to perish.[18] Tagore may be right, because technological production cannot keep pace with expanding acquisitive instincts. Now that development is universally desired, the appropriation of goods on any basis other than universal human solidarity in the face of needs is not a viable ethic. Humankind may be obliged to choose the moral course under pain of collective death. Henry Miller, no friend of morality, thinks that "it is not our religious convictions but the very conditions of our life on earth which will make angels of us."[19] The requirements of human survival, no less than those of justice, dictate universal solidarity. Such solidarity is incompatible with competition among grossly unequal competitors, and it presupposes the abolition of domination structures.

Worldwide development cannot succeed unless solidarity is optimized. Concretely, this means that present rules governing differential power and influence must not remain in force. These rules favor those societies which already "domesticate" others who struggle against the vulnerability characterizing underdevelopment. At present levels of consciousness, underdeveloped classes and nations reject "solidarity" with a system that victimizes them or with "donors" of aid whose own interests are further advanced by that very aid. As Galbraith remarks ironically about the United States:

> [W]e are led, as a nation, by our present preoccupations, to adopt numerous of the least elegant postures of wealth. Though we have much, and much of the remainder of the world is poor, we are single-mindedly devoted to getting more . . . . We do, each year, provide some aid for others. But first we have a prayerful discussion of whether or not we can afford the sacrifice. . . . The nineteenth-century plutocrat who devoted his energies to expanding his already considerable income, who wanted by his competitive position in the plutocracy to live on a suitably ostentatious scale, who found, as a result, that his income was never entirely adequate, who came to the aid of the poor only after a careful consideration of their worth, his ability to spare from his needs and the realistic likelihood of revolt and disorder if he abstained, and who believed withal that God inspired his enterprise and generosity and often said so, was not in all respects an attractive figure. So with nations.[20]

Only by building solidarity among themselves can underdeveloped nations effectively challenge their unenviable lot, thereby hastening the advent of global solidarity. Partial solidarities, however, cannot suffice to promote universal development.

Neither individualism nor collectivism is a sound principle of development. The first renders justice, the second integral human growth, impossible. Some optimal blend of innovation and risk, allied to projective identification with group interests by social creators, is required if the development process is to construct solidarity.

6.

BASIC OPTIONS

Any classification of development strategies risks oversimplification. Much confusion results from debating at levels of generality which render comparisons meaningless, as when one argues for an urban versus a rural strategy or one aimed at growth over redistributive equity. It is evident that any development strategy must embrace both urban and rural policies, both growth and distributional dimensions. It matters greatly what basic images underlie one's diagnosis of underdevelopment as a condition, and one's understanding of the nature of development as a process. Marshall Wolfe, formerly a social planner with the United Nations Economic Commission for Latin America, formulates three basic images of the development process, each of which reflects a preferred strategic path.[1]

A first image is that of a straggling procession of countries scurrying in vain to "close the poverty gap." Most weaker nations and poorer masses fall behind, and both their absolute and relative positions worsen. In the denigrating language used by some Western writers, these nations constitute the "soft" states which "can't make it."[2] Many reasons are adduced for probable failure: the "trickle down" of development benefits takes many decades; growth promotion policies worsen the lot of all except the highly productive "modern" minority; international and national policies do not directly attack poverty or mass unemployment; growth itself is but a "modern" mask to perpetuate inequitable privilege systems. The diagnostic image of the straggling procession suggests policies aimed at "closing the gap."

The second image portrays development as a living pyramid. Countries, classes, and interest groups at the top of the pyramid hold their lofty position because they rest on the shoulders of majorities whom they exploit. The pyramid is not immobile, however; it is a living structure in constant movement caused by the endless jostling of groups competing for top position. This pyramidal image applies both to domestic class relations and to the international distribution of wealth, power, and influence. Moreover, it lends itself to both conservative and revolutionary interpretations. Conservatives endorse the image both as a true portrait of what is, and as a legitimate defense of what ought to be. Revolutionaries concede that the pyramid exists but deny its legitimacy. Consequently, they seek to alter the configuration of the social structure so drastically that no minority privileged group, old or new, can rise to the top. Their goal is to stratify society in egalitarian fashion so that there will exist no "top" where some privilege group can gain solid footing. Each group's development strategy flows from its own diagnosis, resulting in a decision either to engage in stable, incremental problem-solving, or to subordinate all problem-solving to the radical transformation of power structures.

Wolfe's third image presents the development process as an apocalypse: the Great Ascent is headed not toward the Promised Land of Development but toward the Bottomless Pit of Catastrophes—ecological, biological, political. Those who hold this view stress limits to the carrying capacity of the ecosystem; they see alarming threats from rapid population growth; they fear global destruction through radioactivity, nuclear demolition, or the use by state agencies of biotechnologies for purposes of social control in ways destructive of human freedom. This third imagery rejects two basic assumptions shared by the other two views, namely, that long-term growth in production is desirable, and that technology has an unlimited capacity to solve all problems, even those it helps create. The third view prescribes strategies consonant with its diagnosis and posits criteria for deciding which developmental tasks are primordial. It stresses renewing depleted resources, achieving zero population growth, and harnessing technology to a steady-state economy.

All diagnoses of development and strategy prescriptions center on value judgments about what a good, or a better, human society is.

For some, a better society is one in which greater access to opportunity, if not to more tangible benefits, is created; for others, the goal is effective equality in modes of greater or lesser participation; for still others, the basic aim is to assure the planetary survival in modes which preserve human liberties. The three images are not mutually exclusive, nor are they always found in their pure state. Nonetheless, this typology helps to focus our attention on classifications of development strategies which transcend purely ideological or programmatic preferences. In 1972 Mahbub ul Haq, erstwhile World Bank strategist, Pakistani Planning Minister, and creator of the Human Development Indicator, predicted that "the days of the mixed economy are numbered. The developing countries will have to become either more frankly capitalistic or more genuinely socialist."[3] Perhaps Haq is right, but the evidence of comparative development performance reveals no correlation between the ideological system adopted by a poor country and its ability to close the gap, or between the degree of internal class stratification and a country's degree of success in solving its ecological problems. Thus, although the People's Republic of China introduced great class equality in the Maoist period, socialist Algeria failed to do so.[4]

More crucial than the formal ideology any society espouses, however, is whether it conceives of development merely as the pursuit of certain benefits or as the quest of these benefits in a certain mode. *How* benefits are to be obtained is as essential to defining development as the fact that benefits *are* obtained. This is not to deny the importance of benefits sought—greater material welfare, higher productivity, more efficient institutions. Yet it matters enormously how gains are sought: whether in a pattern of high, or of low, dependency on outside powers; whether in an equitable distributional mode, or in ways which enhance the privileges of favored minorities to the detriment of needier masses; whether in a paternalistic, impositional style, or in ways which progressively empower the populace to choose its targets and the instruments to reach them. The values invoked here refer to the mode of developmental change, not to its targeted content. Diverse images of development suggest diverse modal policies even when agreement exists as to the desirability of the goals or content of effort. Central questions affecting the mode of development are:

- Which institutional arrangements best promote the goals of development (political centralization or decentralization; what degree of coercion in planning)?

- What relative roles are to be assigned to political leaders, experts, technicians, and "the people?" This decision affects the degree of elitism or technocracy of the developmental effort.

- What time spans are deemed tolerable before targeted gains are effectively reached?

- What measure of self-reliance or dependence on the outside is permitted or encouraged?

- Is priority given to material or to moral incentives? If to a mixture of both, in what proportions?

- Is the organizing principle of mobilized social effort some form of socialism, a variant of neo-capitalism, or novel indigenous approaches distinct from both?

The answers given to these questions by a given society form a systemic whole which constitutes, in effect, that society's development strategy. Although decisions taken on all these points are important, it is pedagogically useful to focus on a limited number of them, specifically: integration with outside systems and the choice of overarching incentive systems in formulating policy. For illustrative purposes, these two are now examined in detail.

Integration with Outside Systems

No Third World nation has successfully pursued a fully autarchic course. Even during the Mao years, China, notwithstanding its continental size and high degree of economic self-sufficiency, could not exclude all contact with the outside world.[5] Similarly, although Burma (now called Myanmar) in the 1960s adopted a policy of excluding foreign investors and tourists, the country still needed to export rice and oil to outside markets.[6] Moreover, Tanzania and Guinea-Bissau did not interpret their respective doctrines of self-reliance to mean exclusion of ties to other countries, to international agencies, or to world markets.[7] Important differences of degree are nonetheless discernible among nations: some are more highly integrated with outside systems than others. At times, links are one-sided, as in the case of Cuba's ties with the Soviet Union before 1989. Algeria, on the contrary, provided an example of wide diversification, deliberately sought, in its linkages with other countries.

By tying its development fortunes to an industrialized power or by striving to achieve competitiveness in world markets, a nation commits itself, often irreversibly, to certain industrial priorities or to large-scale industrialized agriculture over other alternatives, to certain patterns of consumer-goods production favoring the privileged classes, to promoting export over meeting internal demands, and to certain patterns of technological choice. This is so because the "rules of the game" set by the world market or by hegemonic great powers are biased in favor of obtaining development benefits in modes of large-scale competition, orientation toward higher purchasing power, and of a rapidly shifting "competitive edge" on the strength of changing technology.

More importantly, the decision to seek global integration necessarily relegates the concern for social equality to second rank, behind competitiveness. The reason, as Myrdal explains, is that:

> . . . the theory of international trade was not worked out to explain the reality of underdevelopment and the need for development. One might say, rather, that this imposing structure of abstract reasoning implicitly had almost the opposite purpose, that of *explaining away the international equality problem*.[8]

The existing global economic order is uncongenial to the pursuit of equity within developing countries because it is lubricated by forms of competition based on comparative efficiency. And, according to the capitalist, neocapitalist, and even socialist calculus of efficiency (to the degree that socialist economies "compete" in the world arena), values of equity and equality are treated as "externalities" not to be "internalized" in a cost-benefit calculus. Therefore, whenever a national development plan in some poor country requires a high degree of integration with the global or regional export market, a whole gamut of supportive infrastructure investments is *ipso facto* rendered necessary in order to assure competitive efficiency. Choosing integration implies selecting technology which is capital-intensive and of standardized international quality. It also signifies plant scales opposed to the requirements of small and medium industry, as well as an agricultural policy which favors small minorities within the agricultural sector—this to the detriment of the poorest and least productive.[9] Also implied are an employment policy which provides training and subsidies to small numbers of skilled and professional personnel—to the neglect (at least relative) of large numbers with lesser skills—as well as monetary and fiscal policies ill-suited to produce equitable redistribution inasmuch as subsidies favor "efficient" export sectors.

Poor nations ought to practice self-reliance in choosing their development strategies in order to gain freedom from servility to previously existing models. One of the highest priorities of a self-reliant strategy is to organize the economy in ways that free people from manipulation by the market. The heart of "self-reliance" is the commitment to creative innovation and adaptation in the light of local constraints, values, priorities, and heritage. Any nation pursuing a self-reliant strategy of development must institutionalize its critique of prevailing outside models. It must also adopt criteria for choosing technologies and modes of their utilization drawn from outside the technological market place. Not that foreign technologies are excluded on principle, but only those types of technology which foster locally defined goals will be imported. In many traditional rural localities nature is still deeply respected.

Schumacher contrasts the "self-balancing, self-adjusting, self-cleansing" attributes of nature with technology that recognizes no self-limiting principle as to size, speed, or violence. He concludes that "in the subtle system of nature, technology, and in particular the super-technology of the modern world, acts like a foreign body, and there are now numerous signs of rejection."[10] Because modern industrial societies are no model for export, Third World nations do well to experiment with new "community technologies" which enhance self-reliance in small local groups.[11] Their desires are prompted by the need to reduce the vulnerability any country experiences as a result of integrating with outside market forces. The quest for self-reliance in development models and in sources of capital and technology is motivated by the desire to reduce unacceptable forms of dependency. If the prevailing mode of exchange with others is interdependence with high reciprocity, there is correspondingly less "need" to be self-reliant. But if interdependence is characterized by differential strength or bargaining position (that is, by low mutuality or reciprocity), then a higher degree of self-reliance becomes desirable.

Nevertheless, self-reliance is not an absolute principle, nor must it be interpreted to mean excluding outside influences. Moreover, even where national planners do not choose self-reliance as their primary policy, it is possible within limited sectors (let us say, industry, agriculture, or housing) to champion a self-reliant approach which will have important repercussions on selection and modes of technology adopted. Only in recent years have national development planners begun to integrate science and technology policies with their central value choices and the corresponding development strategies. In the past, technology policies were either abandoned to the workings of existing technology market channels or dictated by local or sectoral actors in economic decisions.[12] Thus, if a housing ministry favored unaided self-help public housing utilizing inexpensive technologies, sectoral policy was shaped with little regard for macroeconomic options. The degree of centrality assumed by integration to outside markets or self-reliance as an organizing principle of developmental effort is crucial. Where integration is the basic option, higher degrees of conformity to technological patterns dominant in industrialized countries are unavoidable. In contrast, where self-reliance is the primary mode of development, greater leverage exists for reducing conformity. Self-reliance exacts sacrifices in efficiency; conversely, although it may improve efficiency, higher integration may exact sacrifices in terms of social justice and lead to excessive industrial concentration or vulnerability to price fluctuations over which national decision-makers have little control.

Other things being equal, if a less-developed country subscribes to the image of a procession of nations struggling to "catch up" to the developed, it will *ipso facto* be influenced by a powerful bias in favor of choosing integration (via aid, trade, imported technology, and the adoption of international standards) as its basic option. If, on the contrary, its primal image is revolutionary convulsion, self-reliance will hold an important place in its basic development strategy. Practical constraints of a strategic, economic, geographical, or political nature may sometimes overrule this preference. This was the case with Cuba, which for thirty years (1959-1989) chose to become highly integrated—militarily, financially, politically, and technologically—to the Soviet Union.

The third image, multiple apocalypse, tends strongly toward the basic option of optimizing at all levels both self-reliance and control over growth. Similarly, if one adopts a frontal attack on mass poverty and unemployment as one's basic strategy, a strong bias exists in favor of lesser integration with international markets and greater local inventiveness to correct factor distortions inherent in technology imported from rich countries. In every case, limits exist beyond which neither efficiency nor equity can be fully ignored. Because reality constantly imposes compromises, no country plan is fully consistent with its basic options. Moreover, unexpected events (abrupt rises in import prices or disastrous floods) can suddenly force relatively self-reliant nations into more "integration" with the outside than they had planned. Nonetheless, any nation's decision-makers must ultimately attach primary importance either to integration or to self-reliance. In large measure, the degree to which they blend the two depends on the overarching incentive systems at work in their societies.

Incentive Systems: Typology

Incentives are the rewards and penalties held out to induce or deter a given behavior. Rewards constitute positive incentives, and penalties negative incentives. Incentives offered vary widely from one institution to another. An extended family invokes kinship loyalty to move relatives to support ailing members. Social clubs, religious groupings, professional associations, and other voluntary organizations appeal to the solidarity of members to elicit contributions in money, labor, or materials. Political parties and ideological movements, in turn, summon masses to action on the basis of what Sorel[13] calls a "myth," *i.e.*, some powerful idea capable of galvanizing people into action and sacrifice. Corporations, in contrast, usually hold out material benefits—stock options, free housing, a chauffeured limousine, or cash bonuses—as incentives to recruit or retain desired personnel.

Such terms as "appeals to," "offers," or "holds out" refer to incentives which are *objective*. *Subjective* incentives, on the other hand, are the motivations which move, or fail to move, subjects to respond to promised rewards or threatened penalties. Another important distinction is that between material and moral incentives.[14] A *material* incentive is some palpable thing held out as a reward or punishment; positive material incentives comprise such goods as money, services, or concrete prizes, whereas negative material incentives are imprisonment, fines, or the deprivation of some good. *Moral* incentives, in constrast, are non-material rewards and penalties: honors, status awards, ostracism, public humiliation.

Incentive *systems*, as distinct from individual incentives, are a society's overall package of rewards and inducements and its array of penalties and deterrents.[15] Incentive systems operative in most Third World countries are biased to favor:

- aggregate growth, most of the benefits of which go to privileged groups, to the detriment of equitable growth where gains are widely shared by the neediest populace;

- manipulative decisional processes which disempower those most affected by decisions; and

- a foreign model of rationality which exacts unnecessary human suffering and massive cultural destruction.

This mismatch between incentive systems and the true developmental aspirations of a nation's populace is reversible, although new incentive systems that foster equitable development must be negotiated.

Incentives as Policy Instruments

All national societies resort to both moral and material incentives to motivate citizens to contribute to their developmental goals. What distinguishes one nation's incentive system from another's is the specific combination of the two types of incentive and the relative weight assigned to each.

By ideological choice, socialist nations assign priority to moral over material incentives and to collective over individual incentives. Nevertheless, moral incentives do not correlate directly with command economies; nor, conversely, do material incentives correlate directly with market economies. All societies use both material and moral incentives as well as both individual and collective incentives. However, one type of incentive dominates in accord with the organizing principle of each economic system. As Karl Mannheim explains:

> Competition and co-operation may be viewed in two different ways: as simple social mechanisms or as organizing principles of a social structure.

> Competition or co-operation as mechanisms may exist and serve diverse ends in any society, preliterate, capitalist, and non-capitalist. But in speaking of the capitalist phase of rugged individualism and competition, we think of an all-pervasive structured principle of social organization.[16]

This distinction applies with equal force to the incentives which dominate in a given economic system. Material incentives serve as the organizing principle of a market system while co-existing alongside moral incentives functioning as social mechanisms subordinate to that organizing principle. Mannheim further notes that:

> This distinction may help to clarify the question whether capitalist competition—allegedly basic to our social structure—needs to be maintained as a presumable activating force. Now, one may well eliminate competition as the *organizing principle* of the social structure and replace it by planning without eliminating competition as a *social mechanism* to serve desirable ends.[17]

Social mechanisms play a corrective role by compensating for failings in the orgainizing principle of the basic system. Welfare payments to unemployed workers play this role in the United States, where the primordial organizing principle governing work is a labor market obeying the "law" of supply and demand. If, however, imperfections in the system result in unemployment, the transfer payments mechanism is activated to mitigate the damaging effects of the untrammelled working of the basic principle. The converse occurred in centrally planned economies where, in order to assure full employment, jobs were given to everyone. If, however, there was not enough work for all to perform, certain people were paid for doing nothing. These disguised welfare payments regulated or corrected the inefficiencies attendant upon the workings of the original organizing principle of this system. In effect, both systems subsidize a category of persons who, in terms of pure economic efficiency, are non-productive.

An analogous relationship is found in the interplay of moral and material incentives. Every nation adopts as its primary incentive system a package of dominantly moral or material incentives, and it utilizes the other type of incentive to perform regulatory, compensatory, or complementary functions. In the United States, voluntarism, a system of freely contributed goods, operates alongside the market where goods are bought and sold. Churches, schools, hospitals, political parties, and philanthropic organizations appeal to individuals and corporations to donate money, time, talents, and material for socially beneficial uses. In the United States economy, voluntarism constitutes a "third system" working alongside the dominant market sphere (the first system) and the government sector (the second system).[18]

Inasmuch as no single category of incentive can satisfy all needs, every society must resort to both types. What distinguishes one society from another, however, is its organizing principle or dominant incentive system. Within capitalist societies, the dominant system of incentives is material, based on market competition and responding to supply and demand forces. On the other hand, in socialist societies rewards and penalties are decreed by political authorities on the principle that moral incentives enjoy primacy.

Moreover, all societies rationalize their resort to ancillary incentives in terms of the logic underlying their dominant system. Thus the provision of individual material incentives to peasants and business entrepreneurs in present-day China is officially presented as supporting the basic socialist nature of the economy.[19] Similarly, in the United States, appeals to voluntary contributions are justified as being fully compatible with the dominant material incentive system which drives the economy.

The Dual Role of Incentives

Incentives play a dual role in society. On the one hand, they mirror the dominant values of any social system and reproduce that system's structures of production, power, and wealth. A small tribal society in which no hierarchy exists bestows status awards as well as material prizes on those individuals who share goods with fellow hunters or food-gatherers, those who protect the integrity of the rituals that bind the society together, and those who successfully negotiate or do battle with strangers. In turn, large-scale peasant societies, pledged to stability and order, reward those who protect their laws and legitimize their social roles. Early industrializing societies heaped acclaim and wealth upon captains of industry, explorers, and practical inventors. Thus do incentive systems reproduce the societal patterns governing the distribution of wealth, power, and legitimacy.

Nevertheless, certain incentives do not reinforce the dominant values, priorities, and stratification systems of a given society; on the contrary, they promote change. To illustrate, proscribed activities have always rewarded those who feared not to violate the rules of society—criminals, pirates, smugglers, and traitors. Social deviants create new incentives that counter the thrust of a society's legitimate formal incentives. In short, incentive systems constitute a fluid domain in constant process of re-negotiation.

Beyond the Material/Moral Dichotomy

Most debates on economic policy assume polar opposition between material and moral incentives. This dichotomy is obsolete, however, and obscures both the real practice of nations and the policy options open to them. The radical opposition between material and moral incentives had its origins in the ideological battle between capitalism and communism. The motor force driving capitalism is the pursuit by all economic actors of individual self-interest, defined exclusively in terms of material benefits. In the theory of capitalism, therefore, there is no room for moral incentives. "There is no capitalist theory of non-profit making enterprises and non-consumable goods," writes Lewis Mumford. "These functions exist accidentally, by the grace of the philanthropist: they have no real place in the system."[20]

The reverse occurred in Communist lands, where ideological values favored social justice over economic efficiency. This preference called for the elimination of exploitation and the subordination of the individual quest for material well-being to socially determined collective objectives. The notion that social good emerges from the untrammeled play of private egotisms within a competitive market arena is alien to communism. What is postulated instead is the duty to design societal structures which assure maximum equality, not merely of opportunity but of results. In collective philosophy, individual gains yield priority to collective goals. No attempt was made by Communist theorists to reconcile the legitimate demands of the community with the requirements of individual persons, viewed as no less legitimate. They contended that personal and individual well-being would be assured automatically once society's collective structures were made right. In order to relegate personal self-seeking to a secondary place in economic domains, these theorists elevated moral incentives to pre-eminent rank as the principal engine of economic effort. It was the moral commitment of a populace to the ideal of constructing a society without alienation that was assumed to move individuals to work, invest, produce, and distribute in the socially most efficient manner.

The purist thinking and terminology favored in both camps has little bearing, however, on the concrete practice of real societies of both ideological persuasions.

Although Communist governments spoke the rhetoric of moral incentives, they acknowledged the potent attraction of material incentives by assigning exclusive material privileges—chauffered automobiles, free recreational homes, subsidized foreign travel, and privileged access to luxury stores off-limits to other consumers—to their party faithful. Even within non-elite classes, numerous material incentives were given—usually in illegal and clandestine fashion—to those who circumvented official prohibitions and regulated prices for certain transactions. A large black market flourished not only for foreign currencies and forbidden luxury goods, but for such everyday services as electrical and plumbing repairs, housing construction, and auto repairs. Notwithstanding their rhetoric about the primacy of collective moral incentives and the illegitimacy of individual material incentives, Communist societies made ample resort to the latter as rewards to elicit necessary economic behavior.

A parallel but inverse force is at work in capitalist societies, which pay ritualistic homage to the centrality, if not to the exclusive validity, of material incentives. Nevertheless, these societies offer moral incentives to induce even profit-seeking corporations to donate resources to socially beneficial causes. More importantly, many economic transactions supposedly carried out in the name of rational maximization of material interest are in reality conducted for less tangible reasons:

e.g., to perform a favor to a friend or relative, to win the goodwill of someone. In *Economy and Society: Constraint, Exchange, and Gift,*[21] the French economist François Perroux reveals how pervasive are culturally sanctioned forms of non-profit exchanges in the conduct of capitalist "business." Business firms rely heavily on citations, awards, testimonial banquets, commendations, and the granting of honorific titles—moral incentives all! Here too the practice belies the rhetoric of exclusive reliance on one type of incentive.

Some blend of material and moral incentives is found in all societies because *both are necessary.* Excessive reliance on moral incentives leads to intolerable levels of inefficiency, absenteeism, and waste. Moral incentives alone do not work because human beings are self-centered and, as Garrett Hardin insists, there are limits to altruism.[22] Consequently, no public policy which ignores psychological motivations in human behavior can succeed. On the other hand, undue reliance on material incentives, although perhaps efficient in narrow terms of self-interest or profitability of individual firms, is inequitable in wider societal terms. It leads to the exploitation of workers, the irresponsible waste of non-renewable resources and environmental destruction. Many social values not reducible to profit-making have thrust themselves upon capitalist societies as necessary in order to provide a balance to the exclusive pursuit of material interests.

A community of the good life cannot arise around market competition alone: moral invocations of values, such as solidarity, mutual responsibility, and loyalty to causes lying above mere interest, are also needed. The "common good" is something more than the aggregated interests of individual members in any society. Moral incentives are needed to provide a cement holding together a delicate tissue of social relations. There are limits to altruism in human individuals, it is true, but it is no less true that humans also have vital needs for altruism and its expression—in friendship, associative endeavors, and disinterested giving.

The growing quest for non-alienating styles of life in advanced industrial capitalist societies serves as evidence that "Man does not live by bread alone."[23] In these societies, one observes a growing repudiation of the exaggerated materialism which undergirds the mainstream definition of the good life. That rejection remains marginal, however, and merely breeds small counter-cultural communities until moral incentives, along with material incentives, find their central place as policy instruments which normatively guide economic activity in society at large.

It is not only material and moral incentives that must be combined in diverse patterns. Individual and collective incentives must also be blended if the true beneficiaries of development are to be effectively reached.[24]

Incentives for Whom and for What?

Incentive systems simultaneously mirror the society in which they operate and because of their high malleability, act as agents of change in that society. Two factors explain incentives' high degree of malleability. First, in most societies *objective* incentives are not well matched to *subjective* incentives or motivations which *de facto* elicit behavior from their members. The second reason is that economic actors are activated by mixed motives of narrow egotism and wider altruism; and the two motives are constantly shifting in their weighted combinations.[25] Consequently, unidimensional incentives designed to move to action will be viewed at different times as unpersuasive to these actors. Moreover, few societies explicitly design a coherent over-arching system of incentives for rewarding and deterring the whole gamut of individual and institutional actions they deem essential to their public purposes. Consequently, *ad hoc* incentives are constantly being created or improvised to satisfy specific perceived needs. And no normative body exists, similar to national academies which preside over the purity and legitimacy of a language, to assure coherence among all incentives tried. Not surprisingly, therefore, different institutions within national society—and at times the same institutions themselves —transmit contradictory signals regarding the behavior to be encouraged or deterred by their incentives. Thus universities urge students to strive for success according to prevailing competitive standards of success within their society, while at the same time preaching to those same students the duty to define their personal success in terms of helping others less fortunate than themselves or of subordinating their career goals to the demands of moral virtue. National societies behave likewise in their presentation of overall incentives: they simultaneously incite their members to pursue narrow self-interest and to practice community altruism. Rarely do their specific incentives harmonize the two sets of messages.

Incentives are the key to equitable development because they provide a margin of space for negotiating the optimal combinations of material and moral rewards/deterrents. Indeed, one may most fruitfully view material, moral, and hybrid incentives as lying on a continuum where readjustments and altered weightings are constantly occurring. As in the larger realm of development itself, the two principal normative questions needing to be posed are reducible to the purposes and the beneficiaries of a strategy: development and incentives *for what* and *for whom*?

7.

FOUR PATHWAYS TO DEVELOPMENT

Basic options are translated into specific strategies. No consensus exists, however, as to what strategies should be adopted to pursue development. The economist Keith Griffin has evaluated six strategies: monetarism, open economy, industrialization, green revolution, redistribution, and socialism. He assesses the performance yielded by each strategy in different countries on six registers: (1) resource utilization and income level; (2) savings, investment, and growth; (3) human capital formation; (4) poverty and inequality; (5) role of the state; and (6) participation, democracy, and freedom. Griffin's inconclusive findings lead him to declare: [T]here is no best path to development.[1]

There is indeed no single best path to development, applicable everywhere and at all times. Nevertheless, there exist four different general orientations that guide the choice of the particular strategies catalogued by Griffin. These are *growth, redistribution, Basic Human Needs,* and *development from tradition.*

Growth

Growth strategists aim at maximizing aggregate economic production: their central assumption is that social energies must be galvanized around the task of "creating a bigger pie." It is useless to redistribute wealth or assets through revolutionary or reform measures, they argue, for this is tantamount to redistributing misery. Their goal is to create new increments of wealth as fast as possible. The principal means for achieving this goal is to marshall domestic *savings* to the maximum degree, or if these are insufficient, to secure foreign capital in diverse forms (investment, loans, grants) and apply it to productive *investment* to increase production. Growth advocates recognize that rapid economic growth results not only from a widened base of productive assets, but also from greater productivity in the utilization of the factors of production. Because they view technology as the greatest single multiplier of productivity, they place great importance on incorporating modern technology to productive processes.

Whatever inequalities result from concentrating on growth are judged by growth strategists to be unavoidable. Either the benefits of growth will trickle down to poor people at some later time or, if they do not, corrective welfare measures to assure equity can be adopted by political authorities. These measures range from progressive taxation, subsidized food and social services for those unable to pay, to social security schemes and safety nets to protect vulnerable and non-competitive people from the consequences of their failure in economic arenas. Growth proponents however, do not address the problem of how to get welfare policies voted by ruling classes whose economic power gives them a disproportionate voice in political decisions as well.

Redistribution with Growth

Advocates of redistribution with growth[2] adopt the principle that distributive justice—the abolition of mass poverty and great inequities in wealth—cannot result from trickle-down growth processes or from welfare policies. They contend that equity, together with growth, must be planned as a direct objective of development strategy. Accordingly, the goal of planners and politicians becomes not to maximize economic growth, but to optimize it in the light of parallel equity objectives. Within this paradigm, one finds a changed view of the role attributed to investments in education, job creation, health, and nutrition. Such investments are not viewed primarily as consumer expenditures but rather as productive investments. Nutritious food and ade-

quate health services, it is claimed, not only improve the living conditions of people benefiting from them; they also add productive wealth
to the nation's work force, leading to decreases in idleness caused by
illness or absenteeism and to increased economic demand among the
poor classes. Defenders of this approach argue that a fairly high level
of economic growth is fully compatible with ethically just performance
in domains of distribution. In essence, redistribution is a corrective
strategy aimed at making the pursuit of growth less socially destabi-
lizing.

Basic Human Needs

The Basic Human Needs (BHN) approach is an important variant of the redistribution-with-growth model.[3] BHN goes further than
redistribution by specifying the quantifiable *content* of redistribution
or equity. For BHN strategists, the priority task of development thus
becomes neither to maximize nor to optimize aggregate growth, but
rather to satisfy a cluster of basic needs felt by the poorest segments
of the nation's population, those lying under some "poverty line." This
cluster of basic needs includes goods and services relating to nutrition, health, housing, education, and access to jobs. The BHN paradigm also differs from the redistribution-with-growth approach in that
it does not necessarily assume that equity is always or necessarily
compatible with high rates of economic growth. If basic needs can be
met with little or no growth, so be it, they say; in any event, true
development is not measured by growth.

The BHN model of development usually incorporates two additional elements in its policy prescriptions: an emphasis on local and
national self-reliance and a preference for styles of decision-making
and problem-solving which induce non-elite populations to participate. Thus, although the two notions are conceptually distinct, BHN
strategies tend to merge into Alternative Development Strategies
(ADS). Alternative development strategies are proposed in order to
provide alternatives to approaches based on growth (with little equity), efficiency (with little new job-creation), high levels of resource
transfers (which tend to increase dependency), and elitist decision-
making (which does not allow poor people to participate in decisions
and which often runs roughshod over their cultural values).

Even under the BHN formula, however, the ultimate *goals* of development are accepted as being those already manifest in industrial nations: economic welfare and improved material conditions for large numbers of people, technological efficiency, and institutional modernity. The distinctive claim made by BHN advocates is that the best means to achieve these goals is to target scarce resources as a first priority toward providing for the poorest. The masses of poor people, they insist, are the most important development resource, more crucial than favorable climate or fertile soil, mineral deposits or heavy rainfall, abundant capital or sophisticated technology, efficient institutions or a large pool of managerial experts.[4] Once poor people are fed, housed, clothed, and made healthy, it is claimed, they will then work dynamically to achieve the other developmental priorities.

Development from Tradition

The development-from-tradition approach or "endogenous self-determined development" stands as a radical alternative to the three pathways outlined thus far.[5] The central premise of this paradigm states that the goals of genuine development, and not only its means, must not be borrowed from countries already "developed." Any such mimetic development is judged to be spurious and distorted. For the defenders of tradition as the values matrix of modernity, the goals of a form of development suited to a particular society should be sought from within the latent dynamism of that society's value system—its traditional beliefs, its meaning system, its local institutions, networks of solidarity, and popular practices. Given that culture's understanding of the significance of life and death, of the meaning of time and frequently of an eternity beyond time, and of how human beings ought to relate to the forces of the cosmos, certain ideal images of the good life and the good society emerge. Not that modern ideas, behavior, and technology are to be repudiated on principle, but rather that they must be critically examined in instrumental fashion to determine whether or not they can contribute to the sound human development of individuals and communities. Only if change agents from "the modern world" discern, respect, and build on the latent dynamism of traditional values can the modern "cargo" of goods and services they bring prove to be genuinely developmental.

Traditional values themselves are not immune to criticism, however. Even Gandhi, a staunch champion of development from tradition, in evaluating the caste system or the spiritual authority of Brahmins in India, recognized that modern notions of rational inquiry and democratic equality of persons before the law can lay bare the inhuman characteristics of many ancient practices. It becomes essential, therefore, to confront traditional images of the good life and the good society with modern alternatives to see which are more truly developmental.

8.

PARTICIPATION

The political redemocratization occurring in recent years in Asia, Latin America, Central Europe, and the ex-Soviet Union has radically challenged the development strategies pursued in numerous countries during periods of dictatorial rule. The cry for greater political freedom is paralleled by demands for more equitable development policies. Dictatorships resort to high degrees of coercion to impose development policies conceived at the summit, and they distribute the fruits of those policies mainly to a limited circle of privileged clients and allies. On both counts, voice and benefits, the majority of a nation's populace is excluded. Not surprisingly, therefore, that majority seeks to change both its political rulers and their development strategies. Hence new forms of non-elite participation in the transition to equitable development strategies become necessary.

Participation is variously defined. For Ivan Illich,[1] participation is deprofessionalization in all domains of life—schooling, health care, transportation, planning—so as to make "ordinary people" responsible for their own well-being. A similar view of participation was held by the late Indian educator J. P. Naik.[2] The strongest claim that participation is superior to elite decision-making, however, comes from the Brazilian pedagogue Paulo Freire. For Freire,[3] the touchstone of development is whether people previously treated as mere *objects*, known and acted upon, can now actively know and act upon, thereby becoming *subjects* of their own social destiny. People who are op-

91

pressed or reduced to the culture of silence do not participate in their own humanization. Conversely, when they participate, thereby becoming active subjects of knowledge and action, they begin to construct their properly human history and to engage in processes of authentic development.

Although these general images of participation are little disputed, crafting a precise operational definition of the term proves difficult. Most definitions are either too narrow or too broad, too strict or too loose. Nevertheless, the working definition proposed by Marshall Wolfe proves to be highly useful in development matters. Participation, for Wolfe, designates "the organized efforts to increase control over resources and regulative institutions in given social situations, on the part of groups and movements hitherto excluded from such control."[4]

Typology

Inasmuch as participation comes in many forms, clarity is served by classifying these.

Participation as Goal or as Means. In practice, participation is never valued solely as a goal by those who engage in it. Over time, the goal ceases to be prized unless it also displays some instrumental merit as a means. Nevertheless, as one emphasizes the teleological or instrumental quality of participation, diverse criteria for its assessment emerge. Instrumentalists judge participation favorably to the degree that it leads to "better" decisions or actions; teleologists, on the other hand, grant only secondary importance to efficiency. Thus political militants, committed to egalitarian participation on ideological grounds, accept the practice of "wasting time" by engaging in full consultation, whether or not the practice proves effective. For them, participation is primarily a goal. On the other hand, technical problem-solvers frequently advocate popular participation on the grounds that it is the best way of getting the job done or of achieving lasting results. Evidently, problem-solvers are here treating participation primarily as a means. It is best, however, to view participation as a hybrid reality, simultaneously an end and a means. This Freire does when discussing agricultural extension in an essay on "Extension or Communication."[5] Agricultural extension, he explains, ought to be true communication or reciprocal dialogue, not the mere issuance of "communiqués" by expert agronomists to peasants. Therefore, extension agents must accept that "time be wasted" in order to engage in active dialogue with the final utilizers of the knowledge being "extended." Participation here is clearly valued both as means and as end.

Participation Classified According to Its Scale. At times, participation exists within small arenas, for example, the domestic affairs of a family when children and spouses all have some voice in decisions. Or the arena of participation may be confined sectorally, as when school teachers in collegial fashion are given the opportunity to shape the curriculum but not the budgets of their respective departments.

Depending on the scope of the arena or field in which participation occurs, its impact on development will vary accordingly.

Participation's Originating Agent. Participation originates in three distinct sources. It can be induced from above by some authority or expert, generated from below by the non-expert populace itself, or catalytically promoted by some external change agent. When they initiate participation, however, these diverse social actors pursue quite different objectives.

Elite groups, governmental or other, usually seek to gain some measure of social control over the process and the participating agents. Matters are different, however, when participation is spontaneously generated from below. In most cases, participation springs from below during a crisis, and in response to some perceived threat to a community's identity, survival, or values. With no prior plan, perhaps even with no precedent (although research into oral histories suggests that many traditionally "passive" communities of exploited people have been in the past active "communities of struggle"),[6] some hitherto passive group mobilizes itself to protest, to resist, to say NO.

In *The Rebel,*[7] Camus lays bare the dynamics by which an oppressed group's refusal to accept its condition is always the latent bearer of all affirmations of possible new orders. To say NO is to open up possibilities for saying YES in a multitude of ways. Those who begin by saying NO to their oppressors soon feel the need to utter a YES or two of their own. Thus even the spontaneous mobilization of a powerless group to defend itself against exploitation bears within it latent seeds of organization for multiple new developmental actions.

Unplanned or spontaneous mobilization does not, however, exhaust the gamut of possibilities covered by the term "participation from below." Bottom-up participation may also result from deliberate initiatives taken by members of a "community of need" to obtain, or pressure others to obtain, some benefit from society at large or some particular group therein. Unlike state-initiated participation, which usually seeks to increase production or elicit new inputs, the type generated from below seeks consumer benefits or a greater share of the pie, that is, some greater output.

A third originating source of participation is the catalytic action of third-party external change agents—technicians, community organizers, or militants of some movement. Such change agents usually adhere to ideologies which consider self-reliance in poor people to be a desirable goal. Accordingly, they see their own activation of participation by the masses as an act of "facilitation" or "pump priming," destined to disappear after the people awaken to their dormant capacities to decide and act for themselves.

Although both types of participation originate *outside* the populace in question, intervention by third party change agents differs in important respects from top-down participation induced by the state or other elite groups. Like the form initiated from below, third party participation usually aims at empowering hitherto powerless people to make demands for goods, not to contribute their resources to someone else's purposes. In most cases, moreover, external facilitators are not content to help a populace mobilize; they also want it to organize. Mobilizing leads to joint action around some discrete, limited objective seen as urgent or important; organizing, on the other hand, is a longer-term pattern of collective action which postulates the need to meet and build solidarity even in the absence of specific tasks to conduct. The broader purpose of organization is to make people conscious of their strength —actual or potential—precisely *qua* group. That strength is to be utilized by a group not only to resist injustices, but also to gain a deeper understanding of its situation and to consider alternative plans of action. Mobilization does not always or necessarily lead to organization; organization, in contrast, usually requires prior mobilization.

Participation Classified According to Its Initiation. Different types of participation exist according to when they first occur—at the moment of diagnosing a problem, of selecting one among many possible courses of action, or of implementing a selected action. A patterned sequence culminating in final action is discernible, and at any point in the sequence, a non-expert populace may "enter in" and begin to share in its dynamics. These sequential moments are:

- initial diagnosis of the problem or condition;

- a listing of possible responses to be taken;

- selecting one possibility to enact;

- organizing or otherwise preparing oneself to implement the course of action chosen;

- self-correction or evaluation in the course of implementation; and

- debating the merits of further mobilization or organization.

The quality of participation depends on its initial entry point. Therefore, if one wishes to judge whether participation constitutes authentic empowerment of the masses or merely manipulation of them, it matters greatly when the participation begins in the overall sequence of steps.

Is participation necessary for development? From the typological analysis just presented, it follows that different kinds of development require different forms of participation. A "people-centered" development, which assigns priority to the satisfaction of basic human needs among the poor, to job creation, self-reliance, and the active preservation of cultural diversity, obviously requires a form of participation in which non-elites play an active role in the diagnosis of their own problems. If, on the other hand, a top-down, growth-oriented approach to development is adopted by a particular country, it is most likely that whatever participation does occur will not be generated by the people themselves from below. Rather, participation will be imposed by the government for the purpose of rallying the populace to implement activities planned for it. In this case, bottom-up participation will generally be confined either to resistance against imposed plans and projects, or to micro "do-it-yourself" activities. As for participation launched by outside change agents, the two decisive variables are the realm in which it operates—diagnosis, the selection of options, implementation of activities chosen, subsequent evaluation—and how quickly it phases out.

Lessons of Experience

Experience has shown that it is relatively easy to achieve participation at micro levels of activity where homogeneous values and interests are easily found and mobilized. The small scale facilitates the active involvement of all those concerned. Hundreds, if not thousands, of cooperatives, associations, and community development organizations have prospered in Third World countries.[8]

It is also relatively easy for participation to remain authentic, *i.e.*, not to degenerate into manipulation by leaders if it confines its operations to the modest arenas in which it began. In effect, such participation creates islets of social organization which obey their own rules of problem-solving irrespective of dominant rules governing society at large.

Participation of some sort is likewise easy to obtain when it is induced by power wielders at the macro level. Strong governments easily "mobilize" large masses to lend the appearance of support to their policies or leaders. Elements of coercion, threat, and fear are clearly at play here. Although such "participation" is easy to promote, only with great difficulty can it achieve authenticity. Authenticity means vesting true decisional power in non-elite people, and freeing them from manipulation and co-optation. In cases of "pseudo-participation," moreover, it is almost impossible to move from mobilization to organization which can truly empower people and transfer voice to them.[9]

The most difficult form of participation to elicit and sustain is also the most indispensable to genuine development. This is participation that starts at the bottom and reaches progressively upward into ever-widening arenas of decision- making. It is that form of participation which is initiated, or at least ratified, by the interested non-elite populace at an early point in the sequence of decision-making. It matures into a social force which may form a critical mass of participating communities progressively empowered to enter into spheres of decision or action beyond their immediate problem-solving arenas.

The itinerary followed moves from micro to macro arenas. Numerous successful micro operations never expand beyond their initial small scale. Many others, although they may grow to achieve "critical mass," do not successfully resist being repressed, co-opted, or marginalized. The supremely difficult transition is precisely that which takes a movement from the micro arena to the macro without dilution or destruction.

Participation: A New Conceptualization

Participation, both as an instrument of development and as a special mode thereof, has not yet been adequately conceptualized. Existing theories of participation do not link it centrally to the core decision-making processes which shape national development strategies.[10] Consequently, participation is considered either as lying outside these processes or as subordinated to them by those who control the "real" dynamics of macro social processes. Certain recent experiences in participation, however, reveal it to be capable of entering into the very inner sanctum of developmental decision-making, by conferring a new voice in macro arenas of decision-making to previously powerless communities of need. These new avenues suggest how participation as a strategy may be conceptualized in a novel fashion.

Participation is best conceptualized as a special kind of *moral incentive* enabling hitherto excluded non-elites to negotiate new packages of material incentives benefiting them. In the pursuit of their development goals, governments hold out various moral incentives, ranging from threats to exhortations, promises of praise or designation as hero or model worker, to denunciation as an enemy of the nation, ostracism, and deprivation of honorific titles. Participation can be fruitfully regarded as a moral incentive within the particular context of a mixed system of social incentives. A "mixed system" combines material and moral incentives. The new element in the mix proposed here is participation, which takes the specific form of expenditures in time, interest, energy, and resources by non-elite people as their means of gaining power to negotiate a new package of material incentives for themselves.

In nearly all cases, incentive systems are designed by elites and held out as enticements to different categories of citizens. In new patterns of participation now discernible in several Third World countries, however, the elites' previous monopoly of the design function is being challenged by the hitherto powerless people most directly affected by the incentive packages in question. "Communities of need," which have struggled to mobilize and organize themselves at some micro level of problem-solving close to their own concerns, are now gaining entry into larger macro arenas of decision-making and beginning to play new roles as decisive actors in these arenas. More specifically, their leaders' appeals to invest time, attention, energy, and resources in participation are now portrayed to the people as their passport to influence higher macro realms, where decisions of crucial importance to their welfare are made.

Conclusion

Participation, or some active role-playing by intended beneficiaries, is an indispensable feature of all forms of development. Even technocratic or dictatorial regimes, which monopolize decisions as to what and how much people will consume, need to win some minimal acceptance of their decisions. At the very least, the populace must avoid boycotting the consumer goods in question, or actively resisting decisions reached through strikes or civil disobedience. It is therefore the nature and quality of participation as gauged by the criteria analyzed above, which largely determines the quality of a nation's development pattern. Where the populace has a voice in diagnosing its problems—where, in other words, it is actively involved in development decisions and actions from the beginning—development has a solid chance of centering on basic human needs, of attending to job creation, of offering opportunities for the consolidation of local and regional autonomy, of promoting patterns of interdependence of a horizontal type, and of respecting cultural integrity and diversity.

Conversely, where participation makes its appearance late in the sequence of decisions and actions, it is likely to be inauthentic, marked by manipulation or overt coercion, and to elicit patterns of development not chosen by the affected populace. If equity, respect for human rights, and the empowerment of local populations in ways consonant with their values—together with increasing output, raising productivity, and achieving institutional and technical modernization—are taken as development objectives, then a policy bias in favor of authentic participation correlates highly with genuine development. Ultimately, a vital connection exists between democracy and development, although, as the social historian Barrington Moore warns, there are limits to participatory democracy, political or economic.[11] Moreover, there is no way of fully suppressing the three-way tensions that pit the state's effort to control participation against attempts by grassroots movements to shape governmental decisions as well as attempts by powerless non-elite populations to gain some measure of control over their own destiny. In short, participation is no panacea for development. Its dual nature as both goal and means implies unending compromises between the antagonistic requirements of efficiency and equity.

Further ambiguities appear when participation initiated by one actor, the state, is "taken over" by another, the affected populace or some mobilizing third party. In such cases, the usual pattern is that the language of participation, which both parties want to preserve, may mask some unavowed manipulation by one of them around conflicting goals. To illustrate, the government may seek increased production or diversified agricultural production, whereas the rural co-operative it "aids" may take as its goal some measure of local, countervailing power against the government and the freedom to pursue its own traditional forms of agriculture.

Limits exist as to how much participation can occur and what goals it can achieve. Even generalized participation within a society cannot eliminate the need for government to take some non-participatory decisions and actions aimed at endowing a nation with infrastructure of various kinds or producing competitive international exports. Participation taken as a vital component of development strategy performs three vital functions:

(1) It guarantees government's non-instrumental treatment of powerless people by bringing them dignity as beings of worth, independent of their productivity, utility, or importance to state goals.

(2) It serves as a valuable instrument for mobilizing, organizing, and promoting action by people themselves as the major problem-solvers in their social environments. Poor people need not wait for some political patron, state agency, or beneficent

philanthropist to bring them salvation in the form of a new road, electricity, a school, or a supply of fertilizer. At the local level, participation enables people to do things for themselves.

(3) It acts as a channel through which local communities or movements can gain access to larger macro arenas of decision-making. The strength and solidarity won at local levels of problem-solving serve as springboards of credibility for hoping that some voice in larger decisions affecting material incentives—sectorally, regionally, or nationally—is possible. Consequently, the contributions in time, effort, energy, and resources made by local populations serve as moral incentives for them to improve the material rewards they will receive in the future.

The main lesson learned from the experience of developing countries pursuing a dominantly material incentives policy on the one hand, or on emphasizing moral incentives on the other, is that moral incentives work best when joined to a parallel package of material incentives. Moral incentives in the form of exhortations or appeals to donate time or resources for others are widely perceived by the target population as coercive. This is the reason why moral incentives alone probably do not produce good results. Conversely, a one-sided reliance on material incentives may be efficient, but it does not yield much equity. A more fruitful approach consists in discovering, or creating, new combinations of the two types of incentives.

Special problems confront governments or other elite agencies seeking to promote, induce, or foster participation. Such past efforts as the Cultural Revolution in China or the SINAMOS program in Peru after the populist revolution of 1968 do not leave analysts optimistic.[12] In growing numbers of Third World nations, nonetheless, newly democratic governments are searching for ways to enter into participatory alliances with grassroots groups already initiated to the practices of participation. Such cooperation is difficult for many reasons, not least of which is the distrust of government embedded in participatory movements and organizations which have had to resist repression and co-optation. Moreover, even well-intentioned governmental agencies suffer from the occupational hazards of bureaucracies, defining success by their capacity to survive, to process a trouble-free problem, or to achieve results within a specified period of time. Another lesson gleaned from the experience of participating communities is that gestation times for success are long and unpredictable. Yet bureaucracies are not designed to relate to the administered populace in a mode that respects these long gestation periods.[13]

Consequently, the stance of governmental agencies seeking participation should be more passive than active. Negatively, this stance consists of not impeding the entry into macro arenas of those participating groups previously operating in micro arenas. More positively, however, such agencies ought to create a free space, as it were, for neophyte participants to win legitimacy and voice in negotiation processes. Legitimacy and freedom do not suffice, however; participating groups also need information, documentation, expertise, and funds to conduct the discussions and studies needed to serve as effective negotiating partners in arenas where incentive packages are designed. Technical and political elites (partners) enjoy such resources; parity requires that their poorer partners likewise have access to them. Successful experiments in empowerment of local communities to shape larger decisions affecting them always contain some component of training to enable local people to master larger issues which transcend the boundaries of their immediate problems.

Participation was launched mainly as a defense mechanism against the destruction wrought by elite problem-solvers in the name of progress or development. From there, it has evolved into a preferred form of "do-it-yourself" problem-solving in small-scale operations. Now, however, many parties to participation seek entry into larger, more macro arenas of decision-making. Alternative development strategies that center on goals of equity, job creation, the multiplication of autonomous capacities, and respect for cultural diversity—all these require significant participation in macro arenas.[14] Without participation, development strategies will be both undemocratic and ineffectual. Without the developmental participation of non-elites, even political democracy will be largely a sham.

PART III

ETHICAL STRATEGIES:
ILLUSTRATIVE SECTORS

9.

TECHNOLOGY FOR DEVELOPMENT

In 1811 strange bands of masked men made their appearance around the English textile town of Nottingham. They roamed the countryside by night, shattering looms, weaving machines, and other factory equipment which had stripped them of their livelihood as craftsmen and brought competition and uncertainty to their lives. These "technological guerrillas" swore an oath not to reveal the names of fellow members in their secret society, professing allegiance to a leader known as Ned Ludd, a mythical Robin Hood figure who fired the imagination of the working classes. At first the Luddites,[1] as they were called, did not commit violence against people but only against machines. In 1812, however, a band of them was shot down by soldiers acting on behalf of an employer named Horsfall, who was later murdered by the Luddites in revenge. By 1813 severe government punishments—hanging and exiles—had decimated the ranks of the Luddites and although riots later flared up sporadically, the movement was shattered. To this day, the name Luddite remains symbolic of any movement which protests the dehumanization of life by instruments of technology.

Social critics in the Third World accuse Western technology of destroying their cultural values, addicting their poor people to wasteful consumption, and keeping them dependent on outside suppliers of technology. Nevertheless, most developing nations ardently desire

modern technology: it is their passport to modernity, their member-
ship card into the twentieth century. Yet technological optimism—the
belief that technology can abolish human misery within one generation—can be dangerous. Technology never operates in a vacuum: it
is created and used within concrete social settings and in order to
achieve certain ends, gaining some competitive advantage in warfare,
in political bargaining (by using the threat of war), and in trade. And
specific groups acquire a vested interest in promoting certain forms of
technology.

Creating and Destroying Values

To its users, modern technology brings new freedom from old
constraints imposed by nature, traditions, and rigid social patterns.
Dams, pesticides, and irrigation systems render farming communities
less vulnerable than before to the whims of nature—floods, droughts,
and insect infestations. Transistor radios, sewing machines, electric
water pumps, and bicycles not only reduce the drudgery of tedious
work, but also release women and children from ancient bonds of
conjugal or parental authority. Industrial technologies, thanks to their
demands for qualified mobile workers, likewise break down traditional
occupational patterns. But modern technologies also introduce new
determinisms into the lives of those who adopt them. The same factory workers who gain freedom from parental constraints or village
taboos as they enter into the urban wage system must now punch
time-clocks, catch buses on tight schedules, and bow to innumerable
pressures imposed by modern life. It is impossible to analyze
technology's dual role, of simultaneously creating new freedoms and
imposing new constraints, without first identifying the values most
deeply imbedded in Western technologies: specific conceptions of
rationality, *efficiency*, and *problem-solving*.

Rationality. For Westerners nurtured on scientific attitudes toward
evidence and familiarity with technological applications, "to be rational" means to view any reality as something which can be broken
down into component parts, analyzed, reassembled, manipulated in
practical ways, and measured in its effects. It is not "truth," in its
ancient meaning of correspondence between perception and some fixed
permanent essence or nature that matters to moderns, but rather veri-

fication—that is, observation and measured proof that something is what it appears to be. Westerners live and think on the historical level of verifiable facts. But many cultural communities in developing nations have lived on the mythical level and continue to view myth as no less real than history. Moreover, they are convinced that the West also has a profound need for meaning, myths, and symbols. And, they add, perhaps Western societies are so highly susceptible to ideological and symbolical manipulation—to fads—because they operate in a vacuum of myths.

Efficiency. The usual justification for introducing some concrete item of technology is that it is more efficient and more productive than manual work. "Efficiency" and "productivity" are terms which express a relationship, some proportion between inputs and outputs. Hence, if smaller inputs yield larger outputs, the process is said to be more efficient. Many diverse measures of efficiency exist. On the input side, one may compare how much labor, capital, land, money, time, or fatigue goes into producing something. And on the output side, one may measure the value, the quantity, the utility, and the impact of what is produced. In general, Western societies have adopted narrow models of efficiency: they have compared only the goods *directly* produced with the input instead of assessing the total results, including *indirect* effects, of their inputs. This failing is now widely acknowledged. And thanks to a better understanding of technology's overall effects on environment, on patterns of congestion, and on the use of time, many decision-makers have now begun to redefine the proper array of relevant considerations to take into account if one is to have a truly accurate "cost-benefit analysis" or "technology assessment." Thus no manufacturing process can be judged efficient if it pollutes the surroundings, forces people to live in crime-ridden or ugly agglomerations, or psychologically alienates workers with boring routine.

The narrow Western conception of efficiency contrasts sharply with contrary practices still prevalent in many developing countries, where people calculate economic or technological efficiency in ways which "internalize" (take into account) such values as religious duties, kinship obligations, artistry, and recreation. The general practice of Westerners, on the other hand, is to "externalize" (exclude) such values from their efficiency equation. The clash among of these divergent approaches to efficiency explains much of the tension and cultural destruction that results when Western technologies are applied indiscriminately in other societies.

Problem-Solving.   Technological modernists take a different approach to problem-solving than do traditional populations. Technocrats adopt a detached stance and treat any problem as an object to be analyzed, broken down into modules, and manipulated in a certain sequence. Nothing is sacred to them: the earth, and nature itself, are there to be mastered—and altered in the process! Traditional societies still assign high value to respecting nature, to observing rules of propriety in dealing with fellow-workers, and to preserving harmony with cosmic forces. Consequently, they often refuse to experiment with new solutions, preferring to follow inherited traditions.

The Impact of Technology Transfer

While Western technology promotes certain values of rationality, efficiency, and problem-solving, it also threatens or destroys other key values when "transferred" to Third World contexts. These are identified as follows.

Neglecting Needs.   Western technologies have evolved historically in a way that biases them in favor of large-scale, high-capital, low-labor, and standardized processes. These biases run counter to such important development goals as the need to launch numerous small-scale dynamic projects providing employment to large numbers of unskilled people, and which are not too costly for resource-poor countries. Moreover, most Western technologies presume the existence of purchasing power in the hands of a large pool of buyers. In most developing countries, however, the buying power of the needy masses is minimal. Therefore, the goods and services which large multinational corporations are best at producing with their technologies are the kinds that only the middle and upper classes and the rich can afford. The "basket of consumer goods" produced by multinationals matches the wants (or in economic terms, the preferences) of the privileged, not the needs of the poor. For this reason, one must prefer production by the masses (because it gave them jobs and incomes) to mass production (occurring in large factories with expensive tools that eliminate much human labor). Development is not simply economic growth but the sustainable improvement of living conditions for those in greatest need. Western technologies foster aggregate economic growth more readily than they promote the just distribution of development's benefits.

Cultural Damage. The "technological system" rewards successful problem-solvers in competitive arenas. These disproportionate rewards can easily lead them to become insensitive to the social and cultural damage they may cause in practicing their expertise. Not that traditional cultures are to be idealized, for there is much to condemn in the traditional double standard which treats women as inferiors along with a superstitious approach to hygiene. Nevertheless, many traditional strengths, indigenous values, and local institutions harbor a latent dynamism for change which is not sufficiently respected by conventional practitioners of "technological approaches." Most Third World populations depend on their traditions and indigenous values for their identity, their cultural integrity, and a sense of meaning to their lives (and death!). Too often technology destroys the symbols these people need to make sense of what is happening to them; it violates their relationship to nature, their friendship and kinship bonds operating independently of money considerations or of merit systems, and their artistic satisfactions derived from ritual celebrations which moderns easily condemn as economically "wasteful."[2]

Technology transfers across national borders are not value-free technical actions, but conflict-laden political transactions. Consequently, the total impact of a technological innovation on a society is more important than isolated results such as increasing production or creating new wealth. One always needs to ask: New wealth is created *for whom* and *at what cost* to human values? And *with what consequences* on the fabric of society at large?

The modern technology system simultaneously creates and destroys values. Yet no society can do without technology, which is indispensable to abolish misery, eliminate onerous work, and create new resources. The road to modernity necessarily passes through technology. But can modern technologies be harnessed to human ends?

Harnessing Technology to Human Ends. In judging the merits of a given technology, one must ask what purposes it serves, what interests it reinforces, what societal transformations it presupposes. The problem is not technology itself but the successful management of it, which requires wisdom and clarity as to the kind of society desired and the ways in which technology can help construct it. Several requirements must be met if technology is to be placed at the service of truly humane values.

A Wisdom to Match Our Sciences.   Wisdom is that unity or simplicity of understanding achieved after complexity has been overcome. Unity or simplicity which has not yet confronted complexity is not wisdom, but naïveté. Western societies, deeply immersed in empirical complexity and practical multiplicity for three centuries, have not yet discovered a unity—or wisdom—around which to organize their societies. As the sociologist Daniel Bell observes,[3] U.S. society is disjointed: economic life obeys one set of rules, political life another, and cultural life still another. Citizens in "developed countries" are overwhelmed with information overload and they experience future shock.[4]

Since the eighteenth century, modern societies have specialized in the pursuit of knowledge and largely abandoned even the very quest after wisdom.[5] Not surprisingly, they now find themselves ill-equipped to forge a synthesis of their vast scientific knowledge and conquests: they lack a wisdom to match their sciences. Developing countries, in turn, still live off residual traditional wisdoms, but these have become largely dysfunctional because they have not yet confronted that new complexity which is the challenge posed to them by modern science and technology. These ancient wisdoms were formulated at a time when human aspirations were relatively static, when social change occurred very slowly, and when each worldview faced little challenge from competing visions and made absolute claims upon people's belief and loyalty.

Today, in contrast, every belief system must come to terms with the existence of plural ideologies, the relativity of secular values, and new modes of "rationality" vehicled by modern science. On the one hand, modern problem-solvers have been too narrow and "reductionist" (reducing the whole of reality solely to those parts of it which they could observe empirically) in their approach to traditional values. On the other hand, only now are traditional wisdoms beginning to be tested in the crucible of a new struggle with conflicting meaning systems, and normative images of the good life and the good society. There is only one way out of the impasse: modern science and ancient wisdoms must come to dialogue with each other with mutual respect and formulate new unifying principles around which to organize disparate realities into some meaningful whole.

Appropriate Technology

The terms of the debate between advocates of so-called appropriate technology and advanced technology are often wrongly posed. National leaders should not choose one unique "appropriate technology," but rather make an appropriate choice of wide range of technologies. This requires that any government or industrial enterprise know clearly what range of technologies are available. National leaders must constantly advert to their development priorities, their resource capabilities, the possible effects of different technologies on income distribution, unemployment, and environmental soundness, and cultural survival. It is in accord with these considerations that appropriate choices are to be made.

At times, the use of inferior materials and less-trained people is preferable—even if the resulting product quality is lower—to spending large sums of money or creating unemployment by adopting other kinds of technology. There is a difference between simply putting all of one's eggs into the "appropriate" technology basket and choosing a whole range of appropriate technologies sector by sector, industry by industry, product by product.

Technology transfer may be likened to learning how to cook from a recipe. Let us imagine that A is a very good cook, whose proudest achievement is a perfect soufflé. On the other hand, B has tried making soufflés but they never come out quite right. No matter how many recipe books B reads for preparing soufflés, he/she never gets them right. In this case, technology transfer will occur not when someone gives B a better cookbook, but when A in observing B trying to make a soufflé advises, "This is what you are doing wrong," and proceeds to show B how to do it right. Such ongoing supervision of the process comes closer to capturing the essence of technology transfer. Of course, some minimum preparation is required in the learning partner. If the amateur cook does not even know what ingredients go into a soufflé, A would say, "I cannot transfer cooking technology to you because you are not yet sufficiently familiar with essentials to be a suitable candidate for successful learning."

Accordingly, the first pre-condition for successful technology transfer is that the recipient already know something about the whole process and can take further steps to understand the precise connections among things. Otherwise stated, one must know how to cope with novelty. Second, when the final user has been involved in formulating the technology problem and asking the prior research questions, successful transfer is more likely to occur. If, however, the final user has not shared in formulating the problem, there may be too great a distance between the problem, as it comes out of the research and development process, and the perceptual world of those who have to apply solutions. Whenever an institution with a vested interest in applying a technological solution already exists, a good transfer is more probable; otherwise much effort and money will be wasted. Technology transfer probably works best when answers come in direct response to queries posed by those facing production process difficulties.

Thomas Allen calls attention to the important role played by "technological gatekeepers."[6] After studying various types of private and public bureaucracies to identify who are the intermediaries between general technological information and concrete applications of it to new operations, Allen found that in every case transfer takes place only indirectly. In factories or laboratories, one usually finds a small number of people who are sufficiently detached from day-to-day activities to keep posted on research conducted outside their organization. Nevertheless, these individuals still have enough influence within their firm to persuade managers or engineers to try something new, even if the innovation may at first be expensive or require time-consuming adjustment in work procedures. Such individuals are the "technological gatekeepers."

Technology has now become the major resource for development. Paradoxically, however, technology is also the main policy instrument used by the industrially advanced societies to domesticate Third World development. Consequently, technology is perhaps the most vital arena where cultures and subcultures will either survive or be crushed. The absorptive capacity of these cultures will be tested in the technological arena.

A "Viable" Development Strategy

A. K. N. Reddy from the Indian Institute of Science in Bangalore, a pioneer in small-scale renewable energy and principal author of a UN report on "Methodology for Selection of Environmentally Sound and Appropriate Technologies," declares that if development is to be valid it must take as its objectives:

- the satisfaction of basic human needs (material and non-material), starting with those of the neediest, in order to achieve a reduction of inequalities between and within countries;

- endogenous self-reliance through social participation and control; and

- harmony with the environment.

He further stipulates that "the advancement of differing development objectives of industrialized and developing countries requires the establishment of a New International Economic Order, for it is only such an order that can make these differing objectives *compatible* with each other. Most importantly, Reddy postulates an intimate correlation between technology and a specific conception of development. "It must *not* be assumed," he concludes, "that all available technologies (however modern they may be) and all future technologies (likely to emerge in the guise of 'technological progress') are necessarily consistent with development objectives."[7]

Since development choices are unavoidably normative, it follows that different contents in the "vital nexus" can be discerned in the technology policies of developing nations. In certain cases, their dominant objectives are rapid industrialization, the enrichment of middle classes, the creation of large technical infrastructures, and the acquisition of advanced military capabilities. In such cases, the technology policy is clearly at the service of spurious development. Sound technology policy exists only when the social values and the development strategies from which that policy is derived are themselves just and sound. Obviously, leaders committed to an alienating conception of development cannot be induced to adopt a technology policy which will produce effects other than those contained implicitly in their initial options. Two questions remain fundamental at all times: what kind of development is being sought and at what social cost? Certain preferred technologies reinforce the dominance of certain social values and conversely, certain preferred social values in turn affect the criteria adopted for making technology choices.

Experimenting with Different Technologies

Technology policy works best in societies willing to experiment with different scales and modes of technology. Although some technologies favor given social constellations of values, others reinforce quite different values. Massive reliance on automobiles instead of on bicycles for urban transportation creates a quite different kind of metropolis. One has only to evoke images of Mexico City and Beijing to see the difference. Similarly, the small cottage industries favored by Gandhi in rural India imply a different pattern of working relationships, of mutual help, and of trading complementarities, than those associated with giant factory complexes.

A society's readiness to experiment with different mixes of technological inputs favors those social values not highly congenial to modern scales of technology. Numerous writers[8] call our attention to "diseconomies of scale" attaching to conventional Western technologies—ecological destruction, wasteful use of scarce resources, and a high level of political dependency. It is equally essential to weigh the cultural and psychological diseconomies attendant upon dehumanizing labor imposed upon large numbers of workers. High productivity is but a relative good needing to be balanced against other goods—a creatively satisfied work force, equitable access to resources and to jobs, the subordination of competitive instincts to collaborative needs.[9]

A nation unwilling to experiment with varied technological "optimum" scales and modes will be exposed and fully vulnerable to the powerful conditioning effects channeled by mainstream modern technologies.

Advocates of the "small is beautiful" philosophy plead the merits of "appropriate" technologies suited to poor local conditions. Their critics retort that "small is not necessarily powerful," a crucial point inasmuch as power is one major objective sought by Third World governments aspiring to modern technology. There exists no single scale, mode, or level of technology appropriate to all development

purposes. Even very poor countries may need a whole array of differently scaled and designed technologies in order to meet different goals.
A Haitian central banking official once explained to me that complex
coordinating activities—in this case, rapid transfers of credit monies
from Port-au-Prince to small farmers in isolated mountain villages—
required "high" technological instruments such as computers. The
obvious point is that a national technology policy dictates "appropriate" mixes of technologies located at various points on the twin scales
of size and complexity.

Nevertheless, in many Third World areas a strong case can be
made for sinning on the side of making "small and reversible" mistakes. Most modern technologies are so costly to install and maintain,
so complex to repair, and so inflexible in their requirement of standardized intermediate inputs that their adoption by poor societies risks
being highly wasteful. In technology policy, as in development planning, it is the better part of wisdom to seek solutions to problems in
experimental ways which respond flexibly to lessons learned from ongoing experience. For this if for no other reason, therefore, technology policy ought to favor multiple small innovations over a few larger
ones. Lessons gleaned from the massive introduction of "miracle
strains" of wheat in several Asian countries suggest that ecological
vulnerability to new blights was needlessly courted—all because a
single technological improvement was applied indiscriminately on a
vast scale.[10]

Developers who seek to launch technological practices in ways
that keep cultural and social damage to a minimum should experiment
with a variety of alternative technical solutions. Otherwise the value
sacrifices exacted of societies may be perceived as excessive only
after irreversible commitments (in the form of capital, creation of a
support structure, and training of personnel) have been made to a
given solution. In several Third World countries, experiments are
now under way to determine the least expensive and the most equitable ways of harnessing technology to the needs of poor villagers.
Consultative processes between specialists and the general population are essential to adjudicate competing claims. In Indian villages
where animal dung is undergoing biogasification treatment to produce electricity, for instance, the key equity question is how to bring
electricity to families too poor to own cows and therefore unable to
supply dung. Where electricity has multiple uses—household light-

ing and cooking, the pumping of water in village wells, and the running of machinery in small workshops—how is the distribution of technology's benefits to be made "appropriate" to the full range of villagers' needs? Continued experimentation is necessary if we are to gain sound answers. Flexible experimentation is rendered impossible, however, by initial commitments of large-scale capital, design, and training to single levels of technology.

New Incentive Systems

Managers of public and private firms in developing countries usually have strong reasons for buying technology from international suppliers. They desire the timely delivery of reliable technological goods. And because technology is a powerful weapon in their marketing strategy, they are reluctant to use alternative local technology supplies, not least because foreign technology commands greater prestige in the market place. Firm managers likewise attach great importance to favorable financing terms when they purchase technology. For all these reasons, government policy cannot easily wean them away from their usual sources of technology supply. The single most compelling pressure upon many officials of Third World companies to buy local technology is the shortage of foreign currency as well as their inability to secure easy credits to purchase imported technology. Accordingly, Third World governments wishing to reorient technology demand need to provide concrete incentives for users of technology, if these are to seek other sources of supply.

Government policies frequently rely on negative incentives to achieve greater "indigenization" of technology use. Negative incentives take varied forms: restrictive legislation on technological imports, compulsory registry of licensing contracts, ceilings on technology payments to foreigners, and the requirement imposed on local consumers of technology to prove that indigenous technology is unavailable to them for a particular task before being allowed to import from outside suppliers. In the absence of positive incentives, however, purely negative measures cannot succeed. Unless local suppliers of technology can satisfy the aspirations of firm managers on the demand side—their need for reliable and timely delivers, easy marketability, and credit facilities—restrictive legislation leads to wide-scale circumvention, whether by black market operations or by the disguising of *de facto* foreign purchases. Wherever vulnerable Third World economies are tightly linked to markets responsive to the control of outside forces, it proves difficult *in the short term* to reverse established technology supply and demand circuits. Even in adverse circumstances like these, however, governments can provide supportive incentive systems which at least facilitate the creation of the vital nexus at the micro level.

To illustrate, agriculture ministries can give credits to small farming units, individuals and cooperatives, to develop new technologies using inexpensive materials locally available. Ministries can at least confer legitimacy on the goal of maximum technical self-reliance at local levels by favoring small-scale production units aimed at the satisfaction of priority food needs. They can likewise provide technical advice to researchers and problem-solvers trying to create new sources of technology supply.

The rationale for this sort of government policy is twofold. First, the policy goals of fostering more indigenous technologies in harmony with societal values and with the larger goals of development strategy need to be pursued wherever leverage exists to do so, especially when large numbers of people are directly affected by choices made. New circulatory flows governing indigenous supply and demand of technology can also be set up in industrial and service sectors, but greater freedom of action and a higher probability of initial success are found in the rural sector. A second reason for pursuing leverage points at the micro level is the vital importance of building up a critical mass of relatively self-reliant producer units at the grass roots. Small innovations can be multiplied and the ongoing correction of errors can be realized more cheaply in local projects, especially in rural settings. More importantly, the dialogue between technical problem-solvers and the populace which is essential to a true vital nexus[11] is best achieved in small-scale operations.

Countries lacking the knowledge, the trained personnel, the supportive structures, and the political strength to achieve a fully coherent *national* technology policy can nonetheless make gradual progress toward such a policy by applying the vital nexus at more modest levels, selected localities, or sectors of activity.

Choosing Among Conflicting Goals

The Third World's technological aspirations center around four goals:

(1) Access to the full range of actual and potential technologies.

(2) A fair price structure in international technology markets.

(3) The purchase of technology in ways that favor the optimum use of local resources (materials, human skills, and capital) instead of buying "packages" imposed upon buyers on "all or nothing" terms by outside technology suppliers.

(4) Reduction of their dependence on outside technology innovators, who enjoy a near monopoly on R&D activities.

These four goals are not readily compatible among themselves. The quest for a high degree of technical autonomy may dictate sacrifices in access to the full gamut of existing merchandise. Likewise, a policy of making optimum use of local materials, skills, and finance capital, with the correlative decision to limit technological imports to "core" technology, can weaken the negotiating pressure poor countries can apply to the world pricing system in force. The reason is that many transnational suppliers will simply refuse to sell to purchasers who "break up the package."

These four general goals are attainable only at a price. That price may well be the temporary acceptance of scant progress on one front while efforts are concentrated on achieving greater gains in other arenas. Nevertheless, the careful trading off of gains among several arenas is a useful tactic which renders it easier to establish the vital nexus. Successful trade-offs are impossible, however, unless a prior screening has been made of a society's value priorities and development strategies. If, for example, the creation of jobs is a high priority in development strategy and if most jobs are to go to the poorest among the population, then the decision to maximize the use of local materials, untrained non-specialists, and local currency in technological activities already constitutes the third element in the vital nexus.

10.

DEVELOPMENT ETHICS AND ECOLOGICAL WISDOM

The ecological imperative is clear and cruel: nature must be saved or we humans will die. The single greatest threat to nature—menacing irreversible destruction of its regenerative powers—comes from "development." This same "development" is also the major culprit in perpetuating the "underdevelopment" of hundreds of millions. The task of eliminating degrading underdevelopment imposes itself with the same urgency as that of safeguarding nature. These twin concerns have spawned two ethical streams of protest. Yet almost always the two streams flow in opposite directions: one is concerned with protecting nature, the other with promoting economic justice. This dissonance is tragic because it is the identical pseudodevelopment which lies at the root of both problems. The only antidote to pseudodevelopment is a working ethic of what is generally called "sustainable development," but which is better termed "integral authentic development." Such an ethic joins the two normative streams, linking the concern for environmental responsibility with the drive for universal economic justice.

There can be no sound development ethic without environmental wisdom and, conversely, no environmental wisdom without a solid development ethic. Development ethics must enter into the formulation of environmental policy, and environmental ethics in the formulation of developmental policy. The task of bringing the two ethical streams together, however, faces great difficulties: fundamental problems of language and meaning, disagreements of diagnosis, discordant policy preferences, and conflicting value assessments. These difficulties are compounded because multiple development paradigms vie for legitimacy. There exist antagonistic ways of defining the essential tasks of ethical reflection, and the very terms "ecology" and "environment" often evoke associations irreconcilable with "development."

Environmental wisdom is compatible only with *certain* images of development, and only with *certain* modes of ethical reflection. Similarly, a normatively sound concept of development is consonant only with *certain* conceptions of the environmental or ecological task. What is needed is an overarching framework of dynamic synthesis, a philosophical vision which reconciles the alleged opposition between human freedom and the integrity of nature. To state matters differently, one must articulate a conceptual scheme in which the demands of three distinct ethical values—justice, freedom, and respect for nature—all become *relativized*. No single one of these values has absolute worth; more importantly, each can only be defined and delineated in its proper boundaries with relation to the other two.

The Ecology of Integral Development

Ecology has now become a household word. Here lies illuminating symbolism since in its Greek etymology "ecology" designates the science of the larger household, the total environment in which living organisms exist. Hence, whenever it is faithful to its origins and inner spirit, ecology is holistic: it looks to the whole picture, to the totality of relations. As a recently certified pluridisciplinary field of study, ecology embraces four interrelated subjects: environment, demography, resource systems, and technology. Its special contribution to human knowledge is to draw a coherent portrait of how these four distinct realms interact in patterns of vital interdependence. Ecological wisdom is the search for optimal modes and scales in which human populations may apply technology to resource use within their environments. Ecology, both as an intellectual discipline and as a practical concern, presupposes some philosophy of nature. Traditional human wisdoms long ago parted ways, however, in their fundamental conceptions of nature and of how humans should relate to it. All wisdoms acknowledge humans to be part of nature, subject to its laws and constraints. The common destiny of all natural beings, humans included, is generation and corruption; they are born, grow, age, and die. But certain worldviews, more than others, have elevated humans above their encompassing nature and assigned them a cosmic role of domination over that very nature of which they are a part. This duality is aptly expressed in the interrogatory words which serve as the title of a Sri Lankan publication, *Man in Nature: Guest or Engineer?*[1]

Nature and human liberty have come to be perceived as opposing poles in a dichotomy. There is paradox here, for human beings are not physically compelled to respect nature but they need to do so if they are to preserve the existential ground on which their freedom rests. Because this is so, there can be no ultimate incompatibility between the demands of nature and the exigencies of human freedom, those of environmental sanity and wise resource stewardship. Insoluble theoretical and practical difficulties arise when one does not look at the whole picture. One needs to look at the whole picture in order to transcend numerous apparent antimonies. Chief among these is the supposed contradiction between anthropocentric and cosmocentric views of the universe.

According to Robert Vachon, the Canadian philosopher of interculturalism, Orientals perceive humanity, nature, and the divine not as autonomous realities but as non-dualistic dimensions of life linked and harmonious with all dimensions of being. Vachon brands the oriental vision of reality holistic because it grants priority to totality over opposition or polarity.[2]

Similarly, the opposition between human freedom and nature can be subsumed under a larger whole—namely, "integral development," a normative concept which embraces three elements: the good life, the foundations of life in society, and the proper stance toward nature. The French ecologist Bernard Charbonneau insists that freedom itself is nature and that both form part of a larger whole.[3] Reconciling nature and freedom is a difficult task precisely because emphasizing one or the other has given birth to divergent ethical orientations. Those who stress the integrity of nature obey an ethic, the highest values of which are the conservation of resources, the preservation of species, and the defense of nature against human depredations. Those who stress human freedom frame an ethic with the primary values of justice (taking the form of an active assault upon human poverty, itself branded as the worst form of pollution) and the duty to "develop" latent resources into their actualized state.

Although both ethical orientations adhere to all five values just listed, they rank them differently. A "nature" emphasis locates development and the elimination of human misery below biological conservation and resource replenishment in the hierarchy of values. In contrast, a "freedom" orientation places development and the active conquest of justice in resource allocations above environmental protection or the preservation of endangered species. Nevertheless, all five values ought to enjoy parity of moral status because any long-term, sustainable, equity-enhancing combat against poverty requires wisdom in the exploitation of resources, just as the preservation of species cannot persuasively be held out as a priority goal if the human species is threatened with degrading poverty or extinction. Nature itself is diminished when its human members are kept "underdeveloped"; reciprocally, human members cannot become truly "developed" if their supportive nature is violated.

Perhaps no worldview can successfully integrate the requirements of nature and freedom except around some higher telos or end-value to which both nature and human freedom are subordinate. Since neither nature nor freedom can be taken as absolute values, however, diverse philosophies and religions assign different value weightings to each. Even within specific worldviews, competing interpretations arise as to the "proper" respective weights to be assigned to nature and to freedom. To illustrate, throughout its history Christianity has harbored a tendency toward exaggerated supernaturalism in which the realms of nature and human activity are treated merely as arenas for human beings to test their virtue or to save their souls. On the other hand, there has been a trend toward excessive naturalism in which God's transcendent and mysterious salvation is reduced to being merely a better way of organizing human society. Within Christianity, there have flourished schools of interpretation favoring an exaggerated theocentric humanism which assumes that anything given to man is stolen from God, and an imbalanced anthropocentric theism in which God becomes a glorified projection of popular human values.

The French Christian philosopher Jacques Maritain, taking up a theme defended seven centuries earlier by Thomas Aquinas, considers that neither nature nor human freedom can be properly valued unless the entire realm of historical time and space is seen as a universe of *infravalent ends*.[4] Therefore, human efforts deployed to expand the frontiers of knowledge, to institute justice and fraternity in political institutions, to create and distribute wealth in economic endeavors, and to craft beauty in artistic enterprises are not merely *means* for gaining the ultimate end, blessed union, and happiness with God. These temporal activities are themselves ends, and as such they are intrinsically precious. Nevertheless, the entire order of being represented by human activities in time and space is subordinate to a higher, more absolute, and transtemporal end.

If one bears in mind this transtemporal end, it appears that some kind of anthropocentric vision of the universe is unavoidable. Since nature cannot defend itself, humans must now assume the task. The human exploitation of planet Earth has gone beyond the threshold point where nature can defend and regenerate itself. The symbiosis between nature and the human species so urgently needed can only result from placing human responsibility at the center of the task of conserving nature. Things have gone wrong not because humans held an anthropocentric view of the universe (they could not do otherwise!), but because they erred in defining the value content of their development and freedom. Freedom *from* constraining nature is indeed a positive value, but it is not an absolute one. Freedom *from* constraints is a value because it allows freedom *for* human fulfillment or realization. But that very realization substantively consists in establishing full harmony with nature—with the cosmos, with the whole universe.

The intercultural philosopher Raimundo Panikkar pleads for a radical change in our understanding of relationships between humans and nature:

> . . . a thoroughgoing conversion which recognizes and appropriates their common destiny. As long as man and world remain estranged, as long as we insist in relating them only as master to slave—following the metaphor used by Hegel and Marx—as long as their relation is not seen to constitute both world and man, no lasting remedy will ever be found. For this reason, I submit that no dualistic solution can endure.[5]

Panikkar divides history into three "kairological moments" of

human consciousness: pre-historical, historical, and transhistorical.[6]
These "moments" are not chronologically separate but define qualitatively different attitudes prevailing at given periods. In the epoch of
historical consciousness:

> Man lives mainly in space. . . . The World of pre-historical
> Man, his environment, is the *theocosmos* or *theocosm*, the
> divinised universe. It is not a World of Man, but it is also not
> the World of the Gods as a separate and superior realm hov-
> ering over the human. . . . In the pre-historical mentality, it is
> the World that is divinised (to use historical language). The
> divine permeates the cosmos. The forces of nature are all
> divine. Nature is supernatural. Or rather, nature is that which
> is "natured," born, from the divine. Pre-historical Man's mi-
> lieu is a cosmotheological one. *Harmony* is the supreme prin-
> ciple—which does not mean that it has been achieved.[7]

The second "kairological moment" is marked by historical consciousness in which "Historical time is under the spell of the future
and the guidance of reason. Only the historical is real."[8] As Panikkar
explains:

> The World of historical Man, his environment, is the *anthro-*
> *pocosmos* or *anthropocosm*, the human world, the universe
> of Man. He is not interested in the evolution of the cosmos;
> his destiny has little to do with the fate of the stars or the
> phases of the moon, or even the seasons and the rivers. . . .
> Nature has been tamed and subjugated. It has been
> demythicized and there is nothing "mysterious" about it. His-
> torical Man has overcome the fear of nature. His backdrop is
> *cosmological*. The meaning of his life is not to be found in
> the cosmic cycles, but in the human sphere, the society. Jus-
> tice is the supreme principle—which does not mean that it
> has been achieved.[9]

These two degrees of consciousness, pre-historical and historical,
have not disappeared from the face of the earth but, says Panikkar, "A
third degree of consciousness is coming more and more to the fore."[10]
This is transhistorical consciousness in the form of metaphysical in-

sights and mystical experiences, which have always been in the air but which nowadays gain momentum and change their character.

A new emerging myth situates transhistorical Man in what Panikkar calls the anthropocosmos:

> Pre-historical Man has *fate*. He is part and parcel of the universe. Historical Man has *destiny*. He predestines where he stands. He arranges his own life. Trans-historical Man has *his lot*. He is involved in the total adventure of reality, by participating freely in the portions allotted to him. . . . The World of trans-historical Man, his environment or ecosystem, is the cosmotheandric universe. . . . The destiny of Man is not just an historical existence. It is linked with the life of the Earth and with the entire fate of reality, the divine not excluded. God or the gods are again incarnated and share in the destiny of the universe at large. We are all in the same boat, which is not just this planet Earth, but the whole mystery of Life, Consciousness, Existence. *Love* is the supreme principle—which, again, does not mean that it has been achieved.[11]

The "new innocence" of which Panikkar speaks is neither cosmocentric nor anthropocentric, but brings all together in a "consciousness lived neither naively nor by rational projection into the future."[12] The center is "neither in God, nor in the cosmos, nor even in man. It is a moving center which is only to be found in the intersection of the three."[13]

Authentic development emerges from the living aspirations of communities of need to affirm themselves as truly human. Similarly, a sound active respect for nature is found more solidly entrenched in non-elite populations, who are the repositories of traditional culture, than in the coterie of new experts calling themselves systems analysts, resource planners, futurists, or ecologists.[14] Consequently, respect for tradition is just as essential for sound developmental planning as it is for ecological strategizing. Most traditional wisdoms have normatively stipulated that human freedom and intervention must respect nature. And they have understood, in turn, that nature is an indispensable ally to sustain, support, and provide for the expansion of that same human freedom. An ethic of authentic development is therefore *ipso facto* an ethic of ecological wisdom. Sound development enjoins and practices ecological wisdom, just as ecological wisdom (integrally and comprehensively understood) promotes sound and harmonious human development. What is urged here is not some passive stance in which no human interventions will be made upon nature to promote some sort of economic growth. Rather, the scope and content of that growth will be redefined and renegotiated to assure just and adequate access to essential goods by all, and to protect biosystemic sustainability.

Conflicts over priorities are inevitable. Cruel choices, such as whether to risk irreversibly damaging some ecosystem to satisfy the immediate needs for food or fuel of an impoverished populace, will not be eliminated; and no pre-existing answers, normative and operational, are to be found or discovered anywhere. Correct answers must be negotiated in arenas of decision-making, and via a process engaging the representatives of three rationalities—technical, political, and ethical. It will be understood by all parties, however, that neither developmental nor ecological values may be treated instrumentally, as a mere means to realizing the other. Although neither is absolute, both are end values.

According to the World Bank, the "achievement of sustained and equitable development remains the greatest challenge facing the human race."[15] Nevertheless, equitable authentic human development has yet to be achieved. Therefore, it will not do merely to sustain the kind of development we already have.

The World Commission on Environment and Development (Brundtland Commission) defines sustainable development as "development that meets the needs of the present without compromising the ability of future generations to meet their own needs."[16] This apparently clear definition is fraught with ambiguities, however. As the economist Paul Streeten notes, it is not certain whether one should:

> . . . be concerned with sustaining the constituents of well-being or its determinants, whether with the means or the ends. Clearly, what ought to matter are the constituents: the health, welfare and prosperity of the people, and not so many tons of minerals, so many trees, or so many animal species. Yet, some of the writings on the subject confuse the two. If, in the process of curing ovarian and other forms of cancer, the Pa-

cific yew trees (or even the spotted owl) had to be reduced in number, in order to produce the drug taxol, people's health must be given priority over trees. Of course, some would want to attach end-values to "nature." This view might be called ethical environmentalism in contrast with prudential environmentalism.[17]

To complicate matters further, Streeten adds, the term "sustainable development" has at least six different meanings. It can signify the (1) "maintenance, replacement and growth of capital assets, both physical and human"; (2) "maintaining the physical environmental conditions for the constituents of well-being"; (3) the "resilience" of a system, enabling it to adjust to shocks and crises; (4) "avoiding burdening future generations with internal and external debts"; (5) "fiscal, administrative and political sustainability. A policy must be credible and acceptable to the citizens, so that there is sufficient consent to carry it out"; and (6) "the ability to hand over projects to the management by citizens of the developing country in which they are carried out, so that foreign experts can withdraw without jeopardizing their success."[18]

"Sustainable development" has now become a fashionable mantra or catchword in international policy circles. The Earth Summit (UNCED Rio Conference of 1992) created a new UN Commission on Sustainable Development to monitor progress on fulfilling the prescriptions of Agenda 21, a vast program of measures aimed at assuring environmentally sound growth. And the U.S. President has established a twenty-five-member National Council on Sustainable Development.[19]

In March of 1993, the World Business Academy sponsored a conference in Dallas on "The Quest for Sustainability with Prosperity." But are sustainability and profitability mutually compatible? Perhaps not, for as the economist Paul Ekins observes:

> . . . the dominant trajectory of economic development since the industrial revolution has been patently unsustainable. There is literally no experience of an environmentally sustainable industrial economy, anywhere in the world, where such sustainability refers to a non-depleting stock of environmental capital. It is therefore not immediately apparent that,

on the basis of past experience only, the term "sustainable development" is any more than an oxymoron.[20]

Sustainability requires simple living in which consumption is limited.[21] Prosperity for all, on the other hand, demands endless economic growth, which may render sustainability impossible by depleting resources and polluting the biosphere irreversibly. The burden of proof lies on those who hold that sustainability and prosperity can coexist. The issue cannot be settled, however, until a prior question is answered—What is genuine wealth?

Defining Wealth

(1) Carolina Maria de Jesus was an impoverished single mother of three dwelling in São Paulo's Canindé slum. Her diary, written on scraps of paper as an exercise in fantasizing to escape the squalor of her life, was accidentally discovered by a journalist in 1958 and became an instant best seller in Brazil. In order to forget her troubles, Carolina wrote poems, novels, and plays:

> . . . anything and everything, for when I was writing I was in a golden palace, with crystal windows and silver chandeliers. My dress was finest satin and diamonds sat shining in my black hair. Then I put away my book and the smells came in through the rotting walls and rats ran over my feet. My satin turned to rags and the only things shining in my hair were lice.[22]

Carolina's definition of wealth is disarmingly simple: "[T]he basic necessities must be within reach of everyone."[23]

(2) Gandhi often declared that there are enough goods in the poorest Indian village to meet the needs of all, but not enough goods in all of India to satisfy the greed of each one. Gandhi advocated production by the masses, which brings dignity and livelihood to all, not mass production, which is production by a few reducing the masses to being mere consumers of others' profit-making activities.[24]

(3) Barry Lopez, a student of Native American societies, consid-

ers that:

> Some native ideas could serve us well in this historical moment: that a concept of wealth should be founded in physical health and spiritual well-being, not material possessions; that to be 'poor' is to be without family, without a tribe—without people who care deeply for you.[25]

(4) Georges Perec is the author of *Things*, a novel about the good life as lived by an upwardly mobile consumerist French couple in the 1960s. At the age of thirty, they "make it," succeeding professionally and socially. Yet the book ends on this sardonic note: "They will be well-housed, well-fed, well-clothed. They will have nothing to regret . . . . [it is] the prelude to a sumptuous feast. Yet the meal which will be served to them will be frankly insipid."[26]

(5) Early Fathers of the Christian Church—John Chrysostom, Gregory of Nyssa, and Basil the Great—often preached on the difference between material and spiritual goods.[27] According to them, only such spiritual goods as virtue, friendship, truth, and beauty constitute genuine wealth. Material goods are by nature limited and cannot be shared without diminishing the advantages each one derives from them. In contrast, spiritual goods grow in intensity and in their capacity to satisfy as they are shared. True wealth, they assert, resides in the internal freedom which makes one use material goods instrumentally to meet needs, and as a springboard for cultivating those higher goods which alone bring deeper satisfaction.

(6) The Brazilian economist Celso Furtado condemns transnational corporations for producing a basket of consumer goods tailored to satisfy the wants of the middle and upper classes, rather than meet the needs of the poor.[28]

(7) In 1954 Adolf Berle wrote:

> The really great corporation managements have reached a position for the first time in their history in which they must consciously take account of philosophical considerations. They must consider the kind of community in which they have

faith, and which they will serve. . . . In a word, they must consider at least in its more elementary phases the ancient problem of the "good life," and how their operations in the community can be adapted to affording or fostering it.[29]

Berle points to a striking paradox:

Our grandfathers quarrelled with corporations because, as the phrase went, they were "soulless." But out of the common denominator of the decision-making machinery, some sort of consensus of mind is emerging, by compulsion as it were, which for good or ill is acting surprisingly like a collective soul.[30]

(8) The psychologist Erich Fromm observes that people always choose one of two modes of living:

The alternative of *having* versus *being* does not appeal to common sense. *To have*, so it would seem, is a normal function of our life: in order to live we must have things. Moreover, we must have things in order to enjoy them. In a culture in which the supreme goal is to have—and to have more and more—and in which one can speak of someone as "being worth a million dollars," how can there be an alternative between having and being. On the contrary, it would seem that the very essence of being is having; that if one *has nothing*, one *is nothing*.

Yet the great Masters of Living have made the alternative between having and being a central issue of their respective systems. The Buddha teaches that in order to arrive at the highest stage of human development, we must not crave possessions. Jesus teaches: "for whosoever will save his life shall lose it; but whosoever will lose his life for my sake, the same shall save it. For what is a man advantaged, if he gain the whole world, and lose himself, or be cast away?" (Luke 9:24-25) Master Eckhart taught that to have nothing and make oneself open and "empty," not to let one's ego stand in one's way, is the condition for achieving spiritual wealth and strength.

For many years I had been deeply impressed by this distinction and was seeking its empirical basis in the concrete study of individuals and groups by the psychoanalytic method. What I saw has led me to conclude that this distinction, together with that between love of life and love of the dead, represents the most crucial problem of existence; that empirical anthropological and psychoanalytic data tend to demonstrate that *having and being are two fundamental modes of experience, the respective strengths of which determine the differences between the characters of individuals and various types of social character.*[31]

(9) The political theorist Douglas Lummis argues that individual riches are not the only form of wealth:

There are other forms that can be shared in common. But these forms of wealth are more political than economic. . . . Common wealth is not something achieved by economic development but by the political ordering of a community. . . . Common wealth may find its physical expression in such things as public roads, bridges, libraries, parks, schools, churches, temples, or works of art that enrich the lives of all. It may take the form of "commons," shared agricultural land, forests or fisheries. It may take the form of ceremonies, feast days, festivals, dances, and other public entertainments celebrated in common. . . .

A marriage of the ancient idea of *commonwealth* with our presently emerging (or re-emerging) understanding of *environment* could give birth to a promising new notion of what "wealth" really is. . . .

The *problem* of the problem of inequality lies not in poverty, but in excess. "The problem of the world's poor," defined more accurately, turns out to be "the problem of the world's rich." This means that the solution to that problem is not a massive change in the culture of poverty so as to place it on the path of development, but a massive change in the culture of superfluity in order to place it on the path of counter-development. It does not call for a new value system forcing the world's majority to feel shame at their traditionally moderate consumption habits, but for a new value system forcing the world's rich to see the shame and vulgarity of their over-consumption habits, and the double vulgarity of standing on other people's shoulders to achieve those consumption habits.[32]

These reflections on wealth suggest that any ethical judgments we make about wealth and the institutions devoted to creating it need to be rooted in philosophical conceptions about the broader purposes of human existence.

Unanswered Questions

The debate on sustainable development is replete with uncertainties and unanswered (perhaps unanswerable) questions.

Question #1.   Is "sustainable authentic development" (SAD) compatible with a globalized economy? One commentator on recent global and regional trade negotiations (GATT and NAFTA) insists:

The philosophy inherent in these accords is directly opposed to the idea of sustainable economic development promoted in Rio. ECO 92 called for economic development that took into account environmental costs. It envisioned harmonizing economic activity with environmental protection by adapting development to fit environmental needs.

The struggle over environmental concerns is no longer a simple North-South dialectic or balancing of needs between industrialized and developing nations. Neoliberal free trade policies are being pushed by a worldwide corporate elite bent on defining the environment as a trade barrier expressed in dollars. Governments have abetted this transformation by forging agreements that ensure a nation's powerlessness to defend itself against commercial activities that harm its citizens or the environment.[33]

Worldwide environmental sustainability may require economic decentralization or localization, this in recognition of the vast "diseconomies" attendant upon large-scale production, distribution, and consumption.

Question #2.   Is SAD compatible with a high material standard of living, as presently defined and measured, for all human populations? If limits must be placed on growth, or if growth has to be redesigned to achieve what Herman Daly calls a "steady-state" economy,[34] there must be cutbacks in present consumption of the "haves" and in future acquisitive aspirations of the "have-nots."

Such cutbacks run counter to the momentum built up over fifty years in the "revolution of rising expectations." How, then, politically speaking, are they to be achieved? If the example of failed central command economies holds out any lesson, it is that austerity cannot be imposed by coercion. And the reluctance of citizens in developed countries to accept even modest tax increases for deficit-cutting or the provision of necessary social services suggests that sacrifices for the sake of sustainability will not be readily consented.

Question #3.   Is SAD compatible with widening global economic disparities? Does not SAD presuppose, if not high levels of relative equality, at least the abolition of absolute poverty among the world's poor masses? But what realistic prospects exist, either for abolishing absolute poverty or for diminishing global disparities? Aid "fatigue" among the rich has greatly reduced the volume of net resource transfers to the poor. Moreover, the world economy is growing too slowly for any "increased economic pie" to "trickle down" (assuming such "trickle-down" did occur) to spill its developmental benefits onto the world's impoverished populations. For Leonard Silk, the greatest danger is that of falling into a new worldwide depression for, contrary to euphoric expectations at the end of the Cold War, "the peace dividend only shows up in lost jobs and falling incomes."[35] Transnational flows of economic migrations tax national and international absorptive systems beyond present capacity. And growing economic disparities will but exacerbate the problem.

Question #4.   How do strategists promoting SAD deal with the hundreds of millions who have a vested interest in the present non-SAD economic dynamism prevailing in the world? What incentives, what countervailing power, and what persuasive alternative economic interests can dissuade:

- corporations from continuing to place short-term profit ex-traction from natural resources above long-term environmental protection?

- military establishments from continuing their monumentally wasteful and toxic modes of resource use and disposal?

- billions of consumers (actual and potential) from curtailing their use of certain practices in the interests of guarding against remote and uncertain future catastrophes in the ozone or the global climate system?

- politicians from adopting wise measures in the long-term defense of biospheres which, in the short term, consign them to political oblivion?

In the view of one astute economic observer, nation-states are rapidly becoming dysfunctional and irrelevant as world economic actors. The future, he contends, belongs to regions transcending national boundaries and willing to participate in the borderless economies. Restrictions, limitations, and controls on such participation are obstacles to economic success.[36]

Even after the 1972 UN Conference on the Environment (Stockholm) and its latter-day sequel, the Earth Summit (Rio de Janeiro 1992), unsustainable development continues with its momentum unabated, because many powerful economic actors have a vested interest in maintaining this form of development. Neither moral exhortations, nor UN Declarations of Principle, nor alarms sounded over environmental collapse will alter their course.[37]

Conclusion

The essential task of development ethics is to render development decisions and actions humane. It is to assure that the painful changes launched under the banner of development do not result in anti-development, which destroys nature, human cultures, and individuals and exacts undue sacrifices—all in the name of profit, some absolutized ideology, or a supposed efficiency imperative. A comprehensive development ethics that incorporates environmental wisdom is the conceptual cement which binds together multiple diagnoses of problems to their policy implications through an explicit phenomenological study of values.

11.

CULTURE AND TRADITION IN DEVELOPMENT

Poor people everywhere have always understood that economic progress in their society usually benefits others and leaves them more vulnerable than before to forces they cannot control. These forces threaten the very survival of their culture and traditions. As development experts belatedly come to recognize this tragic outcome, they acknowledge that if genuine development is to take place, traditional values and cultures must not be recklessly destroyed.[1]

How can any human community preserve the values essential to its identity and cultural integrity while changing its social conditions to improve the quality of life of its people? Traditional value systems and indigenous cultures are not inert deposits of wisdom or ritual, but vital realities that change through time and continue to provide identity and meaning to people conscious of themselves as actors on a shifting historical stage. Every society formulates a strategy for its survival, for access to resources, and for interpreting the information that becomes available to it. This strategy embraces many values, some of which lie at the core of a community's identity, while others ripple out into ever-widening circles away from this centre on the margins of that inner core. Nevertheless, all these values form part of a patterned whole possessing unity and meaning.

Rationality is not synonymous or co-extensive with modern technology or the scientific method. Many attitudes and actions which moderns judge to be irrational, superstitious, or uncritical are, when properly understood in their true context, fully rational.[2] Every society makes sense of reality on the basis of its information-processing capacities and its effective access to resources. Processes of modernization and development, through increased knowledge and command over resources suddenly introduce dramatic new possibilities in both these domains. More important than the speed at which modern forces or images impinge upon traditional cultures, however, are the social structures and contexts within which changes are proposed or imposed. In the last four centuries, Western technology, using its weapons, manufacturing tools, and electronic artifacts, has introduced modernity to Asia, Africa, and the American continents. Its mode of domination through military and political conquest, slavery, or commercial competition created the social instruments which buttress a pattern of global technological diffusion. Even after slavery and overt political colonialism were abolished, forms of dependence set in place in the golden age of colonial expansion were preserved by the mechanisms of economic commercialism. Consequently, traditional value systems in Third World countries must still wage an uphill fight not only to win recognition from modernizers, but also to protect their own fragile self-esteem. Hence the search for alternative development strategies begins with the restoration of this self-esteem.

Traditional Values and Practices

If they are to survive, traditional values must prove themselves useful to each new generation. They prove useful if they can supply meaning to people's lives, guide their actions in their present environment and circumstances, and provide them with criteria for accepting or rejecting outside influences bearing upon them. Ancient traditions are not received uncritically; on the contrary, each new generation discovers its own reasons for ratifying what its ancestors found to be valid.

Invoking such terms as "indigenous" and "native" values raises many questions. Who are the authentic carriers of these values: the original occupants of a territory, or later arrivals who, either deliberately or by the accidents of history, may have anchored their loyalties in a cultural terrain not originally their own? Moreover, in most cultural communities, there have always existed class and status divisions, each of which possessed its own preferred meaning systems and normative values. How then should change agents decide which indigenous or native values are to be approved or condemned? And what judgement can one pass when history has produced multiple overlays of values and new syncretistic mixes with each new sweep of time, this without ever totally eliminating prior values? And to what extent are indigenous values themselves constantly merging with non-indigenous values to form varied hybrids? And what of traditional community practices?

In many parts of the Third World, especially in rural areas, a small band of privileged notables sets standards of what is culturally accepted or proscribed. Recent debates over community values have usually assumed that elite values are bad or exploitative, so consequently only the values of non-elite masses express the true heart and soul of a populace. But not every person in a local community is either a member of the privileged elite or of the oppressed masses. Many individuals occupy intermediate social positions. Although possessing neither great wealth nor power, they are better off than the masses because they are gainfully employed, thanks to some skill or patronage. Such individuals frequently display a high degree of cultural eclecticism, mobility in their aspirations, and a profound ambivalence as to their own sense of identity. Are they to be included in the roster of local people whose practices should be preserved? In short, the question is: Whose local practices are to be defended in the name of preserving traditional culture?

To speak of cultural identity gives rise to yet another troubling question. On what foundation does identity rest—on one's personal history, an accident of birth, the possession of special ethnic or cultural traits, on free political choice, on the accidents of present geographical location, or on a sense of occupational kinship with some work fraternity? Most people have plural overlapping identities, each of which is partial and no single one of which can make absolute claims upon their loyalties. Besides, inasmuch as social identities are neither static or permanent, these identities sometimes change in the wake of new choices made or new constraints encountered.

It is difficult to identify precisely which core values are central to the innumerable traditions, mores, and modes of living found on this planet. Notwithstanding these complexities, however, most human groups are conscious of belonging to some identifiable cultural community and they regard themselves as the bearers of values essential to that community's identity. More importantly, communities usually view behavior patterns associated with modernity as posing threats to their value scheme of reality. Consequently, it is important to examine how development in its multiple modes affects traditions and, conversely, how these traditions and values shape our understanding of development itself.

As used here, the term "culture" signifies the living sum of meanings, norms, habits, and social artifacts which confer identity on one as a member of some visible community that has its own way of relating to the environment, of identifying members and strangers, and of deciding which values are (or are not) important to it. Among the essential creations of any culture are the definitions it makes of its basic needs and its preferred modes of satisfying those needs. Equally important are the tools communities employ to relate to their natural and artificial environments. These tools include both visible instruments to process materials and organizational principles framed as institutions to govern social interactions. Most writers on basic needs assume that needs are shaped by biological necessities; nevertheless, human needs are to a large extent derived from cultural values. As the anthropologist Dorothy Lee explains:

> . . . either needs are not the cause of all behavior, or that the list of needs provides an inadequate unit for assessing human behavior. I am not saying that there are no needs; rather, that if there are needs, they are derivative, not basic. If, for example, physical survival was held as the ultimate goal in some society, it would probably be found to give rise to those needs which have been stated to be basic to human survival; but I know of no culture where human physical survival has been shown rather than unquestioningly assumed by social scientists to be the ultimate goal. I believe that it is value, not a series of needs, which is at the basis of human behavior. The main difference between the two lies in the conception of the good which underlies them.[3]

Rethinking Development

Most development programs treat cultural values instrumentally, viewing them simply as means to development—that is, as aids or obstacles to achieving ends themselves defined by considerations lying outside those value systems. Development is equated with aggregate economic growth, the creation of modern institutions, and the spread of consumer aspirations and professional ambitions. In the most fundamental sense, however, none of these is development: at best, they may be social changes capable of facilitating genuine development. A totally different concept of development is needed, one derived from within the diverse value systems cherished by living communities. It is from within these values, these networks of meanings, loyalties, and patterns of living, that the proper ends of development and the most suitable means for obtaining it are to be defined.

Traditional values frequently harbor a latent dynamism which can be activated to bring about developmental change in ways that cause minimal harm to the identity and integrity of the populations concerned.[4] Sound development ought to be grounded in traditional and indigenous values[5] since ultimately both economic and social development are means to a larger end, the fostering of human development. Integral human development, however, rests on a secure sense of identity and cultural integrity, and on a system of meanings to which one can give enthusiastic allegiance. These values are so vital that economic and institutional modernization need to be judged in the light of their contribution to these values. Material improvement should not, and need not, be obtained at the price of a general impoverishment of the spirit. This conviction lies behind the search for change strategies which take the traditional values of living communities as the foundation upon which to build humane forms of development.

Cultural Diversity and Standardization

Will economic and technological progress, and its attendant standardization, destroy cultural diversity, a precious heritage since the origins of human history? The *meaning systems* of all societies—their philosophies, religions, symbols, and myths—have brought to hundreds of millions of their members a sense of identity, an ultimate explanation of the significance of life and death, and assigned to them a meaningful place and role in the cosmic order of things. Are these meaning systems doomed to disappear under the steamroller effects of a single mass culture characterized by electronic media, consumer gadgets, occupational mobility, and globally transmitted role models?

Or conversely, will the explosive release of ancient ethnic, racial, and linguistic passions, thanks to political liberations now proceeding apace throughout the world, destroy all possibilities of genuine development founded on universal solidarity? Will we witness a return of intercultural discrimination and of intolerant local chauvinisms breeding wars over boundaries?

Such are the questions which thrust themselves upon those who ponder the futures of culture and development.

All cultures are assaulted by powerful forces of standardization which homogenize, dilute, and relegate diverse cultures to purely ornamental, vestigial, or marginal positions in society.

The first of these standardizing forces is technology, especially communications technology. Television, film, radio, electronic musical devices, computers, and telephones operate cumulatively as potent vectors of such values as individualism, hedonistic self-gratification, consumerism, and shallow-thinking.

The second standardizing force is the modern state, a political institution which is bureaucratic, centralizing, legalistic, and powerfully inclined to assert control over ideas, resources, and "rules of the game" in all spheres of human activity.

The third standardizing force is the spread of managerial organization as the one best way of making decisions and coordinating actions in all institutions. Increasingly, government leaders must function as managers, as must university presidents, foundation presidents, airline officials, and directors of hospitals and scientific associations.

The result of these standardizing influences associated with modernity and development is massive cultural destruction, dilution, and assimilation. The very pervasiveness of these destructive forces, however, gives birth to growing manifestations of cultural affirmation and resistance.

Ethical Visions and Policy Directions

In a pessimistic scenario of the future, cultures and authentic cultural values throughout the world will be bastardized or reduced to marginal or ornamental roles in most societies. In the United States, for example, traditional Indian pow-wows (community meetings for purposes of reaching political and economic decisions, of conducting worship, and ritual dancing) have become mere recreational append-ages for the entertainment of visitors to folklore festivals.

An optimistic scenario, in contrast, portrays humanity as advanc-ing in global ecological and economic solidarity as a responsible stew-ard of the cosmos. Numerous vital and authentic cultures flourish, each proud of its identity while actively rejoicing in differences exhib-ited by other cultures. Human beings everywhere consciously nurture the sense of possessing several partial overlapping identities while relativizing each in recognition of their primary allegiance to the hu-man species. Cultural communities plunge creatively into their roots and find therein new ways of being modern and of contributing, out of their cultural patrimony, precious values to the universal human cul-ture presently in gestation.

Cultural policy actions should aim at making the optimistic sce-nario more likely to result than the pessimistic scenario. Educational efforts and policy measures in such spheres as linguistic strategy, the teaching of history and literature, the promotion of arts, and rules governing court procedures need to be identified and adopted with a view to strengthening the forces of cultural affirmation while counter-ing the standardizing forces described above.

Transcultural contacts and exchanges ought to proceed according to a fusion model of interaction. Fusion models of cultural interaction are opposed to two contrasting extremes: violent assimilation of one culture and passive surrender of weaker cultures to stronger ones. Fusion in cross-cultural encounters presupposes mutual accultura-tion. The key to success is the elimination of all triumphalism and the acceptance of reciprocity. This approach has vast implications at two levels: the epistemological stance adopted in transcultural dialogue and rules governing practical decision-making. Simply stated, part-ners to cultural exchanges must come together as equals having a common purpose.

Accordingly, both within nations and in international arenas, plu-ralistic development strategies are needed. Economic growth is a le-gitimate development objective. So too are distributional equity, the institutionalization of human rights, the pursuit of ecological wisdom, and the fostering of authentic cultural diversity. In all societies, this is why policy, programmers, and project planners must negotiate some optimal mix of these diverse (and at times conflicting) development objectives. No single objective can be made absolute or given reductionist hegemony over the others.

An Illustration: Cultural Resistance in Latin America

What are the dynamics of cultural resistance, and how may one assess future prospects for the survival of cultural diversity in Latin America?

It is preferable to speak of "living communities of culture" instead of "cultures." The latter term evokes something abstract, whereas the former suggests vital societies animated by their values. Living communities of culture possess three characteristics:

- a common system of signifying and normative values. Signifying values assign meaning to existence, normative values supply behavioral rules as to how life should be lived;

- some shared basis for people to identify themselves as members of a single group: a common territory, history, language, religion, race, or ancestors; and

- the will to be primarily self-identified as a member of a given community.

Although it is their community of culture that confers their primary identification and value allegiance to members of society, individuals may also maintain secondary identities and loyalties. Indeed, cultural communities themselves usually possess several partial overlapping identities and loyalty systems. In addition to such factors as religion, race, history, and language, other bases for identification likewise exist. Individuals may identify themselves functionally as belonging to a worldwide fellowship of scholars, athletes, or musicians. Or they may identify themselves on the basis of some shared interest as soccer fans, bird watchers, or photographers.

Certain general characteristics have shaped Latin America's diverse cultural communities. Latin American demography is formed from three basic elements: native Indian ethnicity, an African component, and European races (mainly Spanish and Portuguese). A fourth component comprises diverse immigrant groups—Japanese, Chinese, Italian, German, Swiss, Korean—who have come to Latin America in the last century and a half. Four and a half centuries of racial miscegenation have left today's Latin American communities with a culture lacking a clear identity. Identity is fluid and fragile, not fully integrated and forever oscillating between self-definitions as Indian, European, or of mixed race. Latin America's cultural communities are dualistic in other ways as well. The literary dichotomy of Ariel and Caliban captures this duality well—Latins as both idealistic and materialistic, simultaneously dreamers and pragmatists. And Latin American culture groups are at once outward- and inward-looking. As they look outward they are mimetic. In the nineteenth century, they imitated French philosophy (Comte's positivism) and British social mores. In this century, the dominant cultural model is the United States. At the same time, however, Latin American cultural communities remain intensely inward-looking. Throughout the continent endless debates rage over what it means to be distinctively Bolivian, Guatemalan, or Venezuelan. One finds everywhere an abiding pre-occupation with the internal boundaries of cultural definition!

Moreover, the role played by geography in shaping Latin America's collective psyche is immense. Its cultures are profoundly marked by vast distances, large spaces, huge stretches of land, sky, and terrain—mountains, deserts, forests.

A common attitude toward politics and governments is likewise discernible across the varied gamut of Latin American cultures. Most nations gained their independence through revolutionary struggle and, not surprisingly, the stance people have toward government remains one of suspicion. They instinctively adopt an adversarial posture toward governments, even those they have freely elected. As Argentina's Jorge Luis Borges puts it, "the Latin American is a person, not a citizen. The State is impersonal: The Latin only conceives of a personal relationship."[6]

Toward a Theory of Cultural Survival

Survival is a minimum collective goal of every human society; individuals also depend on society to satisfy needs related to esteem and freedom. By definition, non-developed societies are unable to maximize material satisfactions and those psychological satisfactions in which enjoyment presupposes an abundance of goods. On the other hand, they may be able to optimize the satisfaction of survival, identity, solidarity, and esteem needs. Since existence rationality concerns survival and need-satisfaction under present capacities for processing information, suitable means must be found enabling members of one society to process more and more varied information than before.

In addition, whether they are rooted in the scarcity of resources or in rigidities of the allocation system, old resource constraints must be overcome. Because the core values of all existence rationalities aim at nurturing survival, basic esteem, and freedom, core values should not be challenged frontally. Frontal attacks unduly threaten basic identity. If change is to be welcomed, therefore: (a) new capacities for handling information must be generated; (b) vital resources not previously available must be made available; and (c) the alien rationality implicit in "modernization" must be re-interpreted in terms compatible with traditional existence rationalities.

Whenever one culture group impinges upon another, several dynamisms come into play. Each community of culture possesses a different "index of survivability," a different capacity for assimilating change without losing its identity and vitality. Some culture groups can withstand far-reaching changes in their value systems, institutions, and ways of life without losing their identity, whereas others collapse under a lesser barrage of imposed change. History records that cultural communities can preserve their identity over long periods of time even under conditions of extreme duress, thanks to "secondary adaptation." Secondary adaptation occurs when an oppressed community of culture exhibits subservience in its surface behavior, an apparent servility which lulls the dominant cultural group into complacency and lessened repressive vigilance.

At a "secondary" or covert level, however, the oppressed group engages in cultural resistance: in code language, it affirms its sense of identity and pride, mounts educational campaigns against domination, and at times even organizes open revolts. African communities in Northeast Brazil practiced secondary adaptation behind the cultural "mask" of such "innocent" activities as *capoeira* and *candomblé*. Plantation slaves in the United States South educated themselves, organized, and resisted behind the "mask" of folk-tale sessions and the singing of spirituals. For enslaved communities, compliance serves a defensive function allowing them to "elude" the dominant system and to avoid being imprisoned by the definitions and roles larger society imposes on them.[7]

In all pre-modern societies a vital nexus links signifying to normative values.[8] Modernity shatters this nexus, and not all societies can survive the assault.

Cultural Resistance

In times of rapid change, it is difficult to maintain cultural integrity, particularly among subnational groups. One conspicuous effect of the spread of Western technology is the homogenization of lifestyles. Standardization is evident in airports, hotels, industrial parks, residential suburbs, supermarkets, clothing, consumption habits, and aspirations.

As modern technology is transferred to societies other than those of origin, it imposes its logic of uniformity on modes of work. Practices relating to work and leisure are far more constitutive of a culture than such external features as dress, music or artistic wares. As one former member of the British Parliament notes, "Culture, after all, is about people and patterns of everyday life—not monuments and souvenirs."[9] Certain uniformities may be inevitable in modernization processes but, as they make their choices, development planners should beware of the high price in cultural dilution exacted by standardizing modern technology. In order to preserve cultural diversity, planners should select work-related technologies which protect that diversity. Their decisions have great bearing not only on the quality of work and its meaning in people's lives,[10] but also on their patterns of consumption, the degree of urbanization deemed acceptable in their societies, and the scale of the institutions they will choose. These are the vital arenas where the battle for cultural survival will be won or lost. This is not to suggest that the fine arts are unimportant, but simply that they are easily relegated to the periphery of cultural values when technology sets the pace in daily living. Nowhere do the values vectored by modern technology so quickly assert their primacy as in the behavior of business and professional elites. Not only their language but their dress, ethical codes, and stylistic preferences rapidly become modeled on those of rich-world counterparts. Standardization is not always to be regretted! Nevertheless, since these elites constitute "significant others" which masses imitate in their aspirations, one is less than sanguine about the long-run viability of a plurality of rich cultures.

On the streets of La Paz, one still meets peasant women in traditional garb walking alongside bankers wearing pin-striped three-piece suits. Although such residual and picturesque signs of cultural diversity may coexist, the deeper question remains: whose values dominate in the planning of school curricula or television programming? Will the Bolivian peasant woman's children be more powerfully influenced by the banker's new values than the latter's children will be by the old Quechua values shared by the grandparents of both?

Technology transfers impose a high price in cultural destruction. This price can be minimized by deliberate policy measures only if the danger of cultural homogenization inherent in technology transfers is recognized. Moreover, resistant cultures are often the victims of generalized psychological, behavioral, and linguistic discrimination, at times even of physical marginalization as they are relegated to the boundaries of some territory.[11]

Three conditions must be met if cultural resistance is to succeed.[12] First, if they are to defend their authentic identity, threatened communities must become plural cultures. They need to revitalize their own modes of living, their economic and legal systems, their language and traditions. Old traditions are constantly being altered because, at any given time, traditional societies contain in their midst a number of deviant members who challenge their culture's basic values. How living communities come to terms with deviants is an important cultural datum. The most basic sense in which a cultural group under attack must become pluralistic, however, is that it must in some way become modern, at least to the extent of coming to understand modernity's values, institutions, modes of knowing, and definitions of problems.

Pre-modern cultures cannot resist modern technology and its underlying rationality unless they critically understand that technology and that rationality, unless they also harness some of technology's preferred instruments to turn them against their originators, to "fight cultural fire with fire." Cultures at risk must learn how to use the media and legal systems of modernity as well as the political power and the economic mechanisms by which wealth is circulated in modern societies. At least in this limited sense, every culture must become a plural culture.

The second condition of successful resistance is that a community of culture must possess a minimal economic base which gives it some measure of control over the speed and direction at which it will develop its resources. No cultural community can gain mastery over its destiny if it is lacking minimum economical security: it will be thrust into the role of an eternal supplicant of resources, to be tolerated only on the wider society's terms.

A third requirement of cultural resistance is that communities in jeopardy must play some political role. An active political role may be necessary to defend the community's right to settle disputes among its members according to its own legal procedures, to protect itself against discrimination in society at large, or to conduct schooling in its own language. A community may also need to wage political combat in order to define its status *vis-à-vis* the state. Even if communities of culture do not engage in overt political activity, they may need to conduct public education campaigns in order to gain psychological respect from the institutions of society—and from mainstream cultural groups as well as citizens at large.

Cultural Differentiation

A general worldwide process is at work in which cultural communities in growing numbers seek a differentiated identity. Cultural communities, especially subnational groups, strive to project their primary identity as distinctive culture groups because they feel a need to construct a sphere in which they are the dominant actors, in contrast to larger spheres in which they operate as inferior subcultures. It is a reassuring source of esteem to be a majority population in one sphere even if that sphere is a small one. Thus a Guarani with a cultural identity recognized by society at large is not simply a minority Indian who happens to be a Paraguayan.

Many culture groups, which in the past have not actively projected their identity, now seek to reverse the earlier assimilation. Formerly, economic or political necessity forced many groups to accept a level of cultural assimilation to larger societies, which they now contest. Only by re-asserting their differentiated cultural identity can Quechuas in Bolivia, Mapuches in Chile, and Brazilians of African origin press collective claims upon society. The global trend favoring collective claims poses troubling questions for social theorists, however. As Flora Lewis asks:

> Is the individual the only definition which democracy allows, or should diversity be institutionalized? Ethnicity is a human, cultural and social reality that cannot be wiped out. . . .

> Should it also be a legal reality within a society? If so, are hierarchies tolerable, based on numbers? on property? on history? on the assertion of inherent superiority?[13]

As modernization penetrates ever more deeply into all aspects of life (school, family, work, recreation), cultural communities seek a differentiated identity for still another reason: in order to distinguish themselves from the *passe-partout* culture of modernity founded on homogenized technology and consumption. Consumerist images are necessarily mimetic and standardized. Thirty years ago young people everywhere, if they wished to be modern, listened to the Beatles; they now listen to Michael Jackson and Madonna. Modern technology imposes itself in uniform fashion and a highly standardized managerial ethos is gaining sway worldwide. Indeed, technology itself is rapidly displacing other cultures and imposing itself as a culture in its own right.[14]

Alongside growing differentiation, an emerging global culture is in gestation. Thanks to the internationalization of production, the collapse of national barriers under the assault of freely circulating goods, images, information, money, and people, no physical locale can any longer serve as the exclusive home ground of a single culture. The impulses of acculturation flow everywhere, rapidly and pervasively. People everywhere are coming to view themselves as members of the wider human family. Mayan farmers in Guatemala, rubber tappers in Rondônia (Brazil), and Argentine cattle ranchers all sense that they belong to a larger human community. It becomes increasingly difficult for any of us to define ourselves solely as citizens of a particular nation, adepts of a particular religion, members of a particular linguistic or racial group. Media technology, penetrating deeply into the inner recesses of our consciousness, makes us aware that the destinies of other human beings on our planet relate to our own lot. A global culture is in gestation.

Future Prospects

What are the prospects for the survival of diverse vital communities of culture in Latin America? Groups whose existence centers on nomadism may find it impossible to survive as lands become more densely populated and as pressures upon shrinking natural resources grow at a geometric rate. Perhaps the best that can be gained is that such cultural communities can "buy time" to make gradual adjustments to new forms of existence they may adopt in the future.

Small dispersed populations may also find it impossible to survive as coherent vital cultures. A minimum number of people is required if a culture is to maintain itself and its institutions at a bottom threshold of genetic and social vitality. Other cultural communities, however, may successfully develop dual identities, value allegiances, institutions, and behaviors in ways that protect their fundamental values and identity. On what terms will they survive, however? Will it be as economically viable and culturally integral units living in isolation, or on the margins of national societies to which they are politically attached? Will they carve a niche in the dominant societies enveloping them to live therein as vital small enclaves, as Mennonites have done in Paraguay and Miskitos in Nicaragua? Or will they avoid ethical and behavioral assimilation but nonetheless function with ease in the midst of an alien wider cultural milieu, thus exhibiting the prismatic effect whereby modernity is refracted behaviorally in terms of culturally specific social organization and living patterns?[15] This range of prospects—itself not exhaustive—exists as possibilities for culture groups in general. But one would not hazard a guess as to which particular cultural communities in Latin America can survive under one or another set of conditions just outlined.

Some Latin American cultural communities may quite possibly survive in ways that embody neither the optimistic nor the pessimistic scenario outlined in earlier pages. Such cultural groups may reject development, consumerism, and modern technology altogether, and find ways of subsisting, perhaps at a modest level of well-being, while preserving distinctive religious, ethnic, linguistic, and artistic patterns of life. It is possible that the development enterprise itself, with the trappings of modernity attached to it (specialized institutions, large-scale activities, urban settlement patterns, an exploitative approach to resources) will prove unsustainable in the long term. In this scenario, groups which can survive with some measure of cultural vitality are communities devoted to pre-modern agriculture in the mode of tribal, ethnic, or extended family solidarity. The normative value system of such communities could successfully place limits on their members' desire for goods and services. These societies might even generate a modest surplus of wealth to be used for artistic achievements in music, painting, sculpture, architecture, dance, recreation, or sport. Moreover, present-day nation-states in Latin America might conceivably split up into a larger number of decentralized national entities or subnational bioregions, each enjoying considerable degrees of autarchy.

On purely rational and evidential grounds, and given the forces at work to destroy and dilute cultures, the pessimistic scenario appears the more likely. But history is full of surprises: many important long-lasting patterns of events which occur were not predictable at an earlier time. These unexpected outcomes may not necessarily be irrational, but their rationality is not manifest before the fact.

Conclusion

The forces operating to dilute, assimilate, and destroy cultural communities are so great that the future of many of them is uncertain. Authentic cultural diversity, expressing diverse modes of being and of social organization with integrity and vitality, is doomed unless the positive value of such diversity is recognized. Development planners at every level must incorporate the active defense of cultural diversity into their decisions about resource use. Such active defense must not be treated as a mere externality in the cost-benefit equation.

12.

ETHICS OF AID

The ethical frame of reference for debates on "aid" is the promotion of greater justice within and among nations. Genuine assistance presupposes cooperation, however, and as Samir Amin observes: "The essential condition for cooperation [is] real equality between partners," for in its absence, aid is but a form of "social imperialism."[1]

The key to achieving development lies not in receiving external "aid" but in actions taken by developing countries themselves—their mobilization around the creation of just and humane social structures. Nevertheless, global institutional arrangements, such as the workings of the international market or patterns of aid, can either impede or foster efforts at development. Resource transfers may discourage efforts by host countries to institute greater justice by unduly rewarding individualistic entrepreneurs or by blocking structural reforms. Even in the best of circumstances, external aid is merely a stimulant and supplement to the mobilization of resources of low-growth countries. Frequently, however, external suppliers of "aid" support governments hostile to social justice or structural reforms aimed at allying higher productivity to greater distributive equity. Not surprisingly, therefore, many Third World nations have come to view "aid" as a poisoned gift. The UN Charter of Economic Rights and Duties of States declares that "International cooperation for development is the shared goal and common duty of all States. Every State should cooperate with the efforts of developing countries to accelerate their economic and social development by providing favorable external conditions and by extending active assistance to them."[2] Suitable resource transfers are welcomed, provided they are not used as an instrument of social control over recipients or do not unduly favor the economic interests of suppliers.

Even within rich industrial countries, the benefits of economic growth have not "trickled down" to the poor. Mass poverty, high unemployment, and inequitable class structures cannot be reversed except by radical changes in the "ground rules" governing access to basic resources. Thus do the new terms of reference used in development debates also prove normative for discussions of "aid."

New patterns of collaboration must be invented which build creatively on tensions between *self-reliance* and the continuing need for *assistance*. Inasmuch as diverse motives and interests propel "givers" of assistance, large "aid" programs can never be totally compatible with the aspirations of resource-poor countries. Since donors render assistance out of their own perceived interests, these interests cannot fully coincide with the developmental needs of those assisted. Partial convergence of interests is possible, but only the improved bargaining position of those in need can win them better terms, even in "concessional" resource transfers.[3]

Donor nations differ widely in their philosophy of "aid." Those with no colonial past and no interest in establishing economic hegemony more easily embrace a rationale which stresses the welfare of the poor, the transformation of economic structures in favor of greater equity, and grassroots participation in funded programs. Accordingly, "aid" documents published by the governments of Sweden and Canada project a different image of development than those issued by the United States or France. Nevertheless, there always remains something intrinsically unpleasant about "needing help" from outsiders. This is the reason why "aid" debates are fruitful only to the extent that they employ the language of distributive justice, of priority basic needs, and of solidarity.

The Context of Aid

Three conditions affect development assistance: (1) rapid changes occurring in the International Economic Order (IEO); (2) aid's lesser importance than the total influence of one country's presence on another (the impact of its military and diplomatic activities, trade relationships and tariff arrangements, corporate investment and technology exchanges, cultural penetration, tourist and migratory flows, and debt structure); and (3) the involvement of many actors in "assistance" (bilateral government agencies, multilateral institutions, foundations, philanthropic organizations, non-governmental organizations, and corporate firms). The relative importance, the norms, and constraints that govern the workings of these disparate "aid-givers" are not uniform; neither are the expectations host countries have of the benefits each can bring to them.

A Changing International Order

Rich countries criticize the present global order because juridical structures of national sovereignty have grown dysfunctional in a world where plurinational decisions decisively affect the circulation systems governing world flows of finance, trade, investment, technology, and information. Moreover, although inflation, unemployment, and economic recession affecting many nations are not subject to control by purely national policies, no binding mechanisms exist whereby national policies can be harmonized. Poor countries, in turn, denounce the present IEO as biased in favor of industrialized countries. To illustrate, most technological research and development is conducted in "developed" countries, and technology is sold to them at exorbitant prices, in ways that discourage optimal use of local resources and lead to intolerable dependency. Developing countries seek something more than greater economic efficiency: namely, equity and distributive justice.

The final shape of the evolving IEO remains unpredictable and in the wake of concerted Third World demands for structural change in international arrangements, hard bargaining will surely continue.

The relative power of contending stewards of the transition to a new IEO—the U.S., the European Union, Japan, or an alliance of the three—is reflected in patterns of development "assistance." Great powers have a vested interest in tying "aid" to their own geopolitical objectives in order to "domesticate" Third World aspirations. And notwithstanding their denunciatory political rhetoric, many Third World elites benefit from this system since they too are committed to perpetuating the present global exchange system. If, however, transnational corporations become newly mandated as the efficient economic managers of world resources, "aid" itself will become just another business transaction responsive to the purchasing power of those who can pay for goods, and not to the priority needs of those who cannot. Therefore, no ethically valid solution to developmental assistance issues can be expected, except in peripheral and incidental ways, unless some measure of "global populism" gains sway in the evolutionary process presently shaping a new IEO.

Total Impact of Country Presences

Aid is usually a relatively minor ingredient in one country's over-all impact upon another. In many cases, government arms sales to military dictatorships negate the beneficial effects of financial and technical assistance for development. Rich "aid givers" often contra-dict their formal "aid" policy by punishing the governments of less developed countries when these adopt measures to curb the economic depredations of private investors. The massive presence of tourists from rich country A can do more to "push" host country B into a mass consumption pattern of investment that A's "aid" program designed to foster basic needs development for the poor masses.

It is the overall relations between countries that set the range of possible "good" aid relationships, not the converse. When "aid" is supplied purely for reasons of immediate interest, little likelihood ex-ists that it can avoid being manipulative. Ultimately, only two defen-sible justifications for providing development "assistance" exist: (1) a *moral* basis positing a duty in justice on the rich to effectuate equi-table resource distribution in the world; and (2) a *manipulative* basis using aid both as carrot and stick to buy United Nations votes, mili-tary bases, economic favors, or ideological allegiances. Much rich country aid has failed because it has attempted to present its geopo-litical interests as ethically noble and, conversely, to justify its philan-thropic instincts on the grounds that it is supportive of its national security or brings economic advantage.

In real-world politics, however, even morally based aid has al-ways been selective. Socialist countries have preferred to express their solidarity—an eminently moral virtue—with kindred socialist nations. And the aid provided by economically liberal states is fueled by greater moral indignation over "scandalous poverty" in pro-capitalist societies, even if these are not very liberal. It is apparent that politics still finds itself in a state of ethical infantilism. Social virtues are demeaned, however, if they are practiced only where compatible interests are found. Notwithstanding great progress in the technological capacities of the human race, its political wisdom remains embryonic. Yet, as the sociologist Irving Horowitz observed:

> The study of power is the beginning of sociological wisdom—but the essence of that wisdom is that power resides in men. Hence the existence of power is a less significant area of study than the human uses made of power. Men define power; they are not necessarily defined by it. This, at any rate, is the liberating task of the social sciences.[4]

Norms of Development Aid

Because no easy or quick solutions to underdevelopment exist, many students of social change fear apocalyptic violence bred by the despair of poor masses reacting defensively to the indifference or callous manipulation of the rich. Nevertheless, even so uncompromising a critic of "aid establishments" as Tibor Mende—he calls them "mercenaries of the status quo"—sees grounds for hope. He considers that under certain conditions, "the rich world may even be moved to a new dimension of tolerance: to the compassion of disinterested solidarity capable of being helpful without trying to deflect people from their chosen path."[5] In order for this to happen, however, Mende concludes that "rules, norms, and methods would have to be devised, made acceptable and acted upon."[6] Indeed, there are no preexisting rules or norms governing *proper* attempts to lend development assistance. And it proves difficult to imagine ethical prescriptions which are not mere palliatives to present deficiencies.

Priority of Needs

The political and economic priorities of "donor" countries cannot easily be made to match the needs of poor countries receiving "assistance."[7] Resources allocated in accord with donors' priorities rarely fulfill optimal development purposes. Some overlap of interests between donors and recipients of resources transfers can no doubt exist; but development requires, above all, launching and sustaining dynamic social processes which bring new dignity and freedom to people while meeting their essential material needs. It follows, therefore, that meeting needs for optimum sustenance, dignity, and freedom must become the first priority of resource transfers. These ends cannot be obtained simply as by-products of other targeted objectives.

Much "aid" literature engages in tortuous debates over the mix of philanthropic and self-interested motivations invoked to justify providing public assistance to developing countries.[8] Although there are limits beyond which the immediate economic and political interests of donors cannot be neglected, clear priority must be given to the needs of recipients. "Aid" cannot be successful—that is, it cannot contribute to genuine development—if it is given primarily as an instrument of a rich country's economic or trade policy, a carrot-and-stick device to purchase ideological or political loyalties or a bribe to fend off potentially violent revolutions of poor masses. Development assistance is not an act of charity or philanthropy, but a rational requirement of any just and equitable pattern of global resource distribution. Distributive justice[9] requires that higher priority be assigned to meeting the basic needs of human beings—wherever they be located geographically—than to satisfying the wants of other resource users. The ethical foundation for providing essential goods to needy people is not "charity" or optional almsgiving, but the collective human obligation to assure a *just* use of essential resources. Both outside and within national boundaries, the rich have no right to luxury goods until the essential needs of all have first been met.[10]

An urgent need exists to institutionalize, in viable operational fashion, the concept of access to resources *upstream*, instead of *downstream*. The imagery conveyed by these words is clear: those who fish upstream with sonar devices deplete the river's fish stock and leave too little for those located further down. Similarly, those who pollute upstream spoil the river for those located below. The same principle holds true for those who lay claim to resources upstream, or early in the sequence of actions that lead to the extraction, processing, and distribution of goods: they acquire a privileged share of the latter. One ethical imperative, therefore, is to achieve progressive movement toward a reconstruction of economic theory and practice which links first claim on resources (*i.e.*, upstream access) to the priority of needs.

This is to say that ultimately the basis for legitimate access is *not* the geographical location of resources within certain boundaries, or the historical accident that one set of actors possesses the superior technology needed to extract or process that good.

The acceptance of this new set of "ground rules" governing access to resource stands as a long-term goal both for the world at large and for national societies. Nevertheless, some partial implementation of it *now* in the domain of "aid" is both necessary and possible. At least some resources of rich nations and classes can be set aside, *on principle*, in response to the essential needs of poorer people living in all nations.

Assisting the Needy

The bankruptcy of conventional aid practices calls attention to the difficulty of assuring that benefits reach the neediest. The usual operations of bureaucracies and of problem-solving managerial hierarchies geared to efficiency all favor the concentration of power, influence, and benefits in the hands of a small number. The principle of *upstream* access to resources must become operative in assistance programs if these are not to continue favoring the already privileged. Given the structural obstacles to distribution of benefits on the basis of highest need, relative success is possible only in societies where the struggle against elitist decision-making is a high priority. It is not enough to plead for equality of opportunity; systemic mechanisms also must be created to assure some degree of equality of outcome. No society has yet satisfactorily resolved the contradiction between political democracy, which presupposes the equality of *rights*, and the capitalist economy, which requires differential economic rewards for competitive efficiency. In turn, policies which are ideologically committed to egalitarianism must struggle to achieve minimum efficiency and a proper mix of "material" and "moral" incentives to economic effort. To the degree that they emphasize economic equality, they tend to overlook political equality. Conversely, liberal regimes tolerate great economic equality in the name of protecting diversity.

The ethical lesson derived from the fifty-year history of aid is that no society or institution can transfer resources in an egalitarian or need-priority manner unless its own practices are themselves egalitarian and geared to basic needs.[11] This explains why the World Bank, notwithstanding its rhetorical declarations, can do relatively little to assure that its institutional loans will reach the poorest 40 percent of the Third World's populace. Bank economists and project managers relate to peer professionals in host countries who, for the most part, act through institutions *not* designed to share economic goods according to the principle of highest need. Bank professionals may be experts at formulating aggregate plans that meet canons of efficiency, cost effectiveness, and credit-worthiness. But they have no "expertise" at reversing the inertia of their own institution and of counterparts to produce a distribution of benefits founded on criteria of need. Hence, there is no effective way in which rich world institutions can "force" poor country governments to spread resources around in ways uncongenial to the overall social incentive systems operating in their own countries.

Accordingly, an initial selection of countries to be "aided" on the basis of political commitment to, and institutional capacity for, distribution funded on prior need may be the only leverage open to "donors." In the real world, however, needy countries prize their autonomy and self-reliance so highly that they are likely to reject "aid" preferred by countries which are not themselves committed to the same priorities. The stark fact is that "donors" and "recipients" have quite different stakes in those operations misleadingly labelled "development aid" or "international resource transfers."

Ethical Dilemmas

No ethics of "development aid" exists apart from a specific philosophy of development and a concrete historical view on ideological and political conflict. It is futile to look for consensus regarding "aid" practices suited to all sound development objectives. By their very nature, development and its instrumentalities (of which "aid" is but one) mirror disagreements over the nature of the good life, the foundations of justice within and among societies, the stance to take toward nature and technology, and the criteria for assigning human costs attendant upon social changes.

The following pages list—in illustrative rather than exhaustive fashion—value-laden questions and answers about "aid," as would be faced by decision-makers committed to the conception of human development advocated in earlier chapters. One measures success not only on *what* benefits are obtained—higher material welfare, let us say, or an improved educational system—but also on *how* or in what mode the benefits are achieved. Are gains won in ways which empower people to exercise greater control over social processes affecting their lives, bring more reciprocity to their social relationships, or lead to institutional guarantees of human rights? Authentic development is not won if a high GNP growth rate is achieved at the cost of totalitarian repression of the masses, cultural bastardization in order to attract foreign investment, demeaning dependency to outside powers, or the gross neglect of essential needs of some mass sector of the population.

This normative vision of development, which bases the obligation of aid "donors" primarily on the demands of social justice and solidarity, is a far cry from the view that "concessional" resource transfers are justified on grounds of national security, economic interests, political advantages, or the purging of guilt feelings by the rich as they practice "charity" by assisting the poor.

Question 1: Should "aid" be given at all?   In a genuinely developed world, aid would become superfluous. Even in present circumstances, "aid" is not the main ingredient of successful development; even when it is necessary or useful, it takes second place behind the internal mobilization of efforts and the overall impact of one country's presence on another. In the present global order, in which some nations are *over*developed and others are *under*developed, "aid" remains a necessary evil.

Question 2: Should "aid" be bilateral or multilateral?   "Aid" cannot avoid being both bilateral and multilateral. Each of these two channels, like that of private voluntary agencies, carries specific advantages and inconveniences.[12] Moreover, neither category is homogeneous. The bilateral assistance provided by the United States, Sweden, and China is governed by contrasting development philosophies, priorities, and measures of success. There is great merit in preserving a pluralism of modes.

The main ethical point is that meeting basic needs of the very poor must be given first priority. Contributions from rich sources are based on the principle that urgent human needs constitute a claim on resources. Therefore, enough "aid" to complement host country capacities must be provided by someone in order to meet minimal conditions of distributive justice in the allocation of the earth's goods independently of ideological, geopolitical, or economic criteria. This leaves unspecified, of course, the exact agent upon whom rests the burden of effectuating the transfer. Nevertheless, it is impossible to avoid recourse to some version of the "ability to pay" principle in assigning responsibilities.

The modality of assistance and its institutional channel are less important than its finality. Bilateral, multilateral, and private assistance must all be judged according to whether they meet, or fail to meet, genuine developmental needs in some sequence of priorities.

Question 3: Should assistance be mandatory?   On grounds of distributive justice, a general ethical obligation exists upon all societies to move in the direction of some global and regional basic resource-sharing on a mandatory basis. Progress will depend largely on which shifts occur within the evolving IEO.

Obviously, no nation or populace can be forced to accept assistance if it judges that assistance damaging to its interests. The key is to restructure transnational relations so that excessive disparities in bargaining power are eventually countered, either by regional functional associations of the weaker partners or by binding legal constraints imposed upon their stronger counterparts.

Until most nations, rich and poor, come to endorse development strategies truly founded on solidarity in exchanges (which can only be reached after much conflict), it is illusory to make other forms of aid mandatory. At best, during the transition period some guaranteed assistance might cover such basic needs as food and medical supplies for the population of the whole earth.

Question 4: How can "donors" guarantee that their "aid" reaches the needy majorities in poor countries?   No ironclad guarantees can exist. If elites in poor countries are resolved to use their privileged positions to appropriate most benefits accruing from outside resources, "donors" will be impotent to prevent this. Conceivably, they may have the power to stop resource transfers completely or to institute partial safeguards which *encourage* a more equitable distribution of their "aid." But for them to insist on guaranteeing compliance by recipients would entail such a high degree of interference with national sovereignty as to be both politically unfeasible and ethically repugnant.

Suppliers of resources can nevertheless apply selective criteria to determine which countries they wish to assist in that portion of their "aid" not allotted to basic needs. Nothing is gained by self-delusion on this point: those who fear intervention inherent in "aid" should condemn all forms of intervention—foreign investment, cultural penetration by media and books, tourist travel, and military influences. Powerful nations cannot avoid impinging on weaker countries by their inaction as well as by their overt actions. What must be judged is the overall impact of their interventions.

Question 5: Should rich nations use their aid programs to champion human rights in receiving countries?   No issue in transnational relations is so knotty as this one. Liberal democracies have not attached the same importance to economic rights as they have to political and civil rights. Conversely, socialist societies have emphasized economic rights but have been unable to promote political, legal, and personal rights. Moreover, basic conceptions of rights change over time and no agreement exists on what constitutes the ultimate source of human rights—some divine order, "natural" law, positive law, or some merely rhetorical assertion that wins political support.[13]

No nation—particularly a rich and powerful one—can force others to respect one category of rights (political or civil) if its own overall impingement on poorer societies interferes systematically with progress in the obtention of economic rights. Comprehensively understood, human rights embrace personal inviolability, legal and political rights, as well as economic rights. They are best promoted by a society that says to others: "Act as I act, not as I say."

Although ethically speaking, it is a good thing to do battle on behalf of comprehensive human rights, no strategy of promoting rights can succeed unless it deals comprehensively with rights.

"Aid" is a weak instrumentality for promoting human rights. In minimal ethical terms, however, "donors" have a duty to refrain from providing resources that are used to violate personal rights (*e.g.,* training in police or military torture, or mass repression). And it is ethically justifiable for grantors of assistance to withdraw resources to signify their opposition to gross violations of rights in other countries.

Question 6: Is military assistance ethically justified?   Although it powerfully affects the direction taken by developing countries in their approaches to social change, military assistance rarely contributes to genuine development. In most nations, the military constitute the most technologically modern class, the one most directly in touch with international exchange circuits, and the only group possessing effective veto power over civilian politics and ideologies they do not favor. The abolition of militarism as a dominant social phenomenon is a long-term goal which admits of no easy solutions. Meanwhile, "developed" country governments should make it as onerous as possible for arms merchants to sell weapons across national borders, by curtailing their own sales stringently and by taxing private exports prohibitively. Such measures will succeed, however, only if international agreements are reached to police contraband arms traffic. A single standard should govern arms exports to rich and poor countries alike. Considerable moral indignation is expressed in rich world circles over sales to less developed countries on the grounds that these sales obstruct genuine development. This is doubtless true, but it is no less true that by increasing militarization, wasting resources on destructive activities, and exacerbating explosive conflictual situations, arms sales also impede important social objectives in rich countries.

An important ethical principle comes into play here—namely, that partial solutions to systemic evils carry little weight (morally, politically, and technically) unless they are integral parts of a comprehensive strategy. Partial solutions are not separable from their holistic matrix; they cannot be applied to other matrices or merely juxtaposed as *ad hoc* solutions lacking unity. Any concessions made to existing constraints must be viewed as efforts to transform palliative measures into creatively incremental ones within an overall change strategy in which creative incrementalism supports discontinuous social mutations.[14] Partial successes are not to be disdained, but they are validated only if they are followed by continuing efforts to open up new possibilities facilitating the final goal.

Question 7: Should debts of poorer countries be canceled?   Strong theoretical arguments exist in favor of debt abrogation. It is clear, however, that demands from poorer nations will not be met by a policy of generalized relief. The mood of creditors is to argue that "a scalpel is needed, not a broadaxe." By this is meant that each case should be studied on its own merits and that relief should not be allowed to upset the continuity of monetary flows prized by bankers. At best, therefore, some limited cancellation of debt might be granted to the least developed of the less developed. Nevertheless, even debt cancellation helps little unless additional funds are also made available to those in need.

Some larger ethical vision must intervene to help developmental problem-solvers open up new possibilities. In recent years the Old Testament practice of "jubilee years" has found new favor among writers on social justice.[15] The idea is disarmingly simple: Because stocks of wealth tend to accumulate in the hands of those already wealthy, a "jubilee" or remission is to be proclaimed each seven or ten years, at which time basic goods are redistributed on the basis of needs, debts are cancelled, and everyone is given a new start. Cancelling onerous debts owed by poor nations because they have needed to receive "concessional" loans over the years is a twentieth-century functional equivalent of jubilee. It recommends itself both ethically and economically as providing periodic new incentives for fresh starts.

Question 8: Should "aid" be developmental or for relief? This question has long troubled private voluntary agencies. Many of them, previously interested only in relieving victims of natural catastrophes or of war, are now striving to apply their resources in ways which contribute to structural changes of a developmental nature. Nevertheless, it is evident that some resource transfers will always be needed to relieve urgent human suffering following upon natural or social catastrophe. Humanitarian aid is not developmental aid and cannot be given in accord with the same criteria. Both are needed.

These questions highlight the difficulty of knowing, let alone of doing, what is ethically correct in realms of development assistance. Suitable criteria can be drawn neither from a review of what Third World groups demand, nor from the practice of aid donors. The only source of such criteria is a philosophy of development in which essential needs and essential relationships are defined in accord with specific social values.

Conclusion

Donor countries are addicted to periodic development "fads": an exaggerated and short-lived interest, let us say, in infrastructure, human resource planning, population control, integrated rural development, or "green" or environmental aid. However important these issues may be, they are but single elements within a larger whole which is indissociable from questions of dependency, technological vulnerability, ongoing transformations in societal value systems, and perceptions across time and space of different images of the good life. By unduly emphasizing food, basic needs, and quality of life, rich countries regress to an absolute "assistentialist" conception of their relations. "Assistentialist" views of development stress, in unbalanced fashion, the centrality of resource transfers. "Developmental" approaches, in turn, emphasize the need to modernize structures of production and decision-making. And finally, "liberation" approaches center on new ground rules for access, by marginalized or oppressed masses, to resources and to effective power.[16] All three contain elements which must be preserved. Even a refurbished ethic of "aid" must view resource transfers as part of a larger strategy leading to more developmental structures of production and international exchange, as well as more just and value-enhancing systems of power distribution.

Assistentialism is a palliative because it attacks symptoms and not causes of mass poverty, and reinforces an image of Third World nations as mendicants. This view is factually incorrect and psychologically demeaning, since it buttresses the illusion that material wealth confers greater virtue and merit. Most importantly, assistentialism deflects critical thought away from challenging mainstream visions of development in rich societies themselves.

Ultimately, even a sound *ethic* of development assistance is not enough. New *wisdoms* of development are also needed—unifying visions, respectful of cultural and ideological diversity about the meaning of historical change processes. Indeed, no new rules for resource transfers, no crash programs in technological modernization, and no new international economic orders can dispense with the arduous task of creating new developmental wisdoms.

Wisdom will not come from "aid givers" whose own development has proved highly wasteful of resources, ecologically irresponsible, destructive of other cultures, and alienating for their own people. Nor can it come from the less developed nations until they come to grips with social forces which challenge their ancient symbol systems—modern technologies, massive scale, interdependencies, and the plurality of meaning systems. All contemporary societies stand in need of authentic development—that is, more satisfactory ways of defining how a sufficiency of goods can foster the quest for a qualitatively good life, how equity and justice can be translated into "equality of outcome" (and not mere "equality of opportunity"), how responsible ecological management of the planet is to be achieved in ways that assign first priority to abolishing the misery of hundreds of millions of human beings.

If this be the task of development, then no single category of nations is assigned the role of "aiding" others and, conversely, no single category of nations stands solely in need of "aid." Both "developed" and "less developed" will need to practice self-reliance in restructuring their own values, institutions, and behavior while "assisting" others in forging together new wisdoms to match their sciences.

PART IV

EVALUATIONS

13.

MEASURING THE COSTS
OF DEVELOPMENT

Economic development exacts high social costs. Consequently, in order to minimize social disruption, some argue that it should be undertaken only with great deliberation. Thus do they question the orthodox agenda of *rapid* economic growth as the surest route to the elimination of poverty. Clearly, the strategy of implementing major economic structural reforms designed to increase output in agriculture and industry needs to be judged against the high price of social changes attendant upon rapid development.

Social change, especially when associated with industrialization, has always exacted a high price. But the price of *not* developing is also high. As the historian E. H. Carr notes, "the cost of conservation falls just as heavily on the underprivileged as the cost of innovation on those who are deprived of their privileges."[1] The high costs of underdevelopment include the perpetuation, generation after generation of chronic disease, hunger, famine, premature death, and degradation of the human spirit. A painful dilemma is posed for development agents who are conscious of the high social costs of sudden structural changes, yet dedicated to reducing underdevelopment's miseries as rapidly as possible.

The sociologist Peter Berger lays bare the high price of development in *Pyramids of Sacrifice: Political Ethics and Social Change*.

The title is an apt metaphor, as the Great Pyramid at Cholula, Mexico, testifies in stone to "the relation among theory, sweat and blood."[2] The pyramid was built as an altar of sacrifice, and the theory legitimizing its construction was brutally simple: "If the gods were not regularly fed with human blood, the universe would fall apart."[3] Although the Aztecs bear the stigma of being history's chief executioners at Cholula, Berger condemns later generations of leaders everywhere—politicians, military commanders, planners, and revolutionaries, abetted by social theorists—who continue to immolate innocent, usually silent, victims in needless sacrifices to insatiable gods. Berger views development (in both its capitalist and socialist incarnations) and revolution as contemporary Molochs who devour the living flesh of millions, all in the name of a "better life" for *future* generations.

Pyramids of Sacrifice is a *cri de coeur* against the perpetration of monstrous cruelties—and their legitimization by intellectuals—on living generations of men, women, and children in myriad lands. The criminals are the hosts of planners, social theorists, and change agents who purport to speak for the people. The sacrificial tragedy is compounded by the assumption made by experts that their own perception of reality is more correct than that of the masses. Too many development enthusiasts and revolutionaries share with missionaries of old that special blend of arrogance and benevolence, or transformational zeal, which denies to poor people "cognitive respect" for their own perceptions of reality. If any aspiration can be said to be universal, cutting across all lines of cultural space and individual personality, it is that every human person and group wishes to be treated by others as a being of worth, for its own sake and on its own terms and regardless of its utility to others. As Kant puts it, people are to be valued as ends, not as mere means. Planners, revolutionaries, and social scientists must therefore show "cognitive respect" for all populations. This is not the practice of mainstream experts who glibly decree the superiority of their own diagnosis of oppression and misery, and thereafter proceed to prescribe "appropriate" remedies: economic growth, revolution, or socialist transformation. The stakes attaching to these prescriptions are high, and in no way should they be exposed to the risk of a series of laboratory experiments because experts who alter people's lives irresponsibly may damage them beyond repair.

Such warnings remain necessary so long as development keeps

confronting societies in distress with a cruel choice between bread and dignity. A facile slogan may assert that bread can be had with dignity, but the harsh reality is that dignity must often be sacrificed to obtain bread, or that the very aspiration of humans after greater dignity becomes reduced to their quest for more bread. Two truths need to be recalled here: (1) "Not by bread alone does man live," and (2) upon closer examination, the bread may be a stone!

No ethical question is so resistant to easy answers as whether present generations should be sacrificed in exchange for the possible development of future generations. This agonizing question leads many close to despair. Two authors, Barrington Moore and Robert Heilbroner, end their foray into the history of social change on a note of rational pessimism tempered by a transrational appeal not to despair. As much human suffering results from trying to "improve mankind," they conclude, as from cynically exploiting it.[4]

The reluctance of these authors to justify sacrificing present generations in order to prepare a better future for their children is the symptom of a more generalized disaffection among believers in progress. All facile optimism and easy belief in the ineluctable upward movement of history must now be rejected, as much also the very imagery of improvement and evolutionary (or revolutionary) emancipation of the human race. Nevertheless, it would be puerile to react by swinging to the other side of the pendulum, since any serious view of history grasps the irreducibly *tragic* nature of social change.

Social science, development theory, and revolutionary action have all failed to deliver their promised "cargo" of blessings at tolerable human costs. The initial mistake consists, however, in assuming that genuine development can be gained at a "tolerable" human cost. This is why today's change agents need to engage in an unemding struggle against present structural injustices (with their train of alienation, misery, and underdevelopment) so as to construct history while bearing witness to transcendence. Most men and women today still live in conditions far below those objectively demanded by human dignity. It is a fact, however, that throughout human history, innumerable generations have always been "sacrificed."

Table 1 presents two indicators of underdevelopment's human costs. To illustrate, of 23.9 million children born each year in sub-Saharan Africa, approximately 8.1 million die before they reach their first birthday. If these countries had the infant mortality of high-income industrialized countries, the annual mortality of infants would be approximately 4.9 million. This mean that due to underdevelopment, 3.2 million infants die *each year* in sub-Saharan Africa alone.

Table 1: THE HUMAN COSTS OF UNDERDEVELOPMENT		
Countries Grouped by National Income per Capita	Infant Mortality Rate per Thousand Live Births	Life Expectancy at Birth in Years
Low- and Middle-Income (less than $2,690):		
Sub-Saharan Africa	15	52
East Asia & Pacific	8	68
South Asia	10	60
Europe & Central Asia	10	70
Middle East & N. Africa	8	64
Latin America & Caribbean	7	68
High-Income Economies ($12,210 - $36,080)	9	77
SOURCE: The World Bank, *World Development Report 1993*, New York: Oxford University Press, 1994, pp. 162-163, 212-213.		

Such "mathematics of suffering" may appear to be morbid, but they lend essential perspective to the human costs of economic *underdevelopment*. Most of the world's populations live in conditions of poverty where the effect on the dignity of individuals, the degradation of their very being, cannot properly be measured. Accordingly, one must contrast this cruel and persistent poverty with the high social costs attaching to efforts at ending poverty. In the past, the human costs of economic development have been very high, it is true. But it does not necessarily follow that these high costs are an unavoidable part of all industrialization or agricultural modernization processes.

There are several reasons why industrialization is not a painless process. First, in many countries there is the need for radical changes in social structure, which often can be brought about only by a social revolution of greater or lesser violence. The old order fights to maintain its dominance while the new order defends itself against counter-revolutionary menaces. And the period of revolution is not restricted to the time of open civil war, but continues until the inhibiting features of the old social structure are eradicated.

A second, closely allied, reason why industrialization is not painless is the need to socialize people into new habits and values. Peasants must be transformed into factory workers by teaching them new kinds of discipline. People must be convinced that new ways of doing things can be good and beneficial—a difficult endeavor. The labor discipline required in an industrial society is alien to the habits of a pre-industrial society, and it is no easy thing to convince people of the need for new discipline by persuasion alone. Even when the need for discipline and change is understood, it usually is not willed ardently enough. The passage from one set of habits and values to another is therefore difficult and often requires some resort to compulsion. In the Soviet Union during the 1930s, this compulsion took the form of *explicit coercion* by the state police power to expedite the movement from individual to collective farms and to enforce factory discipline.[5] In capitalist countries, the *implicit coercion* of the market mechanism, under which most must sell their labor where and when they can, transferred labor from rural to urban areas and imposed discipline through the threat of starvation and unemployment.[6]

A third reason why industrialization is painful is the need to increase the rate of capital accumulation, a process which involves widening the margin between consumption and total output. Although low consumption levels prevail in underdeveloped countries, these cannot be raised substantially in development's early stages. The need to limit consumption in favor of capital accumulation can cause a rise in social discontent. The poorer classes will feel that after fighting for the recent revolutions or reforms they are entitled to its fruits. The middle classes and upper classes will resent the curtailment of their former privileges and "luxury" consumption. To keep this unrest from upsetting the development plans or from leading to counterrevolution or the reversal of reforms, a powerful government policy of coercion may sometimes be needed. However, although it enables capital to be accumulated, coercion also increases the social cost of accumulation. Development is not a smooth evolutionary process of change. On the contrary, writes the economic historian Alexander Gerschenkron, "the happy picture of a quiet industrial revolution proceeding without undue stir and thrust has been . . . seldom reproduced in historical reality."[7] The changes required to initiate economic development are more likely to resemble a gigantic social and political earthquake.

Nevertheless, on balance, the *human costs* attendant upon development are probably lower than the *human costs* attaching to continued underdevelopment. It is particular historical circumstances, and not the development process itself, which seem to account for the major share of these human costs. Hence the task facing development agents becomes one of finding ways to minimize inevitable social costs accompanying economic development efforts and to agree upon standards for evaluating the acceptability of these costs relative to the potential benefits of the process.

Quite possibly no adequate answer exists inasmuch as all relevant normal moral standards in this matter are so ambiguous. The problem can nonetheless be understood more clearly by a brief discussion of two factors affecting moral judgments.

The first factor is that "objective conditions control the environment in which behavior takes place."[8] One obvious example is the state of war. Restrictions on civil liberties are usually judged to be more acceptable in wartime than in times of peace. In Donald Bowles' cryptic phrase, ". . . death of a political enemy on a battlefield is approved, the domestic execution of a political prisoner is disapproved."[9] A program of economic development is akin to a war on poverty; as such, it is an "objective condition shaping the environment in which ethical judgements are made." Under this "objective condition," akin to a state of war, policies to restrict luxury goods consumption—for example, to mobilize underemployed labor for projects such as reforestation, or to control population movements from rural to urban areas—are to be judged differently than if they were pursued during "peacetime."

A second factor affecting ethical judgements is the recognition that evaluating the social costs of economic development is a highly complex task. Humanity faces a perplexing dilemma here. On the one hand, the failure to overcome underdevelopment *allows* untold human suffering to continue. On the other hand, the process of overcoming these human costs through speeding up development will most likely *generate* some new costs; and the faster the old human costs are overcome the more severe are the new ones. In addition, there is the danger that the centralized power needed to generate rapid development will be used to consolidate personal power and establish enduring totalitarianism.

Berger pleads for "solutions to our problems that accept *neither* hunger *nor* terror."[10] His *caveat* need not necessarily deter us, however, from pursuing both authentic development and genuine revolution. By definition, neither authentic development nor genuine revolution can erect success into an absolute value. In his study of the history of rebellions and revolutions, Albert Camus discovers the de-absolutization, or relativization, of goals to be an ethical law of social change. In his words:

> Rebellion itself only aspires to the relative and can only promise an assured dignity coupled with relative justice. . . . A revolutionary action which wishes to be coherent in terms of its origins should be embodied in an active consent to the relative. It would express fidelity to the human condition. . . . Uncompromising as to its means, it would accept an approximation as far as its ends are concerned. . . . Absolute freedom mocks at justice. Absolute justice denies freedom. To be fruitful, the two ideas must find their limits in each other.[11]

The same ethical law holds for the pursuit of development as for revolution. Yet, the qualified pursuit of both may remain as an urgent duty because prevailing structures of underdevelopment perpetuate both hunger and terror.

14.

OBSTACLES TO DEVELOPMENT

In his 1920 study *The Acquisitive Society*, the economic historian R. H. Tawney laments: "Industrial communities neglect the very objects for which it is worthwhile to acquire riches in their feverish preoccupation with the means by which riches can be acquired."[1]

And Galbraith graces the frontispiece of *The Affluent Society* with a phrase drawn from Alfred Marshall, declaring: "The economist, like everyone else, must concern himself with the ultimate aims of man."[2] Teleological reflection on ultimate aims is no mere luxury, however, to be indulged only by a few philosophically inclined specialists. Willy Brandt, speaking for the North-South Commission, presents development as a life-and-death issue for humanity at large.[3]

If development is so urgent and important a task, however, why has a successful assault on global poverty not been mounted? The answer may lie in the tragic nature of history. The ultimate ethical question in development may well be whether it is futile to strive to improve the lot of one billion human beings who live in "absolute poverty," that condition of life, so characterized by malnutrition, illiteracy, disease, squalid surroundings, high infant mortality, and low life expectancy as to be beneath any reasonable definition of human decency.[4]

"Realists" invoke historical fatalism to justify their policy inaction or timid palliative solutions in the face of global poverty. It is more constructive, they argue, to preserve existing imperfect social orders than to experiment with risky new social arrangements in vain hopes of constructing better systems. There is, admittedly, some semblance of truth to their contention that efforts to build new systems often result in worse disorders. Indeed, no utopian magic wands can be waved that will make institutions serve the poor. Yet all of moral history has been written by human agents who resist the paralysis induced by too "objective" a view of the difficulties lying in the way of structural change. Ethical agendas are predicated not on accepting things as they are, but on struggling to make them what they ought to be: to create new possibilities is the supreme moral imperative.

Two opposite interpretations of the dictum, "politics is the art of the possible," vie for legitimacy. One reading views politics as an arena of wheeling and dealing within closed boundaries of possibility, what Lyndon Johnson called "horse trading." If political practitioners assume that the boundaries of possibility are fixed once and for all, they will strive to maximize particular gains within these set boundaries. This approach in inevitably conservative, dedicated to system maintenance. A contrary reading defines politics as the art of creating new possibilities. Frontiers of possibility must be expanded both by implosion (pushing the system's limits outwards through pressure from within) and by explosion (rupturing continuities through outside forces pressing in). Reformists, revolutionaries, and progressives favor this second exegesis.

By its very nature, development politics aims at creating new possibilities. The internal exigencies of development call for new structures, new institutions, new criteria for problem-solving, and new ground rules to govern relations between rich and poor, within national borders and beyond them. Therefore, the stewards of present global circulation systems cannot be the architects of genuine development. The ethical task of theorists and practitioners alike is to discover or to create new leverage points for triumphing over the obstacles to development. Of the many obstacles to development, three are especially weighty and merit examination: (1) the bankruptcy of development paradigms, (2) the global paralysis of institutional imagination, and (3) the array of domestic impediments to sound national development.

Bankruptcy of Development Paradigms

Development strategies have failed in three domains: *distribution, employment,* and *self-reliance.*

Distribution. In most Third World countries, conventional strategies have not led to satisfactory economic growth. During the 1980s, the World Bank reports, "[S]ome sixty low- and middle-income economies suffered declining real GNP per capita in constant prices."[5] Even where high growth did occur, it generated massive inequities in the distribution of benefits. General Emilio Garrastazu-Medici, president of Brazil from 1969 to 1974, gives poignant expression to the inability even of high economic growth (Brazil's "economic miracle," a reference to growth rates exceeding 10 percent annually) to create equity. In his lapidary and cruel phrase, "a economia vai bem mas o povo vai mal" ("The economy is going well but the people are doing badly"),[6] Medici concedes that, "Despite six years of revolutionary effort, when we look at the actual conditions of life for the vast majority of the Brazilian people, we are forced to the conclusion that industry may be flourishing but the people are not."[7] By 1989 Brazil's poorest 40 percent of the population received only 7 percent of total income, while the top 20 percent accounted for 67.5 percent with the richest 10 percent appropriating 51.3 percent of the total.[8] What kind of development is this, one must ask, which is good for an abstraction known as the national economy, but bad for the flesh-and-blood people that economy is meant to serve?

Disparities grow wider because small percentage gains in income for the already rich add absolute increments to their income far grater than those accruing even from high percentage increases for the poor. Most studies of distribution measure differences in income and in access to basic social services, such as health care, pure water, housing, schooling, and public transportation to work and market place.[9] Little research is conducted, however, on differences in assets, clearly a more enduring source of wealth disparities than income differences.

Employment. Strategies prescribing industrial growth and high technology have, in the main, failed to create jobs. Numerous ILO studies show that rapid industrialization and growth in GNP do not reduce unemployment.[10] For James Grant, former Director of UNICEF, "the tragic waste of human resources in the Third World is symbolized by nearly 300 million persons unemployed or underemployed in the mid-1970s."[11] Modern industrial and high-technology investments are too expensive to create enough workplaces for large numbers of unskilled workers. And by definition, the labor force of Third World countries is comprised mainly of workers unskilled in industrial and technological tasks, their skills being those of subsistence food-growers and artisans. Policies aimed at mechanizing agricultural production exacerbate the problem, displacing peasants from their livelihood without providing them with new sources of productive work and income. The World Bank describes the mechanisms at work here:

> Because average labor productivity is lower in agriculture than in industry or services, the sectoral restructuring of the labor force initially proceeds more slowly than that of production. As a result, agriculture so far remains the predominant source of employment not only in Low Income countries but also in many Middle Income countries.

> The larger number of workers remaining in agriculture in developing countries has increasingly raised doubts about the adequacy of the industrialization process as a source of remunerative employment.[12]

Production by the masses, in contrast, brings jobs and dignity to large numbers of poor village people unfamiliar with new technologies; in contrast, mass production renders their labor and skills superfluous by concentrating production in large, urban factory units requiring costly technologies and imported raw materials.

Moreover, few developing countries provide incentives to retain their skilled professional workers. The resulting brain drain constitutes a disastrous hemorrhage of a poor nation's trained personnel to rich countries. Still another distortion of conventional industrialization models is the over-concentration of facilities, equipment, and job opportunities in a few large cities. The consequences are widespread pauperization and unemployment in the countryside, and parasitical overpopulation in cities unable to supply jobs and basic services to millions fleeing rural misery.

Self-Reliant Growth. Early development writers posited self-sustained growth as the key component of development. Walt Rostow proclaimed that with rational resource planning and adequate capital investment: "In a decade or two both the basic structure of the economy and the social and political structure of the society are transformed in such a way that a steady rate of growth can be, therefore, regularly sustained."[13]

Few Third World countries have achieved self-sustained economic growth; on the contrary, most depend on recurring infusions of foreign capital and technology. Astronomical debts incurred by Brazil, Mexico, and other countries testify to the failure of growth strategies to lessen dependency on outside resources. Dependency is a necessary outcome of the structural relationships binding poor to rich nations. Global interdependence is rarely horizontal, mutual, or reciprocal; almost always it is vertical, paternalistic, and exploitative. The interdependence of horse and rider is qualitatively different from that of two oarsmen rowing one boat, however.[14]

National and local self-reliance have proven to be elusive goals in development history. Centralized patterns of resource allocation reinforce biases in favor of building a few large hospitals instead of providing primary health care to all, of operating a few prestigious schools for the elite rather than supplying basic education to all, of manufacturing luxury cars for the privileged few instead of providing inexpensive buses for the poor masses. Although theories of self-reliance abound, in practice self-reliance has usually been crushed or ignored.[15] Developing countries find it difficult to conquer greater self-reliance because behind resource transfers a *sequence of dependency* is at work. In early periods of development, poor countries depend heavily on foreign suppliers for capital, technology, managerial skills, and markets.[16] Over time, and as they reduce their dependency on foreign capital, they nonetheless continue to depend on outside sources of technology, managerial expertise, and market access.

Cultural subordination, no less than economic, political and technological dependence, continues to plague Third World countries. Under the steamroller effects of foreign influences, their vulnerable cultural values are rapidly being destroyed or damaged. Throughout the world, as Ivan Illich notes, technical values are displacing *vernacular* or non-elite values.[17]

Reasons for Failure.   Industrial growth models have raised high hopes in their promise, but delivered paltry results in their performance. Two reasons explain this failure.

First, the strategies were exported from industrially advanced countries to societies where cultural, psychological, social, and political soil was uncongenial to them. Most Western agents of change were insensitive to these differences. Introducing the wage system and the commercial mentality, for example, to people who for centuries have lived on the edge of subsistence, shatters their fragile social cohesion. It breaks down constraints which protect vulnerable communities from depredations made by selfish and ambitious individuals. As far back as 1958, Albert Hirschman urged developers not to impose ego-focused images of change on societies favoring group-focused images of change. He warned that: "Considerable care must be taken not to violate the 'image' of change that alone is acceptable. This belief or suspicion, however mistaken, that a project will lead to individual enrichment rather than to collective benefits may easily spell its failure. . . ."[18]

Few change agents, however, have taken care to avoid violating the "image" of change acceptable to communities of need. Too often experts did not propose but imposed their standard solutions. Not surprisingly, *either* their advice was resisted *or* their impositions succeeded in a purely technical sense but damaged local values beyond repair. Sound development can never come through shortcuts that violate the perceptual universe of culture groups. If change strategies are to fall on receptive soils, a proper mix of innovative and cooperative elements is needed. In most cases, however, the circulation systems through which modernity is "transferred" from "advanced" to less advanced societies have proven dysfunctional.

Nevertheless, development paradigms suffer from an even more fundamental defect, one which transcends the faulty circulation systems through which these paradigms flow across cultural borders.

Secondly, mainstream development models are flawed in their very roots—they are vitiated *in radice*. It is not a case of sound development being exported to sites unsuited to receive it, but rather that the very conception of development transferred is itself distorted at its point of origin. Even for the United States or Europe, normatively sound development cannot mean maximum economic growth, uncontrolled urbanization, centralized industrialization, or ever-increasing consumption.[19] The psychologist Erich Fromm warns that *having more* often gets in the way of *being more*.[20] And the social philosopher August Hecksher, commenting on the relentless pressures Americans face to buy and consume, writes:

> It is as if the machine had made its bargain: "I will give you free time in abundance, but in return you must promise to absorb my output." The output of the machine cannot be absorbed during working hours—except in so far as one machine devours another; therefore it is the task of the consumer to make his leisure constantly busier and more active. He must go places; he must equip himself; he must invest in gadgets. The result is that leisure becomes more expensive; and the more time men have, the more money they spend. They must therefore work more, and the life of leisure becomes a constant drive to make additional money in order to be able to enjoy more adequately one's free time. The logical result—which in fact occurs often in practice—is a household full of the paraphernalia of leisure without the time or the energy to make use of them.[21]

Philip Slater, Christopher Lasch, Peter Marin, and other social critics discern an intrinsic connection between excessive competition and consumption and the pervasive alienation which afflict Americans.[22] Louise Bernikow calls loneliness a nationwide disease and epidemic.[23] Surely then, personal and societal development must lie elsewhere than in the pursuit of abundant goods. The U.S. model of affluent growth is being challenged not only on psychological grounds, but on economic and technical grounds as well. Advocates of steady-state growth and a sustainable society point to resource imbalances inherent in a mode of development which destroys nature. Throughout the world a consensus is beginning to form that what is called "development" turns out, upon critical examination, to be a spurious *ersatz.*

In rich and poor countries alike, still another major obstacle blocks the quest for new development models: the worldwide paralysis of creative imagination. Although new institutions and problem-solving approaches are urgently needed, the wellsprings of social invention have run dry.

A Global Crisis of Imagination

As he lamented over the fading glories of the Victorian Age, the poet Matthew Arnold (1822-1888) saw his beloved England "wandering between two worlds, one dead, the other powerless to be born."[24] Arnold's lament accurately depicts the present century's dilemma: today's global institutions are relics of an earlier age and no longer function. They are already dead, but not yet buried. Alternative institutions, although often portrayed in desirable scenarios, do not yet exist; worse still, they seem powerless to be born. Practical problem-solvers concede that radically new long-term structures are needed, but nonetheless expend their energies scurrying from one futile exercise in short-term crisis management to another. This state of "colloidal suspension" between a dying but lingering world and a stillborn new universe induces institutional paralysis in several realms.

Disjointed Phases.   Today's world is marked by a disjunction of phases. While industrial civilization is revealing itself to be empty in rich countries, it still holds out its earlier promise to poor countries, which pursue it more avidly than ever. In 1982, while oil took Mexico to the precipice of financial bankruptcy, economic collapse, and social breakdown, it continued to be hailed as the country's best economic hope for the future.[25] Unwise tourist investments thrust impoverished Caribbean Islands to the brink of developmental failure, yet island governments continue to shirk agricultural development policies and look to tourism as their savior. Many Third World leaders assert that it is now their countries' turn to experience pollution since along with pollution, or so they think, comes industry. They brook no sermons from the rich about limits to growth, for they have tasted just enough industrial growth to know that in its wake it brings power, prestige, and bargaining leverage.

Globalism Versus Nationalism.   Discordant phasing likewise marks the drive toward a new world order. The imperatives of technology, trade, disarmament, and pollution control all point to the need for global problem-solving or governance. Yet nationalism of the narrowest sort—chauvinistic, irrational, short-sighted, and aggressive—flourishes as never before. On the one hand, transnational corporations globalize the production of goods; on the other, their disdain of national boundaries arouses violent nationalistic feelings wherever they operate offshore. So too with international organizations. Notwithstanding their rhetoric about supranational loyalties, they serve as conflictual arenas for ethnocentric vituperation and the promotion of parochial interests. When hiring personnel, these organizations obey thinly disguised "quota" systems and conduct deliberations not in a spirit of transcendent global interests, but in the mode of trade-offs among competing parochial gains. In general, the world's circulations systems, governing flows of trade, capital, technology, and information, operate vertically, not horizontally. They reward superior competition, not priority needs; they promote the domination of strong over weak partners, not the mutuality of interests.

Irrational Forces in History. Irrationality wears many masks. The most familiar is violence, which shreds the fabric of national and international agreements. Actual violence is but the tip of the iceberg, however—the symptom of a deeper structural violence that renders "rational" policy-making impossible. Even under relatively normal and peaceful conditions, development processes are largely immune to rational management. Unplanned results of policies turn out to be more important than those expected. To illustrate, Latin American development policy in the 1960s drew its inspiration from the prescriptions of the United Nations' Economic Commission for Latin America (ECLA). ECLA urged Latin American nations to practice import substitution in order to build up their industries, save foreign exchange, create jobs, and become technologically competitive. By and large, however, dependency has simply shifted its locus. Brazil, Argentina, and other import-substituting nations were soon spending more to buy technology used in manufacturing goods than they had previously spent to import finished goods. Worse still, the basket of goods they produced was designed, as their earlier imports had been, to satisfy the wants of classes with strong buying power, not to meet the needs of poor masses with little purchasing power.

This array of global obstacles to development is matched by a no less formidable array of difficulties at work within developing countries.

Domestic Roadblocks to Development

Developing countries face numerous internal barriers: the vested interests of their ruling classes, the passivity of exploited classes, a dearth of enlightened leaders, and the intrinsic difficulty of moving successfully from local to national arenas of development activity.

Vested Interests.   The Mexican sociologist Pablo González Casanova has analyzed the vested interests linking the destiny of privileged classes in poor countries to that of foreign exploiters—governments, corporations, military forces, and wealthy professionals. "Internal colonialism," as he calls it, "has its roots in the great independence movement of the old colonies. . . . With the disappearance of the direct domination of foreigners over natives, the notion of domination and exploitation of natives by natives emerges."[26]

Traditional privileged classes (the rural aristocracy and commodity exporters), new professionals (engineers, business executives, technicians), clerks serving the ruling classes (intellectuals, bureaucrats), and upper echelons of the military hierarchy all have high stakes in keeping their countries dependent on rich world partners. They correctly perceive that alternative development strategies are a threat to their own power, wealth, social status, and global mobility, all of which depend on their partnership with foreigners. Alternative strategies which meet the needs of the poor, make non-elites self-reliant, and respect traditional values violate the interests of elites and their preferred norms for governing society.

Experience has taught these groups how to employ the rhetoric of structural change and development for the poor while protecting their own favored position. Ruling groups such as these make development policy in most Third World countries, and the bankrupt paradigms denounced above are quite acceptable to them. Indeed, growth models are good for business executives, bankers, and real estate speculators in Third World countries. Because these interest groups are not about to relinquish development's benefits to the masses, their domestic strategy centers on co-opting demands for radical change issuing from below. One favorite instrument of co-optation, or the safe channeling of demands from below, is what the British economist Charles Elliott calls the confidence mechanism or "con mech."[27] Ruling groups in many countries, Elliott contends, establish social mechanisms for just enough upward mobility to allow a few lower-class individuals to gain admission to the "club" of the well-off. In order to defuse potentially radical demands from the masses, elites manipulate the propensity of socially deprived groups to identify vicariously with the few members of their own cohort who climb upward. Elliott bases his theory on empirical studies conducted in thirteen African and Asian countries. "Con mechs," however, are relatively benign devices in the arsenal of weapons used to suppress the poor in Third World countries. Less gentle means include systematic intimidation, repression, torture, and outright annihilation.

Privileged elites in developing countries suffer few qualms of conscience over national development strategies that concentrate benefits in their own hands. Themselves largely Westernized, they embrace the values underlying these strategies. The Third World upper stratum is more attuned to Western business, military, bureaucratic, and technical values than to the traditions of its own populace. It is not enough to describe the posture of this upper stratum, however; one also needs to explain the inertia of oppressed groups themselves.

Passivity of the Exploited. Many writers analyze the oppressed consciousness, whether its cause is traced to overt colonialism, economic exploitation, racial discrimination, or less overt forms of social control.[28] One dismal conclusion common to all such analyses is that oppressed people acquire a vested interest in their own servitude. As a defence mechanism, they internalize the demeaning stereotypes thrust upon them by their master. Over time, this internalized image comes to define their own identity; the stereotype becomes a crutch propping up their own fragile self-esteem. To expel the internalized self-image is a long and painful process. Because they understand this, revolutionary leaders assign high priority to the psychological transformation of their people. A new self-image conferring a sense of worth must replace that of people who are weak, inferior, and worthless. Psychological revolution is a prelude to effective action against external enemies.

Social historians confirm the writings of revolutionary theorists.[29] Barrington Moore's *Injustice: The Social Bases of Obedience and Revolt* analyzes with particular clarity the inertia of oppressed groups.[30] Appeals to revolt cannot succeed unless two prior conditions are met. First, large numbers of oppressed people must become convinced that changes proposed to them can succeed. This conviction is hard to reach because their historical memory reminds them that rebellions are usually repressed, betrayed, or peter out after initial successes. A second condition is that oppressed groups must come to view their present evils as intolerably worse than any alternative, especially one which launches them into the unknown. Nevertheless, exploited people who have survived oppression over a long time no longer view their lot as absolutely intolerable Simply in order to survive they have had to find ways of sublimating or, to use the evocative term coined by the Jamaican sociologist Roy Bryce-Laporte, of making "secondary adaptations" to their conditions.[31] Consequently, the leap into the dark, which they are invited to make by revolutionary mobilizers, is almost always perceived by them as too uncertain and dangerous.

Great leaders must appear on the horizon to help the weak overcome their passivity and accept risk. Such leaders, however, are a rare commodity.

The Dearth of Leadership. Good leaders cannot be mass-produced. What are the qualities needed by development leaders?

The first quality required is an intuitive grasp of the larger historical dimensions latent in local struggles. Gandhi possessed an uncanny ability to see national significance in seemingly modest actions—a salt march to the sea, adopting native-spun Khadi garments, a non-cooperation campaign in a single Indian city.

A second important virtue in leaders is the ability to reconcile multiple class alliances. They identify with and experience the exploitation of oppressed masses as a personal affront to their own personal dignity. Genuine leaders are able to circulate among many interest groups; their appeal goes beyond a single frontier of loyalty, whether founded on class, ethnic group, region, or professional category.

A third trait of development leaders is moral and physical courage. Courage enables them to run risks, to persevere in the face of defeat, to reject temptations to compromise along the way, and to face death unflinchingly. At the very least, symbolic death must be faced in the form of politically suicidal decisions necessary to preserve integrity.

Good development leaders also know how to communicate their own vision of possible success to less imaginative or less experienced masses. Sicily's Danilo Dolci overcame the passivity of peasants who previously thought their Mafia oppressors invincible.[32]

A final quality found in good leaders is the ability to learn quickly from their mistakes. Experimentation and risk-taking of necessity produce errors, but critical reflection on the reasons for the errors can lead one to a more successful next round of activities.

Simply to list the qualities demanded of development leaders is to reveal how rarely such leaders are found. These remarks are not to be construed, however, as an endorsement of Thomas Carlyle's "Great Man" view of history.[33] On the contrary, it is precisely because sound development calls for the mobilization of mass energies that good leaders are needed. Amilcar Cabral, the leader of Guinea-Bissau's independence struggle, observed:

> People do not fight for ideals or for notions inside men's heads. The people fight and accept sacrifices demanded by the struggle to obtain material advantages so as to be able to live in peace and in better conditions, in order to see their lives progress and to guarantee their children's future.[34]

Oppressed people need flesh-and-blood heroes to embody their hopes for a better life and galvanize them into action. Even dictators recognize the importance of personifying national aspirations around themselves. That they could so easily promote personality cults reveals how desperately Third World masses need to vest their hopes in visible leaders. This desperate need is traceable, in large measure, to the paradoxical fact that poor and powerless people often do not know exactly what they need. And although they resent having their needs diagnosed for them by experts, they nonetheless recognize "their own voice in trusted leaders." Leaders must be committed in principle to eliciting from the powerless a creative and critical formulation of their hopes and needs. When this occurs, a dialogue is initiated in which leaders merge with the people and these, in turn, enter into the diagnostic and prescriptive universe of the leaders as if it were their own. All those in leadership positions—educators, technical experts, political organizers—must display that ontological humility which makes them define their own true consciousness as necessarily requiring constant rectification by the consciousness of the masses. Only by adopting this self-definition and this role can leaders protect themselves from the temptation to use their superiority as a pretext for manipulating the masses.

Genuine leadership, thus conceived, is not incompatible with bottom-up development in which non-elites progressively are empowered to define their own needs, organize to meet them, and perhaps even choose to transcend them.

The Transition from Micro to Macro Arenas of Action.   No domestic obstacle to sound development is greater than the difficulty grassroots groups face in "graduating" from micro to macro action arenas. It is relatively easy to launch, and even to sustain, small-scale projects which meet the needs of the poor while allowing non-elites to participate in decisions. What is far more difficult is to preserve these values when a grassroots movement grows in size and takes on responsibility in wider arenas of national strategy.[35] One can create a successful free school for peasants but fail to institute an alternative national educational system for non-elites. Similarly, it is relatively easy to operate a farm cooperative on principles of economic democracy, but enormously more difficult to translate these principles into a sound national agricultural policy.

As E. F. Schumacher insisted, it is true that small is beautiful, but development strategists likewise know that "some big is necessary."[36] Grassroots movements must not become mere havens for disenchanted anti-modernists, a kind of parallel counter-culture, no matter how self-sufficient or viable. On the contrary, their goal is to serve as an alternative development paradigm for the entire nation, to lead it into a new way of being modern, one which safeguards national culture and traditional values. Success, obviously, is far from assured.

Exceptional bottom-up innovations face still another obstacle to success; namely, an unfavorable international climate. The late J. P. Naik, a noted Indian educator and developmental strategist, was convinced that "India could follow a Gandhian path in its national development only if the whole world, or at least the neighboring Asian countries, followed the same path."[37] Unfortunately, the stewards of power and legitimacy in the world at large have a stake in resisting alternative development strategies within Third World countries.

Does this depressing inventory of obstacles to authentic development leave any agenda to ethical strategists and policy actors? Notwithstanding the plethora of counter-development forces at work and the irrationalities of history, this thorny question can be answered by a conditional YES.

Conclusion

Systemic obstacles barring sound development leave only narrow leverage space for the conduct of any ethical *praxis*. Ethicists find it relatively easy to diagnose injustice and exploitation in existing patterns of world investment, technology transfer, income distribution, and land tenure. They likewise have little trouble outlining preferred futures, scenarios, or designs for society. And with modest efforts they can even go one step further and start implementing a strategy for the transition to sound development. That strategy's first step consists of educating the public in order to win their intellectual and political support for a normatively better future. What comes next, however, is the arduous task of conceiving and applying new modes of problem-solving.

These modes of problem-solving must be qualitatively better than the old ones, and they must add up, cumulatively, to structural transformations of global and national systems. Palliatives which merely treat the symptoms of the evils diagnosed are ruled out. Hence the goal is to fashion creatively incremental modes of problem-solving while avoiding palliatives.[38]

Experts are not those best qualified to issue development prescriptions. On the contrary, the message *from below* states that the most basic human need of poor people is the freedom to define their own needs, to organize to meet them, and to transcend them as they see fit.[39]

Development ethicists need not feel apologetic about sharing policy platforms with world bankers, international politicians, or technical experts. If timidity is not warranted, however, humility certainly is. No less than other development professionals, ethicists need to wage war against their own personal, professional, ideological and national vested interests if they are to avoid palliative solutions to global underdevelopment. More than others, ethicists need that quality of which the late L. J. Lebret so often spoke—"intelligent love." Lebret's moral indignation over injustice led him to proclaim the need for prophecy, commitment, and—yes—even love. But it had to be "intelligent love," for love without disciplined intelligence is inefficient, naive, and in its bungling good intentions, catastrophic. And intelligence without love breeds a brutalizing technocracy that crushes people. Ethicists commit an unpardonable sin if they posit a simplistic policy choice: *either* efficiency *or* humanization. Efficiency, indispensable to those who would humanize our anti-developed strategies themselves, must be redefined to serve human values.

15.

DEVELOPMENT OR
ANTI-DEVELOPMENT?

Upon critical examination, much apparent development proves to be "anti-development." Conversely, seemingly modest accomplishments often constitute genuine developmental progress. No assessment of the quality of performance is realistic, however, if it ignores the constraints faced by societies in their efforts to develop. The present chapter traces some of the limits within which development performance and policies may properly be evaluated.

Economic, political, and cultural development are all presumed to be means for obtaining the good life. Consequently, it is possible for material standards of living to improve and for institutions to become modern in the absence of qualitative improvement in society. This judgment rests on what Fromm calls "normative humanism."[1] In order to engage in normative thinking, one need not postulate the existence of a fixed human essence; one has only to grant that societies may foster social health, personal integration, and human fulfillment or, conversely, promote pathological states, disintegration, and the waste of human energies. Unless one wishes to judge a society solely by the number of radios or miles of highway it possesses, one must perforce appeal to qualitative indicators of life and society in determining what constitutes good (or bad) development. Marx considered that the truly wealthy man is the man who *is* much, not the one who *has* much.[2] This distinction applies to nations as well: the truly "developed" country is one whose inhabitants *are* rich even if they do not *have* riches.

Anti-Development

Those societies conventionally labelled as developed are in a good position to assure optimal life-sustenance to their citizens. Their score on the registers of optimizing esteem and freedom, the other two goals of development, may prove less satisfactory, however. Within the United States social critics bear witness to a widespread "alienation of abundance," no less dehumanizing than "alienation in misery."[3] And ecologists assume that a high correlation exists between the internal health of a society and its relationship to environment. As Lynton Caldwell noted:

> A civilization reveals the nature of its internalized goals in the environmental conditions it creates. . . . American treatment of its environments appears to be violently contradictory. . . . Numerous species of wildlife have been eliminated from the American environment, but health-hazardous "pesticides" have been injected into the ecosystem with minimal regard to the full range of their effects; in an effort to eliminate harmful species, beneficial plants and animals have been destroyed. . . . [I]n the United States there is widespread acceptance of certain assumptions regarding man's freedom of choice that handicaps his rational use of whatever freedom he might have to shape his environment.[4]

One of the assumptions which greatly impedes the rational use of freedom is the attachment of Americans to the myth of the beneficence of ever-expanding economic growth and production. Among the most serious problems resulting from obsessive attachment to growth is "the contamination of our society and food chain with deadly pesticides, toxic chemicals, and dangerous radiation. This pollution is killing, sickening, and disabling millions of Americans."[5]

The difference between quantitative and qualitative development has been personally experienced by thousands of Peace Corps volunteers. While sharing the lives of economically "underdeveloped" Africans, Filipinos, Latin Americans, or Nepalese, many U.S. volunteers learned for the first time of the existence of rich human values.[6] The reason why economic development can be a lesser good than a healthy community, let us say, or a culturally rich society is that an industrial economy tends to lose its proper status as a means and to eliminate every sphere of non-economic value from life. A prosperous society whose members are manipulated by an impersonal system is not developed, but distorted. A society suffers from "anti-development" if its "development" breeds new oppressions and structural servitudes. The unholy alliance among what C. Wright Mills[7] calls "the big three"—government, industry, and the military establishment—has spawned a new privilege system in the United States no less anti-democratic than that which characterizes "underdeveloped" societies.

One may object that qualitative defects in a "developed" society do not justify labeling its performance as "anti-development." This objection rests on the assumption that "development" is a purely descriptive label reflecting quantitative conditions expressed in certain levels of economic performance and social efficiency, or in the prevalence of specific attitudes toward time, work, achievement, and secularity. This assumption overlooks the ambiguity of the term "development" which, in its deepest sense, evokes qualitative ideas of maturation, progress toward perfection, justice, greater consciousness, perhaps even greater happiness. It is such an uncritical use of the term that leads many to mistake the means for the ends.

Ultimately, the only ethically justifiable goal of development is to make people happier. That is also the only ethically justifiable goal for not developing. In practice, economic development may make some people happier, others less happy. Those who benefit may do so at the expense of others and, in any case, it is highly questionable whether more goods make people happier.

Development processes as presently conducted reinforce a tendency already rampant within technologically advanced societies toward the absolutization of means. Notwithstanding their private denunciation of the folly of treating development in economic terms alone, many development economists recommend policies which in effect confer primacy on mass consumption as a goal. One serious consequence of this practice is that policy-makers often prematurely relegate precious values to oblivion because they judge them to be incompatible with development. These are such values as personal communion in friendship because it is time-consuming, contemplation of nature because it is useless, communal celebration because it is inefficient.

If we are to assess correctly the effects of development on social values, we must distinguish between two forms of materialism. The first is healthy and guards us against that escapism which treats material wants as unimportant and views misery as the result of fate or the will of gods. Such escapist outlooks hold material things in disdain. Healthy materialism, on the contrary, gives due emphasis to life's physical conditions and grants ethical approval to reasonable acquisitive desires, all the while frankly acknowledging that human virtue cannot consist in closing one's eyes to human suffering. However, there also exists a second kind of materialism which transforms humans into manipulators or objects of manipulation. This brand of materialism reduces a person's being to what that person possesses: worth is measured in monetary terms and is substituted for value. This brand of materialism is at once innocent and deadly, and it feeds on a mindless and insensitive system which allows the quest for abundance to depersonalize life. By its uncritical complacency toward material wealth, it blinds us to the presence of authentic human values within cultures of poverty and affluence alike. Things come to dominate persons. The "immensity of desires paralyzes man," however, if "unlimited desires are dictated by a law of civilization."[8] Authentic development, on the other hand, frees people from the thralldom of misery and satisfies their needs at a pace which allows them to control the dynamisms of their desire.

The French eighteenth-century essayist and dramatist L. S. Mercier declared luxury to be "the executioner of the rich" because exaggerated ease in gaining access to pleasures makes one lose the capacity to enjoy those very pleasures. If, therefore, the spread of development simply makes it possible for all humans to have the same "executioner" as did the rich two centuries ago, then development is clearly a regressive, not a progressive, thing. When commenting on the lot of the rich, Mercier judges that "luxury is to them as much an affliction as poverty is to the poor."[9] Whether a society is non-developed, underdeveloped, partially developed, or highly developed, its members repeatedly make conscious or unconscious choices about the values and vital qualities they seek. The systematic pursuit of economic improvement, social modernization, and cumulative science constitutes one option in favor of a certain definition of human progress and social maturation. One needs to go further, however, and examine the instruments chosen to obtain these goals.

No less important than the goals pursued are the means selected and their consequences on human life. Maslow pointedly warns that "Americans have learned that political democracy and economic prosperity don't in themselves solve any of the basic value problems."[10] Accordingly, anti-development results whenever some basic element of the good life as normatively defined by the interested population itself—its view of optimal life-sustenance, esteem, freedom, and actualization (self and collective)—is diminished instead of enhanced. The danger of losing precious core values in the pursuit of development is not imaginary. On the contrary, under the banner of development, many harmful images of the good life are disseminated throughout the world by ideological and commercial propaganda, unexamined demonstration effects, and cultural transfers of all types. Normative values borrowed from "developed" societies have at times proved to be trivial or dehumanizing. At best, the patterns of modernity displayed by today's "developed" societies represent a mixed blessing which must not be blindly imitated.[11] Developers must invent alternatives both to traditional static wisdoms, which are powerless to satisfy many needs, and to the modern "pathology of normalcy,"[12] which lacks a wisdom to integrate its sciences.

It is a serious mistake to portray high living standards and efficiency as unequivocal goods and to condemn their opposites as unmitigated evils. Progress in one sphere usually entails regression in some other domain. Nations achieve success in such realms as the specialization of knowledge, efficiency at work, and high levels of individual performance only because they sacrifice other values, such as synthesis in knowledge, tolerance of conversation, music and play during work periods, and maintenance of extended family solidarity to provide emotionally satisfying roles to old people. The alternative courses available to underdeveloped societies must not be reduced to the simplistic dyad: either to remain stagnant and "underdeveloped," or to embrace all the ills surrounding current patterns of modernity and "development." According to Douglas Steere,[13] it is possible to obtain industry without ugly cities, greater food production without demoralizing speculation, and education without cultural alienation. So long as one continues to evaluate development in predominantly quantitative terms, however, one cannot devise new forms of social cost-accounting responsive to the qualitative dimensions of development.[14]

One writer[15] goes so far as to suggest that payments should be made by governments to individuals whose psychic security is shattered by a macro-social development in which they are unsuited to share. Underlying this recommendation is a presumptive ethical principle—namely, that compensation for mental damages is due to those who are rendered unhappy because their desire mechanisms have been damaged by a general process over which they lack control and from whose benefits they are excluded. Although this idea is neither juridically nor economically feasible, it nonetheless dramatizes an issue too often ignored when development's costs are appraised. The true costs paid to obtain development are terrifyingly high. What is easily overlooked, on the other hand, is the cost of *remaining developed and maintaining efficiency after development is reached.*

The Chinese philosopher Lin Yutang, reflecting on his country's long history, evokes the high tribute exacted by efficiency. "It is evident anyway," this ancient sage writes, "that the Chinese as a nation are more philosophic than efficient, and that if it were otherwise, no nation could have survived the high blood pressure of an efficient life for four thousand years. Four thousand years of efficient living would ruin any nation."[16] At present levels of technological development, however, a painful tribute would be exacted of efficient societies long before four thousand years had elapsed. Certain "developed" nations may well experience early ruin because they pay too high a price to maintain what is, in fact, "anti-development." Ecologists, biologists, and psychologists warn emphatically of the dangers of narrowly maximizing purely economic goals. Accordingly, development performance needs to be judged not by purely quantitative indicators, but in the light of qualities which relate to intangible values. "Anti-development" can coexist alongside excellent nutrition, high income, general literacy, bureaucratic efficiency, and expanding investment capacities. Since these are all relative goods, much depends on what is sacrificed in order to obtain or preserve them. Like Esau of Old Testament lore, societies are easily tempted to sell their cultural birthright for developmental pottage![17]

Powerful deterministic forces are at work in development processes. Inasmuch as enhanced freedom is one of development's major goals, it is difficult to assess what makes for sound development. It may be that prosperity and happiness for all may be attainable in a technological society only at the price of sacrificed freedom. Yet new structural constraints are imposed on the world by the development processes themselves. Beneficiaries and those left behind are differently affected by these determinisms. An overarching deterministic system exists wherein nations are diversely positioned in their struggle to conquer freedom. Whereas certain possibilities are sealed off from vulnerable nations, other possibilities are denied to developed and underdeveloped alike. Since development takes place in a broad ecological and symbolic context which is massively, albeit not fully, deterministic, central development decisions bear on basic values. It is no less irresponsible to launch societies on irreversible paths in the name of development than it was a century ago to destroy forests, animal species, and farmlands on the naïve assumption that resources would prove inexhaustible.

Another qualitative indicator of development, closely related to a society's degree of civilization, is the capacity of its members to face death. According to the theologian John Dunne:

> . . . the nature of a society, it could be argued, is decided by the relationship which obtains in that society between the living and the dead. In a modern progressive society or in a modern revolutionary society the relationship will be fairly negative, will consist, in fact, in the independence of the living from the dead, but it will nonetheless be decisive, for it will be this relationship of independence which the living have toward the dead that will make the society progressive or revolutionary.[18]

If one uses this criterion to judge which societies are least alienated from reality—including death (which in "developed" countries has become a major taboo)—the ranking of nations is profoundly altered. In his novel *The Plague*, Camus notes with irony that one learns all that is truly important about a city if one knows how its inhabitants work, love, and die. In his later years, Freud held a similar opinion, believing that genuine human development in individuals and societies is expressed in the capacity to live and to work creatively. The point here is not that improved food, housing, and banking services are not good, but that the norms ordinarily used to measure success have been too narrowly material. Many have falsely assumed that the most significant needs of human beings are their material needs.

The healing relativism of evaluative standards disposes us to heed the reminder issued by the anthropologist Claude Lévi-Strauss that: "A primitive people is not a backward or retarded people: indeed it may possess a genius for invention that leaves the achievements of civilized people far behind."[19] Accordingly, for members of "developed" societies wisdom may consist in humility amid affluence. Paul Goodman condemns the Empty Society as but "the obverse face of the Affluent Society. When Adam Smith spoke of the Wealth of Nations, he did not mean anything like this."[20]

Development, as presently conducted in the world, may have led to economic growth, improved living standards for some, and even to a beneficient reduction of fatalism and feudal exploitation in human affairs. But these benefits have not reached the masses of the world's poor, nor have they been obtained in a manner consonant with certain values (*e.g.*, universal solidarity) required for the total ascent of humankind as a whole. Although development goals are proclaimed in lofty moral terms, its agents, both native and foreign, have tampered irreversibly with people's desires before endowing economic systems with the ability to satisfy the new demands they have generated. And members of pre-modern societies have been given the power to exercise death control before gaining control over their lives. For all these reasons, "development" may therefore be in large measure "anti-development."

CONCLUSION

16.

DEVELOPMENT: HISTORICAL TASK
OR OPENING TO TRANSCENDENCE?

Godfrey Gunatilleke, Director of Sri Lanka's Centre for Development Studies (Marga Institute), laments that "political and religio-cultural components are not kept in the field of vision" of experts and are left outside "the development strategy itself." Why this monumental omission, he asks?

> [T]he reluctance of current development thinking to engage in a discussion of these issues ultimately has its roots in a system of cognition, a structure of knowledge which is partial and incomplete. In the development strategies that are propagated it is always the pursuit of material well-being, it is the socio-economic component of development which has primacy. Underlying this bias are the European ideologies of social change and the cognitive systems which grew out of the industrial revolution and enthroned the economist view of society and man.[1]

This reductionist approach to knowledge leads most development specialists to function as "one-eyed giants,"[2] purveyors of science who are bereft of wisdom. They analyze, prescribe, and act *as if* humans could live by bread alone, *as if* human destiny could be stripped down to its material dimensions alone. High indices of suicide in "developed" countries hint at the truth that material abundance may be less essential—even for survival—than is the presence of *meaning*. In order to survive one must want to survive, but how can one want to survive unless one's life has a meaning? Indeed, having a meaningful existence may well be the most basic of all human needs. Richard Falk, who considers that "awe and mystery are as integral to human experience as bread and reason," concludes that "the future prospects of the human species depend upon internalizing an essentially religious perspective, sufficient to transform secular outlooks that now dominate the destiny of the planet."[3]

Most people in developing countries still derive their primary source of meaning from religious beliefs, symbols, practices, and mysteries.[4] And they instinctively sense that neither the promise of material paradise, nor the glorification of political processes, can abolish life's tragic dimensions—suffering, death, wasted talents, hopelessness.

The sociologist Peter Berger inquires why "a theory that sees secularization as inextricably linked with modernity runs into serious trouble." The evidence reveals that "there are vast regions today in which modernization has not only failed to result in secularity but has instead led to reaffirmations of religion." What explains this "reenchantment of the world," occurring long after what Max Weber called its "disenchantment" via processes of secularization? The answer, Berger suggests, may be that:

> [M]odern scientific thought places man in a universe devoid of supernatural presences and modern technology gives him the limited comfort of increasing his control over the universe, limited because it cannot ever change the root circumstances of human finitude and mortality. . . . It may be true that the reason for the recurring human outreach toward transcendence is that reality indeed includes transcendence and that reality finally reasserts itself over secularity.[5]

Another possibility is "that religious resurgences occur for psychological rather than ontological reasons. Reality is indeed cold and comfortless, but human beings seek comfort and, again and again, they will be prepared to embrace comforting illusions."[6] What is im-

portant here is the empirical fact of "the recurring human outreach
toward transcendence."

Within developed industrial countries one likewise detects a thirst
for something that transcends material happiness. According to *The
Economist*:

> . . . [the] late-twentieth century world, with its urge to open-
> ness and equality, is also a world which is starting to think
> that its recent preoccupation with the material aspects of life
> may be incomplete. It therefore needs a church, Catholic,
> Orthodox, Protestant or whatever, prepared to carry the ban-
> ner for the non-material aspects, and to insist that some kinds
> of truth—the non-political kinds—are objective and perma-
> nent.[7]

In the words of Ismail Serageldin, Vice President of the World
Bank:

> . . . it must surely be recognized that all that glitters is not
> gold, and development must mean more than the sheer accu-
> mulation of worldly goods.

> The quest for a broader meaning to development should gen-
> erate questions in the minds of decision-makers and the pub-
> lic at large, questions such as, development for what? devel-
> opment for whom? and are we paying too high a price for
> what we call development?[8]

A similar judgment is expressed by another World Bank officer,
who considers that:

> Science and technology have done their job; properly utilized,
> they can fulfill all the material needs of human beings. The
> standard of living in the United States—roughly $20,000 per
> capita—could, even with improved efficiency, probably be
> sustained for only about one billion people. But with a needs-
> based standard, an income of $2,000 per capita would be
> adequate, and the world's resources could sustain about 10
> billion people at that level of income indefinitely. With ma-

terial needs taken care of, mankind could get on with its job
of spiritual development. . . .

Just as economics is the study of the material well-being of
societies, harmonics is the study of the spiritual well-being of
society. In economics, we deal with trade-offs, zero-sum
games, and interpersonal and intergenerational exchanges. In
this context, if I give away something, I have less of it for
myself; if I use a resource today, I have less of it for tomor-
row. But for some resources—namely knowledge, love, and
beauty—the exactly opposite law applies: the more I give the
more I have, the more the resource is used the greater it becomes. . . .

A society based on harmonism will be more than just a "sustainable society." There have been many primitive societies
which were sustainable. Instead, it will be a sustainable society with a cutting edge of spiritual advancement that will provide the excitement that has been so painfully lacking in recent years. Spiritual advancement is the antidote to the bore-
dom that lies just below the surface of many of the ills of the
modern world.[9]

In the face of growing pleas for a richer and less homogeneous
universe of values, we need to distinguish two modes (instrumental
and non-instrumental) of treating values in social theory, and to analyze how religious belief systems are the vectors of different "coeffi-
cients of insertion in time and history."[10]

How to Treat Values?

Religious and other indigenous values should not be treated by
development agents in a purely *instrumental* fashion. Such values
are not to be seen *primarily* as means—mere aids or obstacles—to the
achievement of goals derived from sources outside the value systems
in question. Even change agents who are sensitive to local values
usually derive their goals from outside the universe of these values:
from development models or the common assumptions of their respective scientific disciplines. Thus, demographers will strive to "har-

ness" local values to their objective of limiting population growth. Similarly, agronomists will search for some traditional practice upon which to "graft" their recommendation to use chemical pesticides. Similarly, community organizers will "mobilize" a population for their political ends around traditionally cherished symbols. All three cases illustrate an "instrumental" treatment of local values. This same approach is that habitually used as well by national leaders, politicians, or technocrats.

The anthropologist Louis Dupree describes the instrumental use of Islam made by Afghanistan's Prime Minister Mohammad Daoud Khan in the 1950s. This example constitutes an almost "pure case" of an "instrumental" use made of religion in the quest for development:

> During the Afghan national holidays (*Jeshn*) in August of 1959, the government of Prime Minister Mohammad Daoud Khan, who had seized power from his uncle in a bloodless 1953 coup, informally ended purdah (the isolation of women) and the *chowdry* or *burqa* (Afghan version of the veil). The king, cabinet, high-ranking military officers, and members of the royal family stood before the march past of the army and the fly past of the air force as they had in past years—but with a radical difference. Their wives stood beside them unveiled. The thousands of villagers and tribesmen (including many religious leaders) in the crowd were stunned, some genuinely shocked. Amanullah [the ruler of Afghanistan, 1919-1929] had tried the same thing, but without the support of the army. In addition, he had issued a royal firman (proclamation) which made unveiling obligatory. The 1959 unveiling, however, was technically voluntary. The king did not issue a firman, and only high government officials were actually forced to display their unveiled wives in public, to set an example for the masses.

> The immediate result of the voluntary unveiling could have been easily predicted. A delegation of leading religious leaders in the country demanded and received an audience with Prime Minister Daoud, whom they accused of being anti-Islamic, of having succumbed to the influence of the Isai'ites

(American Christians) and Kafirs (heathen Russians).

Prime Minister Daoud, normally not a patient man, waited
until the mullahs vented their spleens, and then calmly in-
formed the delegation that the removal of the veil was not
anti-Islamic, and that if the venerable religious leaders could
find anything in the Qur'an which definitely demanded that
women be kept in purdah, he would be the first to return his
wife and daughters to the harem. Daoud knew he stood on
firm theological ground, for several young Afghan lawyers
had carefully checked the Qur'an.[11]

Daoud drew his goals from an exogenous vision of modernity; he
was, in effect, "using" religion to engineer popular compliance with
his modernization program. It is just such an instrumental approach
which ought to be avoided by national leaders and development agents.

The more justifiable stance is *non-instrumental*, one whose initial postulate holds that traditional values harbor within them a latent
dynamism which, when properly respected, can serve as the springboard for modes of development that are more humane than those
derived from outside paradigms. When development builds on indigenous values, it exacts lower social costs and imposes less human
suffering and cultural destruction than when it copies outside models.
This is so because indigenous values are the matrix from which people
derive meaning in their lives, a sense of identity and cultural integrity,
and the experience of continuity with their environment and their past—
this even in the midst of change.[12] A non-instrumental treatment of
values draws its development goals from within the value system to
which living communities adhere. A sound development strategy doubtless requires that these values be critically re-examined in the light of
modern diagnoses of human needs for better nutrition, greater security against the ravages of nature, or the uncertainties attendant upon
unplanned economic production. This re-examination of old values
leads to the formulation of goals for a development appropriate to the
populace in question. A proper strategy presupposes a collective debate around how these traditional strengths, whether visible or latent,
can best be harnessed to achieve humane developmental goals consonant with what is best in those values. The first task is to define the
development goals themselves: only afterwards does one instrumen-

tally "use" local institutions or traditional strengths found in the value system to galvanize people into action.

Such efforts are now deployed by Islamic theorists and practitioners as they search for new approaches to developmental problem-solving within the boundaries of their religious traditions. Because the Koran condemns interest as sinful usury, Islamic banks[13] neither pay interest to depositors nor charge it to borrowers. Nevertheless, since the banks need to operate as viable economic enterprises, they spread the risks flowing from their borrowing and lending. They receive a share of the profits earned by their borrowers and pro-rata shares of these profits are then distributed to depositors. Such payments do not constitute interest (an automatic fee charged for the use of money). The example of Islamic bankers illustrates how a religious norm can alter a "modern" practice, instead of itself being shaped by the dictates of modernity.

Religions, like traditions and indigenous values, come in all varieties and shapes. It becomes essential, therefore, to identify the coefficient of insertion in secular matters inherent in any religious value system.

Coefficients of Secular Commitment

By stigmatizing religion as "the opium of the masses," Marx sought to hasten the demise of "religious alienation" which turned humans away from the tasks of building history on earth. Other-worldly gods and paradises, Marx complained, poisoned men's minds by adorning them with dreams of celestial bliss. He denounced religion for abolishing history by making human destiny reside ultimately outside history. Religious doctrines, he thundered, negate true humanism and perpetuate injustice by offering promises of happiness to people who remain alienated. With the same passion the French surrealist poet André Breton branded Jesus Christ as "that eternal thief of human energies." No contemporary religious believers can ignore the challenge to their values posed not only by Marx and Breton, but by secularism everywhere. The central question they must answer is whether any religion can supply men and women of our day with a convincing rationale for building up history even as they strive to bear witness to transcendence? Stated in different terms, can any religious worldview preach a humanistic philosophy of history which, no less compellingly than did Marxism, incites faith in a transcendent future while making a commitment to present historical tasks an inescapable duty?

The key to the answer lies in analyzing the "coefficient of secular commitment" contained in different religions. Two points are worth noting here: that the coefficient of insertion can be applied to *all* religions, and that a few key arenas of religion can be examined with a view to determining how "serious" about historical commitment any religion (more precisely, any interpretative stream within a religion) is.

The anthropologist and theologian Teilhard de Chardin once compared a contemporary pagan with what he called a "true Christian humanist." The former, he says, loves the earth in order to enjoy it; the latter, *loving it no less*, does so to make it purer and draw from it the strength to escape from it. For Chardin, however, this escape is not an alienating flight from reality, but the opening, or the "issue," which alone confers final meaning on the cosmos.[14] In Berger's words, "The choice is finally between a closed world or a world with windows on transcendence."[15] Chardin insists that no pretext, however subtle or "spiritual" it may appear, justifies inertia in religious believers faced with an array of pressing secular tasks to accomplish, knowledge and wisdom to be gained, greater justice to be forged, creativity and creation to be unleashed, political fraternity to be instituted, and comprehensive human development to be progressively achieved.

A second arena in which a religion's coefficient in secular affairs may be judged is eschatology—the "last things" or the final destiny of human effort. If gods are thought of as dramatic saviors who "bail out humanity" in spite of its sins and errors, humans will be powerfully motivated to "sin by omission"—their ecological responsibilities, their duty to reduce armaments, and their summons to abolish misery and exploitation everywhere. What is crucial, therefore, is the connection between religiously inspired commitment to human tasks and the "final redemption," "nirvana," "bliss," or "absorption into Brahman-Atman." If a religion possesses a high coefficient of insertion in history, that connection is intrinsic and essential, not extrinsic or accidental.

Latin American "theologians of liberation"[16] repudiate all overly spiritualistic conceptions of religion that justify passivity in the presence of oppressive temporal structures. Their writings and the social movements inspired by them are instructive to students of develop-

ment. Liberation theologians embrace the creative tensions which
exist between fidelity to the demands of religious mystery and the
exigencies of full involvement in the creation of history—scientific
and artistic work, political struggle, building a just and prosperous
economy, changing social structures to meet human needs. Building
history and witnessing to transcendence, as these theologians understand the terms, are co-extensive with that wider, more comprehensive view of development called for by Gunatilleke in earlier pages.[17]

No less than other traditional meaning systems can religions turn
away from the challenges posed to them by secularization and, more
particularly, by the requirements of instituting just forms of national
and global development. Therefore, a key strategic question emerges,
namely: *How* are change strategies aimed at development to be *proposed* (and not *imposed*) to a populace whose traditional interpretation of its own religious value system may display a lower coefficient
of insertion in history than might otherwise be possible without violating the essential tenets of that religion itself? The answer lies in
what elsewhere I have called "existence rationality."[18]

Existence rationality is the process by which any human society
applies a conscious strategy for realizing its goals (survival, the defence of its identity and cultural integrity, the protection of possibilities for its members to attain what they understand to be the "good
life," and so forth), given the ability of that society to process information and its effective access to resources. All existence rationalities contain an inner core of values which must not be sacrificed,
along with an outer periphery where, at least on principle, alteration is
admissible. Even the narrow existence rationalities of "traditional"
societies offer considerable scope for change, on condition that proposed alterations reinforce the dominant strategy adopted by the society in question to assure its life-sustenance, minimum esteem (self-
esteem and out-group esteem), freedom from unwanted constraints,
and modes of fulfillment of its own choosing—all of which are core
values.

Independently of the strategy adopted, however, the *legitimacy* of
change agents is vital. Most religions harbor within them, at least
latently, a relatively high coefficient of commitment to human tasks,
even those requiring great changes in symbols, social organization
and normative values. Hence it is a mistake to assume that development is incompatible with religion.[19] On the contrary, mutually re-

spectful encounters between religious values and sound development plans usually prove beneficial to both sides. In the process, escapist and alienating interpretations of religion lose their legitimacy; in turn, development models are challenged to become more humane and to open themselves to a fuller gamut of values, not excluding those which thrust human endeavors into the realms of mystery and transcendence.

Recent experience in Catholic Latin America suggests that notwithstanding initial misgivings, no basic resistance is offered to well-designed population control programs, if these are part of a broader strategy to bring economic and social improvement and a wider range of personal choices to poor populations. More importantly, all traces of upper-class manipulation of the need of lower-class peoples to find social security and joy in numerous progeny must be purged.

History must be constructed by its human agents in ways that leave history itself open to transcendence. In a world of plural religions, philosophies, and modes of knowledge, there exists no single predetermined channel to transcendence.[20] For millions of religious believers—Christians, Muslims, Hindus, Animists, and others—transcendence points to a life after this life, a universe beyond this material world, which alone confers full and final meaning to human efforts deployed in time. Whether historical life be viewed as a testing ground for separating the virtuous from the wicked, or simply as a tragic confirmation of the finiteness of all material things, what matters most are the precise links postulated between this-worldly existence and the transcendent reality which is the object of religious faith. Is transcendence something so qualitatively *other* that nothing accomplished in historical time has any direct or proportionate relationship to the higher values? Or on the contrary, does one's image of transcendence make of collective human effort in time the very prerequisite of triumphant divine intervention as the final crowning of history? Human effort need not be alienated from human tasks by pointing toward transcendence; on the contrary, that effort may draw from its orientation to values beyond itself a new dignity, urgency, and depth. To this extent, therefore, a transcendent meaning system can be a powerfully developmental force: it is the vector of a high coefficient of secular commitment.

Conclusion

In rich and poor countries alike, a growing chorus of voices proclaims that full human development is not possible without regard for essential religious values. They assert that achievements in political, social, economic, technical, artistic, and scientific realms do not exhaust the creativity, beauty, or triumphs of which human beings are capable. Development thus appears both as a grandiose historical task and as a summons—or an opening—to transcendence. The pressing this-worldly imperatives of development will doubtless oblige religious practitioners to change many of their ancient symbols and practices. And conversely, the resiliency of critically tested religious value systems will incite development experts to enrich their own diagnoses and prescriptions for action. Both categories of one-eyed giants may perhaps come to acknowledge that they need each other if they are, jointly, to gain a wisdom to match modern sciences.

NOTES

Preface

1. For a descriptive account of how the author has plied the craft of development ethics in diverse research/planning/action sites—Lebanon, Brazil, Guinea-Bissau, Sri Lanka, Mexico, and Poland—see Denis Goulet, "Ethics and Development: A Development Ethicist at Work," *Research and Exploration,* National Geographic Society, Vol. 8, No. 2, 1992, pp. 138-147.

2. Prepared for such bodies as OAS (Organization of American States), UNESCO, IUCN (The World Conservation Union), Lebanon's Ministry of Planning, USAID (U.S. Agency for International Development), and SUDENE (Superintendency for Development in Northeast Brazil).

3. They have appeared in such journals as: *World Development, International Development Review, Review of Social Economy, Harvard Educational Review, Comparative Political Studies, The Bulletin of Atomic Scientists, Futures Research Quarterly, Human Rights Quarterly, Christianity and Crisis, Cross Currents,* and *Alternatives.*

4. Denis Goulet, *Ética do desenvolvimento,* São Paulo: Livraria Duas Cidades, 1966; and *idem., The Cruel Choice: A New Concept in the Theory of Development,* New York: Atheneum Publishers, 1971.

Introduction

1. Carolina Maria de Jesus, *Child of the Dark,* New York: E. P. Dutton & Co., Inc., 1962; Domitila Barrios de Chungata with Moema Viezzer, *Let Me Speak!* New York: Monthly Review Press, 1978; Hazel Johnson and Henry Bernstein with Raul Hernan Ampuero and Ben Crow, *Third World Lives of Struggle,* Ibadan: Heinemann Educational Books, Ltd., 1982; James D. Sexton, *Campesino: The Diary of a Guatemalan Indian,* Tucson: University of Arizona Press, 1985; and Nancy Scheper-Hughes, *Death Without Weeping: The Violence of Everyday Life in Brazil,* Berkeley: University of California Press, 1992.

2. See, *e.g.,* Christovam Buarque, *The End of Economics?* London: Zed Books, 1993; Justinian F. Rweyemamu, *Third World Options,* Dar es Salaam: Tanzania Publishing House, 1992; David E. Apter, *Rethinking Development,* Newbury Park, CA: Sage Publications, 1987; Erich Fromm, *To Have or To Be?* New York: Harper & Row, 1976; Nigel Dower, *World Poverty: Challenge and Response,* York, U.K.: William Sessions, Ltd., The Ebor Press, 1983; and David J. Pollock and A. R. M. Ritter, *What Kinds of Development?* 3 Vols., Ottawa: Norman Paterson School of International Affairs, Carleton University, 1980.

3. Ray Bromley and Gavin Kitching, Series editors' "Preface" to Gavin Kitching, *Development and Underdevelopment in Historical Perspective,* London: Methuen, 1982, p. vii.

Chapter 1: A New Discipline

1. Most notably François Perroux, in *Économie et société,* Paris: Presses Universitaires de France, 1963; and *L'Économie du XXème siècle,* Paris: Presses Universitaires de France, 1964. Cf. Jacques Austruy, *Le Scandale du développement,* Paris: Éditions Marcel Rivière et Cie., 1965.

2. Gunnar Myrdal, *Asian Drama: An Inquiry into the Poverty of Nations,* 3 Vols., New York: Pantheon Books, 1968. See especially Vol. I, Chapters 2 and 3 entitled "The Value Premises Chosen" and "The Wider Field of Valuations," and Vol. III, Appendix 1, "Diplomacy by Terminology."

3. Benjamin Higgins, *Economic Development: Problems, Principles, and Policies,* revised edition, New York: W. W. Norton & Co., 1968, p. 369.

4. See John Brode, *The Process of Modernization: An Annotated Bibliography of the Sociocultural Aspects of Development*, Cambridge, MA: Harvard University Press, 1969.

5. Denis Goulet, "L. J. Lebret: Pioneer of Development Ethics," Chapter II of *A New Moral Order*, Maryknoll, NY: Orbis Books, 1974.

6. David A. Crocker, *Praxis and Democratic Socialism: The Critical Social Theory of Markovic and Stojanovic*, Atlantic Highlands, NJ: Humanities Press, Inc., 1983.

7. E. Roy Ramirez, *La Responsabilidad ética en ciencia y tecnologia*, Cartago: Editorial Tecnológica de Costa Rica, 1980; *idem.*, "Desarrollo y ética," *Revista Comunicación*, Vol. 2, No. 2, 1986.

8. David A. Crocker, "Toward Development Ethics," *World Development*, Vol. 19, No. 5, 1991, pp. 457-483.

9. *Revista de la Universidad Autónoma de Yucatán*, Edición Especial, Universidad Autónoma de Yucatán, Mérida, Yucatán, Mexico, 1990. This is a special issue devoted to "Ethics of Development."

10. David E. Apter, *The Politics of Modernization*, Chicago: University of Chicago Press, 1967, p. 6.

11. Erwin A. Gaede, *Politics and Ethics: Machiavelli to Niebuhr*, Lanham, MD: University of America Press, 1983.

12. Kenneth Lux, *Adam Smith's Mistake: How a Moral Philosopher Invented Economics and Ended Morality*, Boston: Shambhala Publications, Inc., 1990.

13. James K. Feibleman, *The Institutions of Society*, London: George Allen & Unwin, 1956, p. 61.

14. Amartya Sen, *On Ethics and Economics*, Oxford: Basil Blackwell, 1987; Thomas Michael Power, *The Economic Pursuit of Quality*, Armonk, NY: M. E. Sharpe, Inc., 1988; Mark A. Lutz and Kenneth Lux, *Humanistic Economics*, New York: The Bootstrap Press, 1988; and Daniel M. Hausman and Michael McPherson, "Taking Ethics Seriously: Economics and Contemporary Moral Philosophy," *Journal of Economic Literature*, Vol. XXXI, June 1993, pp. 671-731.

15. Joseph Lebret, René Moreux *et.al.*, "Manifeste d'économie et humanisme," *Économie et Humanisme*, Special Issue, February-March 1942, 28 pp.; L. J. Lebret, *Manifeste pour une civilisation solidaire*, Caluire, France: Éditions Économie et Humanisme, 1959. In 1960

Lebret created the journal *Développement et Civilisations.*

16. L. J. Lebret, "Editorial," *Développement et Civilisations,* No. 1, March 1960, p. 1. Translation mine.

17. L. J. Lebret, *Dynamique concrète du développement,* Paris: Les Éditions Ouvrières, 1959, p. 40.

18. Charles P. Oman and Ganeshan Wignaraja, *The Postwar Evolution of Development Thinking,* New York: St. Martin's Press, 1991. Cf. Paul Bairoch, *Diagnostic de l'évolution économique du Tiers-Monde 1900-1966,* Paris: Gauthier-Villars Éditeur, 1967.

19. L. J. Lebret, *La Montée humaine,* Paris: Les Éditions Ouvrières, 1959; Robert L. Heilbroner, *The Great Ascent,* New York: Harper Torchbooks, 1963.

Chapter 2: Nature and Methods

1. Peter L. Berger, *Pyramids of Sacrifice,* New York: Basic Books, 1974, Chapters V-VI.

2. Denis Goulet, "Three Rationalities in Development Decision-making," *World Development,* Vol. 14, No. 2, 1986, pp. 301-317.

3. Robert Chambers, "Putting 'Last' Thinking First: A Professional Revolution," *Third World Affairs,* London: Third World Foundation for Social and Economic Studies, 1985, pp. 78-94.

4. This section draws from a memorandum to the author by Georges Allo, "Réflexions sur notre tentative d'opérer un rapprochement entre la recherche américaine et la recherche de l'IRFED sur le rôle des valeurs dans le développement," October 25, 1967, 20 pp.

5. Denis Goulet, "Interdisciplinary Knowledge and the Quest for Wisdom," *Research and Exploration,* National Geographic Society, Spring 1991, pp. 131-132; *idem.,* "Interdisciplinary Learning in the United States: Old Problems, New Approaches, *American Studies* (University of Warsaw), Vol. XII, 1992, pp. 7-20.

6. Cf. Denis Goulet "An Ethical Model for the Study of Values," *Harvard Educational Review,* Vol. 41, No. 2, May 1971, pp. 205-227.

7. On vulnerability, see Denis Goulet, "Vulnerability, the Key to Understanding and Promoting Development," Chapter 2 in *The Cruel Choice:*

A New Concept in the Theory of Development, New York: Atheneum Publishers, 1971; also *idem.,* "Development Administration and Structures of Vulnerability," *The Administration of Change in Africa,* E. Philip Morgan, ed., New York: Dunellen Publishing Co., Inc., 1974, pp. 27-58.

8. Celso Furtado, "Nordeste: Novos depoimentos no II ciclo de estudos," *O Estado de São Paulo,* January 26, 1962, p. 12.

9. Robert Heilbroner, *The Great Ascent,* New York: Harper Torchbooks, 1963, pp. 7ff.

10. Jacques Ellul, *The Technological Society,* New York: Alfred A. Knopf, 1965; *idem., The Technological System,* New York: Continuum, 1980; and *idem., The Technological Bluff,* Grand Rapids, MI: William B. Eerdmans Publishing Co., 1990.

11. Irving Louis Horowitz, *The Rise and Fall of Project Camelot: Studies in the Relationship Between Social Science and Practical Politics,* Cambridge, MA: MIT Press, 1974.

12. Le Corbusier, *Quand les cathédrales etaient blanches,* Paris: Librairie Plon, 1937, p. 308.

13. Mark 2:27.

14. Lewis Mumford, *Technics and Civilization,* New York: Harcourt, Brace & Co., 1934, p. 179.

15. Paul Goodman, *The Moral Ambiguity of America: The Massey Lectures for 1966,* Toronto: Canadian Broadcasting Corporation Publications, 1966, p. 12.

16. August Hecksher, *The Public Happiness,* New York: Atheneum Publishers, 1962, p. 61.

17. Goodman, *The Moral Ambiguity, op. cit.,* p. 4.

18. Jacques Ellul, *The Political Illusion,* New York: Alfred A. Knopf, 1967, p. 195.

19. Denis Goulet, "World Interdependence: Verbal Smokescreen or New Ethic?" New York: Praeger Publishers, Overseas Development Council Development Paper No. 21, March 1976, pp. 1-32.

20. John Kenneth Galbraith, *Economic Development in Perspective,* Cambridge, MA: Harvard University Press, 1962, p. 43.

21. Gustave Thibon, *Nietzsche ou le déclin de l'esprit,* Paris: Fayard, 1975, p. 75. Translation mine.

22. Denis Goulet, "Beyond Moralism: Ethical Strategies in Global Development," in Thomas M. McFadden, *Theology Confronts a Changing World,* West Mystic, CT: Twenty-Third Publications, 1977, pp. 12-39.

23. The phrase "means of the means" is used by the ethicist Raymond Polin in a different sense. For Polin, the essence of man consists in his freedom and all the characteristics of humans are merely means to the creation of meaning and value. Among these means, he declares, freedom is "the means of all means." On this, see Joseph J. Kocklemans, "Phenomenology," in Lawrence C. Becker and Charlotte B. Becker, eds., *Encyclopedia of Ethics,* New York: Garland Publishing, Inc., 1992, Vol. II, p. 962.

24. Richard J. Bernstein, *Praxis and Action,* Philadelphia: University of Pennsylvania Press, 1971.

25. Morris Ginsberg, *On Justice in Society,* New York: Penguin Books, 1965, p. 29.

26. Garret Hardin, *Filters Against Folly,* New York: Penguin Books, 1985.

27. Jacques Ellul, *Hope in a Time of Abandonment,* New York: Seabury Press, 1973.

28. Ivan Illich, *Tools for Conviviality,* New York: Harper & Row, 1973.

29. René Dubos, *Man Adapting,* New Haven: Yale University Press, 1978.

30. Robert Vacca, *The Coming Dark Age,* Garden City, NY: Doubleday & Co., 1973.

31. Lamar Carter, Ann Mische, and David R. Schwartz, eds., *Aspects of Hope,* New York: ICI's Center for a Science of Hope, 1993.

32. Denis Goulet, "Makers of History or Witnesses to Transcendence?" in *A New Moral Order,* Maryknoll, NY: Orbis Books, 1974, pp. 109-142.

Chapter 3: A Research Model

1. Georges Allo has described his work in numerous articles and reports:

"Research on Values at the Crossroads of Modern Civilizations," a brochure printed in English and French, Beirut: Institut de Recherche et de Formation En Vue de Développement (IRFED), 1961; "La Recherche de l'IRFED sur les valeurs et les civilisations," *Développement et Civilisations,* No. 13, March 1963, pp. 104-108; "La Recherche de'IRFED sur la rencontre moderne des civilisations," *Développement et Civilisations,* No. 14, June 1963, pp. 113-116; "L'Évolution des valeurs dans une civilisation," *Développement et Civilisations,* No. 20, December 1964, pp. 78-87; IRFED VEC (Valeurs et Civilisations), *Bulletin de la Recherche,* No. 5, May 1963 (this text is an evaluation of the eighteen-month trial run on values research conducted by Allo in the Middle East); "Revolution des valeurs," *Économie et Humanisme,* No. 160, May/June 1965, pp. 3-10; "Les Valeurs dans la rencontre moderne des civilisation," *Développement et Civilisations,* No. 23, September 1965, pp. 80-87; "Pourquoi le développement exige un dialogue entre civilisations," *Développement et Civilisations,* No. 34, June 1968, pp. 61-66; and the entire issue of *Dialogue* (Paris), No. 1, June 1967, 40 pp.

Chapter 4: Goals of Development

1. United Nations Development Programme, *Human Development Report 1992,* New York: Oxford University Press, 1992, p. 2.

2. Frederick Harbison and Charles A. Myers, *Education, Manpower, and Economic Growth,* New York: McGraw-Hill, 1964, p. 13

3. Cheikh Hamidou Kane, *Ambiguous Adventure,* London: Heinemann, 1972.

4. Carolina Maria de Jesus, *Child of the Dark,* New York: E. P. Dutton & Co., 1962.

5. Robert S. Browne, then a professor at Fairleight Dickinson University, in a personal communication to the author dated August 11, 1968. Cf. Browne, ed., *The Social Scene: A Contemporary View of the Social Sciences,* Cambridge, MA: Winthrop Publishers, 1972.

6. David Bidney, "The Concept of Value in Modern Anthropoligy," *Anthropology Today,* A. L. Kroeber, ed., Chicago: University of Chicago Press, 1965, p. 697.

7. Lewis Mumford, *Technics and Civilization,* New York: Harcourt, Brace

& Co., 1934, p. 76.

8. John Kenneth Galbraith, *The Affluent Society,* London: Hamish Hamilton, 1958, p. 259.

9. Erich Fromm, *Escape from Freedom,* New York: Farrar & Rinehart, Inc., 1941.

10. Hannah Arendt, *On Revolution,* New York: Viking Press, 1963, p. 218.

11. Celso Furtado, "Brazil: What Kind of Revolution?" in *Economic Development: Evolution or Revolution,* Laura Randall, ed., Lexington, MA: D. C. Heath & Co., 1964, pp. 36-37.

12. W. Arthur Lewis, "Is Economic Growth Desirable?" in *Studies in Economic Development,* Bernard Okun and Richard W. Richardson, eds., New York: Holt, Rinehart & Winston, 1962, p. 478.

13. *Ibid.,* p. 490.

14. For an illuminating analysis of these processes, see Robert E. Gamer, *The Developing Nations: A Comparative Perspective,* Boston: Allyn & Bacon, Inc., 1982.

15. In Raymond Aron, ed., *Colloques de Rheinfelden,* Paris: Calmann-Levy, 1960, p. 89. The English translation is *World Technology and Human Destiny,* Ann Arbor: University of Michigan Press, 1963, p. 121.

16. *Ibid.,* p. 256. For a profound exploration of the tragic dimension of human destiny, see Jean-Marie Domenach, *Le Retour du tragique,* Paris: Les Éditions du Seuil, 1967.

17. Orlando Fals-Borda, *Subversion and Social Change in Colombia,* New York: Columbia University Press, 1969.

18. On this, see Barrington Moore, Jr., *Reflections on the Causes of Human Misery,* Boston: Beacon Press, 1973.

19. Irving Louis Horowitz, *Three Worlds of Development,* New York: Oxford University Press, 1966, p. 365.

20. *Ibid.,* p. 376.

Chapter 5: Strategic Principles

1. Amartya Sen, *Commodities and Capabilities,* Amsterdam: North Holland Publishers, 1985.

2. Friedrich Engels, "The Condition of the Working Class in England in 1844," in *Engels: Selected Writings,* W. O. Henderson, ed., New York: Penguin Books, 1967, p. 51.

3. Thorstein Veblen, *The Theory of the Leisure Class,* New York: The Modern Library, 1934; cf. Josef Peiper, *Leisure: The Basis of Culture,* London: Faber & Faber, 1952.

4. John Kenneth Galbraith, *The Affluent Society,* London: Hamish Hamilton, 1958, p. 1.

5. These paragraphs are based on the following works: *A Pobreza na Igreja,* São Paulo: Livraria Duas Cidades, *n.d.* (an anthology of writings on wealth by Church figures); Robert Theobald, ed., *Dialogue on Poverty,* Indianapolis: Bobbs-Merrill, 1967; *Maitriser l'opulence,* Paris: Économie et Humanisme, 1964; and P. R. Régamey, *Poverty: An Essential Element in the Christian Life,* New York: Sheed & Ward, 1950.

6. Quoted in Theobald, ed., *Dialogue on Poverty, op. cit.,* p. 60.

7. Gunnar Myrdal, *Economic Theory and Under-developed Regions,* London: Duckworth, 1963, p. 7.

8. Pierre Antoine, "Qui est coupable?" in *Revue de l'Action Populaire,* No. 32, November 1959, pp. 1055-1065. Translation and italics mine.

9. Abraham Maslow, *Toward a Psychology of Being,* New York: D. Van Nostrand Co., 1968, p. 114.

10. The "imperialism of consumption" is probingly analyzed in William Leach, *Land of Desire: Merchants, Power, and the Rise of a New American Culture,* New York: Pantheon Books, 1993. Cf. Paul L. Wachtel, *The Poverty of Affluence,* Philadelphia: New Society Publishers, 1989; and Georges Fagard, *La Richesse,* Mayenne, France: Collection Point Aveugle, 1980.

11. Alfred Marshall, "Principles of Economics," in *Classics of Economic Theory,* George W. Wilson, ed., Bloomington: Indiana University Press, 1964, p. 632.

12. On this, see Denis Goulet, "Voluntary Austerity: The Necessary Art,"

The Christian Century, No. 4, June 8, 1966, pp. 748-753.

13. L. J. Lebret, *The Last Revolution,* New York: Sheed & Ward, 1965, p. 4.

14. François Perroux, *La Coexistence pacifique,* Paris: Presses Universitaires de France, 1958, p. 409.

15. Kenneth E. Boulding, *The Image,* Ann Arbor: University of Michigan Press, 1963.

16. This remark does not prejudge the possibility that other planets may support living beings similar to earthly humans.

17. Willy Brandt, *North-South: A Programme for Survival,* Cambridge, MA: MIT Press, 1980, p. 16.

18. Rabindranath Tagore, *Vers l'homme universel,* Paris: Éditions Gallimard, p. 210, cited in Lebret, *Développement = révolution solidaire,* Paris: Les Éditions Ouvrières, 1967, p. 52.

19. Claude Sarraute, "Un Entretien avec Henry Miller," in *Le Monde,* April 20, 1960, p. 8.

20. John Kenneth Galbraith, *The Affluent Society,* London: Hamish Hamilton, 1958, p. 140.

Chapter 6: Basic Options

1. Marshall Wolfe, "Development: Images, Conceptions, Criteria, Agents, Choices," *Economic Bulletin for Latin America,* Vol. XVIII, No. 1 and 2, 1973; Cf. Wolfe, "Approaches to Development: Who Is Approaching What?" *Cepal Review,* New York and Geneva: United Nations Publications, 1976.

2. Gunnar Myrdal originated the term *"soft states."* See his *Asian Drama: An Inquiry Into the Poverty of Nations,* New York: Pantheon Books, 1968, Vol. 1, pp. 66-67, and Vol. 2, pp. 895-900. For an explicit application, see Franklin Tugwell, "Modernization, Political Development and the Study of the Future," in *Political Science and the Study of the Future,* Albert Somit, ed., New York: Holt, Rinehart & Winston, 1974, pp. 155-173.

3. Mahbub ul Haq, "The Crisis in Development Strategies," in *The Political Economy of Development and Underdevelopment,* Charles K.

Wilber, ed., New York: Random House, 1973, p. 370.

4. On China, see Marc Blecher, *China: Politics, Economics and Society,* Boulder, CO: Lynne Rienner Publishers, Inc., 1986; Al Imfeld, *China as a Model of Development,* Maryknoll, NY: Orbis Books, 1976; Yu Guangyuan, ed., *China's Socialist Modernization,* Beijing: Foreign Languages Press, 1984; Wang Xizhe, *Mao Zedong and the Cultural Revolution,* Hong Kong: Plough Publications, 1981. On Algeria, see William B. Quandt, *Revolution and Political Leadership: Algeria 1954-1968,* Cambridge, MA: MIT Press, 1969; David and Marina Ottaway, *Algeria: The Politics of a Socialist Revolution,* Berkeley: University of California Press, 1970; Gérard Chaliand, *L'Algérie depuis,* Paris: La Table Ronde, 1975.

5. On this, see Nicolas Spulber, "Contrasting Economic Patterns: Chinese and Soviet Development Strategies," *Soviet Studies,* Vol. 15, No. 1, July 1963, p. 13. Cf. John Phipps and Jenelle Matheson, "Basic Data on the Economy of the People's Republic of China, *Overseas Business Reports,* Washington, DC: US Department of Commerce, June 1974, pp. 11ff.

6. See Errol G. Rampersad, "Burma's Economy Is Deteriorating," *The New York Times,* 24 January 1972. Also Stanley Johnson, "The Road to Mandalay," VISTA (Magazine of the United Nations Association of the USA), Vol. 7, No. 3, November/December 1971, pp. 22-29.

7. See Denis Goulet, *Looking at Guinea-Bissau: A New Nation's Development Strategy,* Washington, DC: Overseas Development Council, 1978; Goran Hyden, *Beyond Ujamaa in Tanzania,* Berkeley: University of California Press, 1980.

8. Gunnar Myrdal, *The Challenge of World Poverty,* New York: Pantheon Books, 1970, p. 277. Italics are Myrdal's.

9. For numerous examples, see Raphael Kaplinsky, *The Economies of Small: Appropriate Technology in a Changing World,* London: Intermediate Technology Publications, 1990.

10. E. F. Schumacher, *Small is Beautiful: Economics as if People Mattered,* New York: Harper & Row, 1973, p. 147.

11. On this, see Marilyn Carr, ed., *The AT Reader: Theory and Practice in Appropriate Technology,* New York: Intermediate Technology Development Group of North America, 1985; and Witold Rybczynski, *Paper Heroes, Appropriate Technology: Panacea or Pipe Dream?* New York: Viking Penguin Books, 1991.

12. For details, see Denis Goulet, *The Uncertain Promise: Value Conflicts in Technology Transfer,* New York: New Horizons Press, 1989, pp. 167-195.

13. Georges Sorel, *Reflections on Violence,* New York: Collier Books, 1961.

14. Denis Goulet, *Incentives for Development: The Key to Equity,* New York: New Horizons Press, 1989, pp. 3-4.

15. Joseph J. Carens, *Equality, Moral Incentives, and the Market: An Essay in Utopian Politico-Economic Theory,* Chicago: University of Chicago Press, 1981; and Schlomo Maital, *Minds, Markets and Money: Psychological Foundations of Economic Behavior,* New York: Basic Books, 1982.

16. Karl Mannheim, *Freedom, Power and Democratic Planning,* London: Routledge & Kegan Paul, Ltd., 1951, p. 192.

17. *Ibid.*

18. Lester M. Salamon, *America's Non-Profit Sector: A Primer,* New York: The Foundation Center, 1992.

19. On this, see Orville Schell, revised edition, *To Get Rich Is Glorious: China in the 80's,* New York: New American Library, 1985. Cf. Deng Xiaoping, *Fundamental Issues in Present-Day China,* Beijing: Foreign Languages Press, 1987.

20. Lewis Mumford, *Technics and Civilization,* New York: Harcourt, Brace & Co., 1934, p. 377.

21. François Perroux, *Échange et société, contrainte, échange, don,* 2nd edition, Paris: Presses Universitaires de France, 1963.

22. Garrett Hardin, *The Limits of Altruism: An Ecologist's View of Survival,* Bloomington: Indiana University Press, 1977.

23. The biblical citation is Matthew 4:4. Cf. Ian Miles & John Irvine, *The Poverty of Progress,* Elmsford, NY: Pergamon Press, 1982; and Michael Schluter and David Lee, *The R Factor,* London: Hodder & Stoughton, 1993.

24. Lawrence F. Salmen, "Beneficiary Assessment: An Approach Described," Working Paper No. 1, Poverty and Social Policy Division, *The World Bank,* February 1992, Washington, DC.

25. On this two-fold motivation, see Amitai Etzioni, *The Moral Dimension: Toward a New Economics,* New York: The Free Press, 1988.

Chapter 7:   Four Pathways to Development

1.   Keith Griffin, *Alternative Strategies for Economic Development,* Paris: OECD Development Centre, 1989.

2.   See, *e.g.,* Hollis Chenery *et.al.,* eds., *Redistribution with Growth,* London: Oxford University Press, 1974.

3.   See, *e.g.,* International Labour Office (ILO), *Employment, Growth, and Basic Needs: A One-World Problem,* New York: Praeger Publishers, 1977; World Bank, *Poverty and Basic Needs,* Washington, DC: World Bank, 1980; and Hans Singer, *Technologies for Basic Needs,* Geneva: International Labour Office, 1982.

4.   Typical examples are Albert Tévoédjrè, *Poverty: Wealth of Mankind,* Oxford: Pergamon Press, 1978; and Georges Anglade, *Éloge de la pauvreté,* Montréal: ERCE, 1983.

5.   On this, see Robert Vachon, *Alternatives au développement,* Montreal: Éditions du Fleuve, 1990; Thierry G. Verhelst, *No Life Without Roots: Culture and Development,* London: Zed Books, 1989; and Charles David Kleymeyer, ed., *Cultural Expression and Grassroots Development,* Boulder, CO: Lynne Reinner Publishers, Inc., 1994.

Chapter 8:   Participation

1.   Ivan Illich, *Deschooling Society,* New York: Harper & Row, 1983; *idem., Medical Nemesis,* New York: Pantheon Books, 1976; and *idem., Toward a History of Needs,* New York: Pantheon Books, 1978.

2.   J. P. Naik, *Equality, Quality, and Quantity,* New Delhi: Allied Publishers Private Ltd., 1975; *idem., An Alternative System of Health Care Service in India,* New Delhi: Allied Publishers Private Ltd., 1977; and *idem., Some Perspectives on Non-Formal Education,* New Delhi: Allied Publishers Private Ltd., 1977.

3.   Paulo Freire, *Cultural Action for Freedom,* Cambridge, MA: *Harvard Educational Review* and Center for the Study of Development and Social Change Monograph Series No. 1, 1970; *idem., Education for Critical Consciousness,* New York: Seabury Press, 1973; and *idem., Pedagogy of the Oppressed,* New York: Herder & Herder, 1970.

4.   Marshall Wolfe, *Participation: The View From Above,* Geneva: UNRISD, March 1983, p. 2.

5. Freire, *Education for Critical Consciousness, op. cit.,* pp. 91-164.

6. Orlando Fals-Borda, *Historia doble de la costa,* Bogotá: Carlos Valencia Editores, 1979; *idem., Historia de la cuestión agraria en Colombia,* Bogotá: Publicaciones de la Rosca, 1975.

7. Albert Camus, *The Rebel: An Essay on Man in Revolt,* New York: Vintage Books, 1956.

8. Albert O. Hirschman, *Getting Ahead Collectively,* Elmsford, NY: Pergamon Press, 1984; Robert Wasserstrom, *Grassroots Development in Latin America and the Caribbean,* New York: Praeger Publishers, 1985; Sheldon Annis and Peter Hakim, eds., *Direct to the Poor,* Boulder, CO: Lynne Rienner Publishers, Inc., 1988; and Lawrence F. Salmen, *Listen to the People,* New York: Oxford University Press, 1987.

9. Albert O. Hirschman, *Exit, Voice, and Loyalty,* Cambridge, MA: Harvard University Press, 1970.

10. For a review of theories, see Guy Gran, *Development By People: Citizen Construction of a Just World,* New York: Praeger Publishers, 1983.

11. Barrington Moore, *Reflections of the Causes of Human Misery,* Boston: Beacon Press, 1972, pp. 66-67.

12. See Marc Blecher, *China: Politics, Economics and Society,* Boulder CO: Lynne Rienner Publishers, Inc., 1986; Cynthia McClintock and Abraham Lowenthal, eds., *The Peruvian Experiment Reconsidered,* Princeton: Princeton University Press, 1983.

13. Denis Goulet, "Structural Vulnerability in Administration," in E. Philip Morgan, ed., *The Administration of Change in Africa,* New York: Dunellen Publishing Co., Inc., 1974, pp. 27-58.

14. Bernard Schaffer and Geoff Lamb, *Can Equity Be Organized?* Paris: UNESCO, 1981.

Chapter 9: Technology for Development

1. Malcolm I. Thomis, *The Luddites,* New York: Shocken Books, 1970.

2. Thierry G. Verhelst, *No Life Without Roots: Culture and Development,* London: Zed Books, 1990.

3. Daniel Bell, *The Cultural Contradictions of Capitalism*, New York: Basic Books, 1976.

4. Alvin Toffler, *Future Shock*, New York: Bantam Books, 1979.

5. Denis Goulet, "The Quest for Wisdom in a Technological Age," *Philosophical Studies in Education: Proceedings of the Annual Meeting of the Ohio Valley Philosophy of Education Society, 1985*, Robert J. Skovira, ed., Coraopolis, PA: Versatile Printing Co., 1987, pp. 123-137; and Goulet, "Interdisciplinary Knowledge and the Quest for Wisdom," *Research and Exploration*, National Geographic Society, Spring 1991, pp. 131-132.

6. Thomas J. Allen *et. al.*, "The International Technological Gatekeeper," *Technology Review 72*, March 1971, p. 1.

7. A. K. N. Reddy, Unpublished report entitled "Methodology for Selection of Environmentally Sound and Appropriate Technologies," United Nations Environment Programme, *n.d.*, paragraphs 1.12-1.13.

8. E. J. Mishan, *The Costs of Economic Growth*, revised edition, New York: Praeger, 1993; E. F. Schumacher, *Small is Beautiful: Economics as if People Mattered*, New York: Harper Torchbooks, 1973; Dennis C. Pirages, ed., *The Sustainable Society*, New York: Praeger Publishers, 1977; Hazel Henderson, *Creating Alternative Futures: The End of Economics*, New York: Berkeley Publishing Corp., 1978; and Fred Hirsch, *Social Limits to Growth*, Cambridge, MA: Harvard University Press, 1976.

9. On this, see Thomas Michael Power, *The Economic Pursuit of Quality*, Armonk, NY: M. E. Sharpe, Inc., 1988.

10. P. P. R. Hazell, *The Green Revolution Reconsidered*, Baltimore: The Johns Hopkins University Press, 1991.

11. The "vital nexus" links a society's values to its development strategy and criteria of technology choice. For details, see Denis Goulet, *The Uncertain Promise: Value Conflicts in Technology Transfer*, New York: New Horizons Press, 1989, pp. 43-46, 86-87.

Chapter 10: Development Ethics and Ecological Wisdom

1. S. J. Samartha and Lynn de Silva, eds., *Man in Nature: Guest or Engineer?* Columbo: The Ecumenical Institute for Study and Dialogue, 1979.

2. Robert Vachon, "Relations de l'homme à la nature dans les sagesses Orientales traditionnelles," *Écologie et Environnement,* Cahiers de Recherche Éthique, 9, 1983, pp. 157-160.

3. Bernard Charbonneau, *Je fus, essai sur la liberté,* Pau, France: Imprimerie Marrimpouey Jeune, 1980, pp. 149-156; and *Le Feu vert: Auto-critique du mouvement écologique,* Paris: Éditions Karthala, 1980.

4. Jacques Maritain, *Integral Humanism,* Notre Dame, IN: University of Notre Dame Press, 1973, p. 134.

5. Raimundo Panikkar, "The New Innocence," *Cross Currents,* Spring 1977, p. 7.

6. Raimundo Panikkar, "Is History the Measure of Man? Three Kairological Moments of Human Consciousness," *The Teilhard Review,* Vol. 16, Nos. 1 and 2, pp. 39-45.

7. *Ibid.,* p. 40.

8. *Ibid.*

9. *Ibid.,* p. 41.

10. *Ibid.,* p. 42.

11. *Ibid.,* p. 45.

12. Panikkar, "The New Innocence," *op. cit.,* p. 13.

13. *Ibid.,* p. 14.

14. Denis Goulet, "Culture and Traditional Values in Development," in Susan Stratigos and Philip J. Hughes, eds., *The Ethics of Development: The Pacific in the 21st Century,* Port Moresby: University of Papua New Guinea Press, 1987, pp. 165-178.

15. World Bank, *World Development Report 1992,* New York: Oxford University Press, 1992, "Overview," p. 1.

16. World Commission on Environment and Development, *Our Common Future,* New York: Oxford University Press, 1987, p. 89.

17. Paul Streeten, "Future Generations and Socio-Economic Development—Introducing the Long-Term Perspective," unpublished ms. dated January 1991, p. 3. A shorter published version of this text does not contain the citation given and appears in "Des institutions pour un développement durable," in *Revue Tiers-Monde,* Tome XXXIII No.

130, Avril-Juin 1992, pp. 455-469.

18. *Ibid.,* pp. 1-2.

19. Richard N. Gardner, *Negotiating Survival: Four Priorities After Rio,* New York: Council of Foreign Relations Press, 1992, pp. 42ff. Cf. *New York Times,* June 15, 1993, p. B6.

20. Paul Ekins, "Sustainability First," in Paul Ekins and Manfred Max-Neef, eds., *Real-Life Economics,* London and New York: Routledge, 1992, p. 412.

21. Duane Elgin, *Voluntary Simplicity,* New York: William Morrow & Co., Inc., 1981; Denis Goulet, "Voluntary Austerity: The Necessary Art," *The Christian Century,* 4, 8 June 1966, pp. 748-753.

22. Carolina Maria de Jesus, *Child of the Dark,* New York: E. P. Dutton & Co., 1962, p. 11.

23. *Ibid.,* p. 39.

24. For Gandhi's views on development, see Amritananda Das, *Foundations of Gandhian Economics,* Delhi: Center for the Study of Developing Societies, 1979; and J. P. Naik, "Gandhi and Development Theory," *The Review of Politics,* Vol. 45, No. 3, July 1983, pp. 345-365.

25. Barry Lopez, "The American Indian Mind," *Quest 78,* September-October 1978, p. 109.

26. Georges Perec, *Les Choses,* Paris: Les Lettres Nouvelles, 1965, pp. 128-130.

27. Charles Avila, *Ownership: Early Christian Teaching,* Maryknoll, NY: Orbis Books, 1983.

28. Celso Furtado, *O Mito do desenvolvimento econômico,* Rio de Janeiro: Paz E Terra, 2ª ed., p. 45.

29. Adolf A. Berle, Jr., *The 20th Century Capitalist Revolution,* New York: Harcourt, Brace & Co., 1954, p. 166.

30. *Ibid.,* p. 183.

31. Erich Fromm, *To Have or To Be?* New York: Harper & Row, 1976, pp. 15-16.

32. C. Douglas Lummis, "Equality," in *The Development Dictionary,* Wolfgang Sachs, ed., London: Zed Books, 1992, pp. 49-50.

33. Douglass Stinson, "Sustainable Accords? Free Trade and the Environment," *Latinamerica Press,* Vol. 25, No. 24, July 1, 1993, p. 1.

34. Herman E. Daly, "The Steady-State Economy: What, Why, and How," in Dennis Clark Pirages, ed., *The Sustainable Society,* New York: Praeger Publishers, 1977, pp. 107-130.

35. Leonard Silk, "Dangers of Slow Growth," *Foreign Affairs,* Vol. 72, No. 1, 1992-93, p. 173.

36. Kenichi Ohmae, "The Rise of the Region State," *Foreign Affairs,* Vol. 72, No. 2, Spring 1993, pp. 78-87.

37. For an analysis of obstacles to sound development, see Denis Goulet, "Obstacles to World Development: An Ethical Reflection," *World Development,* 11:7, July 1983, pp. 609-624.

Chapter 11: Culture and Tradition in Development

1. See, *e.g.,* David Kleymeyer, ed., *Cultural Expression and Grassroots Development,* Boulder, CO: Lynne Rienner Publishers, Inc., 1994; Eleonora Masini, ed., *The Futures of Culture,* Paris: UNESCO, Vol. I, 1991, Vol. II, 1992.

2. Denis Goulet, "In Defense of Cultural Rights: Technology, Tradition and Conflicting Models of Rationality," *Human Rights Quarterly,* 3:4, 1981, pp. 1-18.

3. Dorothy Lee, *Freedom and Culture,* Englewood Cliffs, NJ: Prentice Hall, 1959, p. 72.

4. Lloyd Rudolph and Suzanne Rudolph, *The Modernity of Tradition,* Chicago: The University of Chicago Press, 1967; Mirrit Boutros Ghali, *Tradition for the Future,* Oxford: Alden, 1972.

5. On continuities between tradition and change, see Peter Marris, *Loss and Change,* Garden City, NY: Anchor Books, 1975.

6. Jorge Luis Borges, *Otras investigaciones,* Bueno Aires: Emeco, 1960, p. 51. Cited in Alfredo L de Romana, "The Autonomous Economy," *Interculture,* Montreal, Vol. XXII, No. 4, Fall 1989, Issue #105, p. 109.

7. For a detailed analysis, see Roy Simon Bryce-Laporte, "Slaves as In-

mates, Slaves as Men: A Sociological Discussion of Elkins' Thesis," in Ann J. Lane, ed., *The Debate Over Slavery,* Urbana: University of Illinois Press, 1971, pp. 269-292.

8. The vital nexus is analyzed and illustrated in Denis Goulet, "An Ethical Model for the Study of Values," *Harvard Educational Review,* Vol. 41, No. 2, May 1971, pp. 205-227.

9. George Young, "Tourism: Blessing or Blight?" *Development Digest,* Vol. 13, No. 1, January 1975, p. 49.

10. In *Working,* New York: Pantheon Books, 1974, Studs Terkel shows how central the work *milieu* is to people's sense of identity and values. Cf. Charles M. Savage, *Work and Meaning: A Phenomenological Enquiry,* Springfield, VA: National Technical Information Service, U.S. Department of Commerce, 1973.

11. For an analysis of marginalization, see Denis Goulet and Marco Walshok, "Values Among Underdeveloped Marginals: The Case of Spanish Gypsies," *Comparative Studies in Society and History,* 13:4, 1971, pp. 451-472.

12. For a detailed view of how cultural resistance functions, see Thierry G. Verhelst, *No Life Without Roots: Culture and Development,* London: Zed Books, 1990.

13. Flora Lewis, "Rights vs. Rights: When Individuals Identify With Groups," *International Herald Tribune,* Monday, April 2, 1990, p. 6. The centrifugal and centripetal effects wrought by nationalization are analyzed in Michael Ignatieff, *Blood and Belonging: Journeys Into the Ne Nationalism,* New York: Farrar, Straus & Giroux, 1993.

14. On technology as a displacer of cultures, see Jacques Ellul, *The Technological Bluff,* Grand Rapids, MI: William B. Eerdmans Publishing Co., 1990, Chapter VI, "Is There a Technical Culture?"

15. Fred W. Riggs, *Administration in Developing Countries: The Theory of a Prismatic Society,* Boston: Houghton Mifflin Co., 1964.

Chapter 12: Ethics of Aid

1. Samir Amin, "Interview," *Africa,* 1, 1976, pp. 35-37.

2. Article 17, U.N. General Assembly Resolution 3281 (29), December 12, 1974.

3. "Concessional" resource transfers contain a grant element of at least 25 percent (calculated at the rate of discount of 10 percent). See DAC (Development Assistance Committee), *Development Cooperation: Aid in Transition, 1993 Report,* Paris: OECD, 1994, p. 11.

4. Irving Louis Horowitz, ed., "Introduction" to *Power, Politics and People: The Collected Essays of C. Wright Mills,* New York: Ballantine Books, 1963, p. 11.

5. Tibor Mende, *From Aid to Re-Colonization: Lesson of a Failure,* New York: Pantheon Books, 1973, pp. 262-263.

6. *Ibid.*

7. This is especially true in the case of the African continent, where development needs have moved far from donor countries' interests. Thomas M. Callaghy, "Africa: Falling Off the Map?" *Current History,* Vol. 93, No. 579, January 1994, pp. 31-36.

8. Recent critical evaluations include: Roger C. Riddell, *Foreign Aid Reconsidered,* Baltimore: The Johns Hopkins University Press, 1988; Douglas Hellinger and Fred M. O'Regan, *Aid for Just Development,* Boulder, CO: Lynne Rienner Publishers, Inc., 1988; Graham Hancock, *Lords of Poverty: The Power, Prestige, and Corruption of the International Aid Business,* New York: The Atlantic Monthly Press, 1989; Joan M. Nelson and Stephanie J. Eglinton, *Global Goals, Contentious Means: Issues of Multiple Aid Conditionality,* Washington, DC: Overseas Development Council, 1993; and Sarah J. Tisch and Michael B. Wallace, *Dilemmas of Development Assistance: The What, Why and Who of Foreign Assistance,* Boulder, CO: Westview Press, 1994.

9. On the difference between "distributive" and "commutative" justice, see J. Messner, *Social Ethics,* St. Louis: B. Herder Book Co., 1949, pp. 218ff; and John A. Ryan, *Distributive Justice,* New York: Macmillan, Inc., 1942. For a different approach, see John Rawls, *A Theory of Justice,* Cambridge, MA: Harvard University Press, 1971.

10. On the ethical principle of priority allocations of scarce resources, see Denis Goulet, *Ética del desarrollo,* Montevideo: Estela IEPAL, 1965, pp. 307-354; *idem., The Cruel Choice: A New Concept in the Theory of Development,* New York: Atheneum Publishers, 1971, pp. 281-293.

11. John Isbister, *Promises Not Kept: The Betrayal of Social Change in the Third World,* West Hartford, CT: Kumarian Press, 1991.

12. PVOs (Private Voluntary Organizations) and NGOs (Non-Governmen-

tal Organizations) have been praised as better channels of development aid than either bilateral or multilateral agencies. In the past, most PVO and NGO operations have centered on small-scale projects and programs. Not surprisingly, therefore, recent advocacy urges NGOs to "upscale" their ambitions and activities, *i.e.,* to move into macro arenas of development policy, even national and international political lobbying. On this, see Michael Edwards and David Hulme, eds., *Making a Difference: NGOs and Development in a Changing World,* London: Earthscan Publications, Ltd., 1992.

13. See Denis Goulet, "International Ethics and Human Rights, *Alternatives,* Vol. 17, Spring 1992, pp. 231-246.

14. Denis Goulet, *Is Gradualism Dead? Reflections on Order, Change and Force,* New York: Ethics in Foreign Policy Series, Council on Religion and International Affairs, 1970.

15. Arthur Waskow, *Becoming Brothers,* New York: The Free Press/ Macmillan, Inc., 1993.

16. See Denis Goulet, "Development as Liberation: Policy Lessons from Case Studies, *World Development,* 7:6, June 1979, pp. 555-566.

Chapter 13: Measuring the Costs of Development

1. E. H. Carr, *What Is History?* New York: Alfred A. Knopf, 1962, p. 102.

2. Peter L. Berger, *Pyramids of Sacrifice: Political Ethics and Social Change,* New York: Basic Books, 1974, p. 5.

3. *Ibid.*

4. See Barrington Moore, *Reflections of the Causes of Human Misery,* Boston: Beacon Press, 1972; and Robert Heilbroner, *An Inquiry into the Human Prospect,* New York: W. W. Norton, Inc., 1991.

5. See Robert Conquest, *The Harvest of Sorrow: Soviet Collectivization and the Terror-Famine,* New York: Oxford University Press, 1986.

6. See Phyllis Deane, *The First Industrial Revolution,* London: Cambridge University Press, 1965; and Karl Polanyi, *The Great Transformation,* Boston: Beacon Press, 1957.

7. Alexander Gerschenkron, *Economic Backwardness in Historical Per-*

spective, New York: Praeger Publishers, 1965, p. 213.

8. Karl de Schweinitz, "Economic Growth, Coercion, and Freedom," *World Politics,* 9:2, January 1957, p. 168.

9. W. Donald Bowles, "Soviet Russia as a Model for Underdeveloped Areas," *World Politics,* 14:3, April 1962, p. 502.

10. Berger, *Pyramids of Sacrifice, op. cit.,* p. xii.

11. Albert Camus, *The Rebel,* New York: Vintage Books, 1956, pp. 290-291.

Chapter 14: Obstacles to Development

1. Cited in John Bartlett, *Familiar Quotations,* 15th edition, Boston: Little, Brown & Co., 1980, p. 773.

2. John Kenneth Galbraith, *The Affluent Society,* Boston: Houghton Mifflin Co., 1958.

3. Willy Brandt, "Introduction" to Anthony Sampson, ed., *North-South: A Program for Survival,* Cambridge, MA: MIT Press, 1980, pp. 17, 13, and 29.

4. Robert S. McNamara, "Foreword" to *World Development Report 1978,* Washington, DC: World Bank, 1978, p. iii.

5. World Bank, *World Development Report 1993,* New York: Oxford University Press, 1993, p. 305.

6. Cited in Peter McDonough, *Power and Ideology in Brazil,* Princeton: Princeton University Press, 1981, p. 136, footnote 12.

7. Cited in Charles Antoine, *Church and Power in Brazil,* Maryknoll, NY: Orbis Books, 1973, p. 274.

8. World Bank, *World Development Report 1993, op. cit.,* Table 30, p. 297.

9. Mitchell A. Seligson and John T. Passé-Smith, eds., *Development and Under-Development: The Political Economy of Inequality,* Boulder, CO: Lynne Rienner Publishers, Inc., 1993.

10. See International Labour Office (ILO), *Towards Full Employment: A Programme for Colombia,* Geneva: ILO, 1970; *idem., Matching Em-*

ployment Opportunities and Expectations: A Programme of Action for Ceylon, report and technical papers in 2 Vols., Geneva, 1971; *idem., Employment Incomes and Inequality: A Strategy for Increasing Productive Employment in Kenya,* Geneva, 1972; *idem., Sharing in Development: A Programme of Employment, Equity and Growth for the Philippines,* Geneva, 1974; *idem., Generacion de empleo productivo y crecimiento económico: El Caso de la Republica Dominicana,* Geneva, 1975; and *idem., Growth, Employment and Equity: A Comprehensive Strategy for Sudan,* Geneva, 1976.

11. See ILO, *Employment, Growth and Basic Needs: A One-World Problem,* "Introduction" by James P. Grant, New York: Praeger Publishers, 1977, p. 3.

12. World Bank, *World Development Report 1979,* Washington, DC: World Bank, 1979, p. 46.

13. Walter W. Rostow, *The Stages of Economic Growth,* New York: Cambridge University Press, 1960, pp. 8-9.

14. On this, see Denis Goulet, *World Interdependence: Verbal Smokescreen or New Ethic?* Overseas Development Council Development Paper No. 21, New York: Praeger Publishers, March 1976.

15. Johan Galtung, Peter O'Brien, and Roy Preiswerk, eds., *Self-Reliance: A Strategy for Development,* London: Bogle-L'Ouverture, 1980.

16. Denis Goulet, *The Uncertain Promise: Value Conflicts in Technology Transfer,* New York: IDOC, 1977, pp. 38-39.

17. Ivan Illich, *Shadow Work,* Salem, NH: Marion Boyars, Inc., 1981, Chapter 2, pp. 27-52.

18. Albert O. Hirschman, *The Strategy of Economic Development,* New Haven: Yale University Press, 1958, p. 12.

19. On this, see Paul L. Wachtel, *The Poverty of Affluence,* Philadelphia: New Society Publishers, 1989.

20. Erich Fromm, *To Have or To Be?* New York: Harper & Row, 1976.

21. August Hecksher, *The Public Happiness,* London: Hutchinson, 1963, p. 157.

22. Philip Slater, *The Pursuit of Loneliness: American Culture at the Breaking Point,* revised edition, Boston: Beacon Press, 1976; Christopher Lasch, *The Culture of Narcissism: American Life in an Age of Dimin-*

ishing Expectations, New York: W. W. Norton & Co., 1978; and Peter Marin, "The New Narcissism," *Harper's Magazine,* October 1975, pp. 45-56.

23. Louise Bernikow, "Alone, Yearning for Companionship in America," *The New York Times Magazine,* 15 August 1982, Section 6, pp. 24-34.

24. Matthew Arnold, "Stanzas from the Grande Chartreuse," Stanza 15, 1855, cited in John Bartlett, *Familiar Quotations,* revised and enlarged edition, Boston: Little, Brown & Co., 1980, p. 586.

25. Alan Riding, "Taming Mexico's Passion for More," *New York Times,* Business Section, 12 September 1982, pp. 1 and 26.

26. Pablo González Casanova, "Internal Colonialism and National Development," in Irving Louis Horowitz *et.al.,* eds., *Latin American Radicalism,* New York: Vintage Books, 1969, p. 119.

27. Charles Elliott, *Patterns of Poverty in the Third World,* New York: Praeger Publishers, 1975.

28. Frantz Fanon, *The Wretched of the Earth,* New York: Grove Press, 1965; Albert Memni, *The Colonizer and the Colonized,* Boston: Beacon Press, 1991; Paulo Freire, *Pedagogy of the Oppressed,* New York: Seabury Press, 1970; Ronald Segal, *The Race War,* New York: Viking Press, 1967; and Rodolfo Stavenhagen, *Problemas etnicos y campesinos,* Mexico DF: Instituto Nacional Indigenista, 1979.

29. Eric Wolf, *Peasant Wars in the Twentieth Century,* New York: Harper & Row, 1970; John Womack, Jr., *Zapata and the Mexican Revolution,* New York: Vintage, 1968; and Ralph Della Cava, *Miracle at Joaseiro,* New York: Columbia University Press, 1970.

30. Barrington Moore, Jr., *Injustice: The Social Bases of Obedience and Revolt,* New York: Pantheon Books, 1979.

31. Roy Bryce-Laporte and Claudewill S. Thomas, eds., *Alienation in Contemporary Society: A Multi-disciplinary Examination,* New York: Praeger Publishers, 1976.

32. Jerre Mangione, *The World Around Danilo Dolci,* New York: Harper & Row, 1968.

33. See Thomas Carlyle, *Heroes, Hero-Worship and the Heroic in History,* Berkeley: University of California Press, 1993; B. H. Lehman, *Carlyle's Theory of the Hero,* Durham, NC: Duke University Press, 1928.

34. Amilcar Cabral, *Palavras de ordem gerais,* Bissau: PAIGC Secretariado Geral, 1976, p. 34. Translation mine.

35. For a detailed study of one such attempt, see Denis Goulet, *Survival with Integrity: Sarvodaya at the Crossroads,* Colombo: Marga Institute, 1981.

36. I owe this formulation to Johan Galtung, who communicated it to me at a workshop in Enschede, Holland, May 1981.

37. Private conversation with the author, New Delhi, 1977.

38. Denis Goulet, *Is Gradualism Dead? Reflections on Order, Change and Force,* New York: Ethics in Foreign Policy Series, Council on Religion and International Affairs, 1970, p. 34.

39. I owe this formulation of Basic Needs to the Colombian anthropologist Manuel Zapata Olivella.

Chapter 15: Development or Anti-Development?

1. Erich Fromm, *The Sane Society,* New York: Fawcett Publications, 1967, p. 21.

2. Karl Marx, *Die Fruhschriften,* Stuttgart: A. Kroner Verlag, 1953, p. 243. Cited by Fromm, *op. cit.,* p. 223.

3. Terms used by Erich Fromm in his "Introduction" to *Socialist Humanism,* E. Fromm, ed., New York: Anchor Books, 1966, p. ix.

4. Lynton Keith Caldwell, *Environment: A Challenge for Modern Society,* Garden City, NY: The Natural History Press, 1970, pp. 142, 154-155.

5. Paul G. Irwin, "Foreword" to Lewis G. Regenstein, *Cleaning Up America the Poisoned,* Washington, DC: Acropolis Books, Ltd., 1993, p. 9.

6. This is the theme of Lawrence Fuchs, *Those Peculiar Americans,* New York: Meredith Press, 1967.

7. C. Wright Mills, "The Structure of Power in American Society," in C. Wright Mills, *Power, Politics and People,* Irving Louis Horowitz, ed., New York: Ballantine Books, 1963, p. 27.

8. Phrases drawn from George Perec, *Les Choses,* Paris: Éditions Julliard,

1962, pp. 21, 42.

9. Author of *Tableau de Paris,* 1783. Cited in Werner Sombart, *Luxury and Capitalism,* Ann Arbor: University of Michigan Press, 1967, p. 62.

10. Abraham H. Maslow, *Toward a Psychology of Being,* New York: D. Van Nostrand Co., 1968, p. 10.

11. On this, see Khosrow Jahandary, "Modernization Revisited: An Interview with Daniel Lerner," in *Communications and Development Review,* Tehran: Iran Communications and Development Institute, Vol. I, Nos. 2 and 3, Summer-Autumn, 1977, pp. 4-6.

12. A term used by Fromm, *The Sane Society, op. cit.,* p. 15.

13. Douglas V. Steere, in *Development for What?* John H. Hallowell, ed., Durham, NC: Duke University Press, 1964, pp. 213-235.

14. On the difference between quantitative and qualitative indicators, see Denis Goulet, "Development Indicators: A Research Problem, a Policy Problem," *The Journal of Socio-Economics,* Vol. 21, No. 3 (Fall 1992), pp. 245-260. Cf. Thomas Michael Power, *The Economic Pursuit of Quality,* Armonk, NY: M. E. Sharpe, Inc., 1988.

15. Jules Klanfer in *Le Sous-développement humain,* Paris: Les Éditions Ouvrières, 1967, p. 176.

16. Lin Yutang, *The Importance of Living,* New York: John Day Co., 1937, p. 3.

17. Genesis 25:34.

18. John S. Dunne, *The City of the Gods: A Study in Myth and Mortality,* New York: Macmillan Co., 1965, p. 16. Cf. pp. 184-217.

19. Cited in "Man's New Dialogue with Man," *Time,* June 30, 1967, p. 34.

20. Paul Goodman, *The Moral Ambiguity of America: The Massey Lectures for 1966,* Toronto: Canadian Broadcasting Corporation Publications, 1966, p. 12.

Chapter 16: Development: Historical Task or Opening to Transcendence?

1.   Godfrey Gunatilleke, "The Interior Dimension," *International Development Review,* Vol. 21, No. 1, 1979/1, p. 4.

2.   Denis Goulet, "Development Experts: The One-Eyed Giants," *World Development,* 8:7/8, July/August 1980, pp. 481-489.

3.   Richard Falk, "Satisfying Human Needs in a World of Sovereign States: Rhetoric, Reality and Vision," in J. Gremillion and W. Ryan, eds., *World Faiths and the New World Order,* Washington, DC: Inter-Religious Peace Colloquium, 1978, pp. 134, 136.

4.   For a detailed analysis, see Jeff Haynes, *Religion in Third World Politics,* Boulder, CO: Lynne Rienner Publishers, Inc., 1994.

5.   Peter L. Berger, *A Far Glory: The Quest for Faith in an Age of Credulity,* New York: The Free Press/Macmillan, Inc., 1992, pp. 28-29.

6.   *Ibid.,* p. 30.

7.   Editorial, "The Keys to Rome," *The Economist,* 12 August 1978, p. 9.

8.   Ismail Serageldin, "The Justly Balanced Society: One Muslim's View," in David Beckmann, Ramgopal Agarwala, Sven Burmester, and Ismail Serageldin, *Friday Morning Reflections at the World Bank: Essays on Values and Development,* Washington, DC: Seven Locks Press, 1991, pp. 60-61.

9.   Ramgopal Agarwala, "A Harmonist Manifesto: Hindu Philosophy in Action," in *ibid.,* pp. 9-10.

10. Denis Goulet, "Secular History and Teleology," *World Justice,* Vol. 8, No. 1, September 1966, pp. 5-19.

11. L. Dupree, "The Political Uses of Religion: Afghanistan," in K. H. Silvert, ed., *Churches and States: The Religious Institution and Modernization,* New York: American Universities Field Staff, 1967, pp. 203-204.

12. The need for assuring continuity in processes of change is cogently argued by British sociologist Peter Marris in *Loss and Change,* New York: Pantheon Books, 1974.

13. "Basic Islamic Principles Will Shape Iran's Economy in Post-Revolutionary Era," *Business International* (weekly report to managers of

worldwide operations), New York, 16 March 1979, pp. 81-84. In June 1979, Chase Manhattan Bank sponsored a conference for businessmen on "The Reemergence of Islamic Law." On this, see the *Washington Post,* Metro Section, Monday, 14 May 1979, p. C-1. Cf. Elias G. Kazarian, *Islamic Versus Traditional Banking: Financial Innovation in Egypt,* Boulder, CO: Westview Press, 1993. For a scholarly treatment of Islamic approaches to finance, technology, and economics, see Z. Sardar, *Science, Technology and Development in the Muslim World,* London: Croom Helm, 1977.

14. M. B. Madaule, "La Personne dans la perspective Teilhardienne," in collective eds., *Essais sur Teilhard de Chardin,* Paris: Fayard, 1962, p. 76.

15. Berger, *A Far Glory, op. cit.,* p. 142.

16. G. Gutierrez, *A Theology of Liberation,* Maryknoll, NY: Orbis Books, 1973; cf. J. L. Segundo, *The Liberation of Theology,* Maryknoll, NY: Orbis Books, 1976.

17. Denis Goulet, "Makers of History or Witness to Transcendence?" *The Drew Gateway,* 43:2, Winter 1973, pp. 70-90.

18. Denis Goulet, *The Cruel Choice: A New Concept in the Theory of Development,* New York: Atheneum Publishers, 1971, Chapter 9, "Existence Rationality and the Dynamics of Value Change," pp. 187-214.

19. Kenneth P. Jameson and Charles K. Wilber, eds., "Religious Values and Development," special issue of *World Development,* Vol. 8, Nos. 7/8, 1980. Cf. Joseph Gremillion and William Ryan, eds., *World Faiths and the New World Order,* Washington, DC: Inter-Religious Peace Colloquium, 1978.

20. J. W. Richardson and D. R. Cutler, *Transcendence,* Boston: Beacon Press, 1969. Cf. Jerry H. Gill, *Mediated Transcendence: A Post-Modern Reflection,* Macon, GA: Mercer University Press, 1989; and David Chidester, *Patterns of Transcendence: Religion, Death, and Dying,* Belmont, CA: Wadsworth Publishing Co., 1990.

INDEX